THE
COMMUNICATION
CATALYST

THE FAST (BUT NOT STUPID)
TRACK TO VALUE
FOR CUSTOMERS, INVESTORS,
AND EMPLOYEES

MICKEY
CONNOLLY RICHARD
RIANOSHEK Ph.D.

KAPLAN PUBLISHING

President, Kaplan Publishing: Roy Lipner
Vice President and Publisher: Cynthia A. Zigmund
Editorial Director: Donald J. Hull
Acquisitions Editor: Mary B. Good
Senior Managing Editor: Jack Kiburz
Interior Design: Lucy Jenkins
Cover Design: Jody Billert, Design Literate, Inc.
Typesetting: the dotted i

Published by Kaplan Publishing,
a division of Kaplan, Inc.

Printed in the United States of America

11 12   20 19 18 17 16

Library of Congress Cataloging-in-Publication Data

Connolly, Mickey.
   The communication catalyst : the fast (but not stupid) track to value for
customers, investors, and employees / Mickey Connolly and Richard Rianoshek.
     p.   cm.
   Includes index.
   ISBN 0-7931-4904-5 (alk. paper)
   1. Communication in organizations.   I. Rianoshek, Richard.   II. Title.
   HD30.3 .C6546 2002
   658.4'5—dc21

                  2002006709

DEDICATION

■ ■ ■

Dedication from Mickey Connolly

To Fairy Tana Cochran, for her love, integrity,
and wise resilience.

Dedication from Richard Rianoshek

To baby Addie Rose,
whose purity of engagement inspires all.

CONTENTS

■ ■ ■

PART / ONE
Uncommon Leadership, Uncommon Value

PART / TWO
The Cycle of Value: A Conversational Architecture

P A R T / T H R E E
Moments of Truth

FOREWORD

■ ■ ■

Some years ago, as the leader of a high-growth technology operation, constantly trying to expand operations to keep up with demand, I became very interested in the notion of velocity in conversation. It seemed quite obvious that a business would create value sooner if it could reduce its "time-to-resolution," as people often speak of time-to-market in the product development world. What would be the shareholder value of cutting in half decision time frames in a business? What about decisions that should but never seem to get made? What about those decisions that get made too quickly but are obviously not well thought out? Although these problems are endemic to organizations, very little or nothing is done about them!

In our operations, we were adding products and sites—thus greatly increasing complexity—and our ability to manage information in 7x24 interdependent operations across several cultures and regions in the world was being sorely stretched. A particular event brought this home and prompted us to develop communications competence in the organization beyond what already existed. We ran into a critical yield problem on a particular product, and we were creating scrap at an enormous rate. As the sites attempted to diagnose and correct the problem, initial indicators were misleading, which lengthened the time to solve the problem. The way communication was handled, it damaged relationships between sites and organizations, thus rendering us even less capable to solve the next issue!

Although I was disappointed in the time it took to solve the problem, I was even more worried about the reduction in capacity to solve the next issue because of damaged relationships. We were still growing dramatically, so the likelihood increased that the next problem would be even more critical to the business.

During this period, I had been in conversation with Mickey and others about time-to-resolution, and so I invited Mickey and Richard to share their work on high performance collaboration with my staff and the next level of managers. From that initial two-day event, we expanded work with much of the material covered in this book across the entire organization, taking it to the different sites.

Also, about this time, in order to maximize the productivity of the business, we decided to actually create a single enterprise out of the various sites, which required agreement on IT systems, processes, equipment strategy and standards, and a host of other things. It was a daunting task in an organization that had grown to almost 10,000 people around the world, in a high-growth, high-tech environment with a lot of legacy ways of operating.

It was not an easy conversation, as leaders and managers had to give up site prerogatives in behalf of enterprise or system value on the "bet" that that behavior would eventually be in the best interest of their site! Representatives from the sites had to be empowered to commit their sites to strategies and methods in "horizontal forums." To accomplish this effort, we focused on relationships and communications to create worldwide systems and capabilities. We created a system level of performance that has brought hundreds of millions of incremental dollars to the bottom line, by comparing results in an environment where no one was arguing with the scoreboard, but was using the difference in results as a platform for learning and improvement in reducing waste.

The principles and practices in *The Communications Catalyst* have been key to our being able to accomplish such an undertaking. It has been a journey measured in years, not months or weeks. While immediate value can be derived from practicing these principles, our experience indicates that it takes years to become fully competent at applying these practices in difficult situations. The impending era of ubiquitous information, enabled by digitization and the distribution capacity of the Web, will require successful organizations to "process" information even more competently to be successful. If that were not enough, system complexity is increasing as well. Becoming much more competent as leaders and managers at deriving value inside of increasing complexity, ubiquitous information, and faster rates of change presents a very exciting challenge. It's actually a journey fit for a lifetime.

My journey has been of immense value to me, both at work and in my personal life.

I believe very profoundly that valuable conversation causes both learning and enhanced relationships. If there was ever a time when both attributes are sorely needed, it is now.

> Greg Merten
> Vice President and General Manager, Supplies Operations
> Hewlett-Packard Company

ACKNOWLEDGMENTS

∎ ∎ ∎

For whatever value is in these pages, we are indebted to these important people:

Our families have surrendered a precious resource—time—because they thought *The Communication Catalyst* a worthy investment. To Tana, Emma Rose, Guy, Kathleen, and Addie Rose we offer grateful love. To Jim Rianoshek, Tim Connolly, and Judy Connolly, thank you for research, fieldwork, and our unshakable mutual faith.

Members of our extended Conversant community have been crucially supportive. Julie Naster orchestrated all of our efforts, staying true to the principles of our practice every step of the way. Trese Black, Mary Rianoshek, and Allison Corsi provided timely research and heartfelt support. Sue Rhodes did key research and made elegant suggestions that gave us a more reader-friendly manuscript. Julie, Sue, Jane Ellen Seymour, Dianne Dickerson, and Jim Motroni shared their insights from working with real clients facing real challenges. David Goldsmith inspired us all with his passionate devotion to increasing the valuable impact of our practice. Due to their work, we have a reality-tested book we can all stand behind.

Bill Boyar, our attorney, client, and friend, provided crucial and timely support (as always).

To Guy Villavaso and Larry Foles, thank you for enduring friendship and wondrous food (some of the research was highly pleasurable).

Many of our clients have made important contributions. In particular, we owe much to Greg Merten, Bill Boyar, Ruth Rodriguez, Jim Reinhart, Al Miksch, Bob Hiebert, Joe Rubin, Ron McKinney, Stan Hill, Susan Bowick, Susan Burnett, Will Fleissig, Dave Rhodes, Chiqui Santos, Dave Young, and Tom Koby for their time-tested, valuable partnership.

Extraordinary teachers have shaped our thinking. Take care: they may well not agree with some of what we say, so blame nothing on them. The intellectual prowess and vigilant integrity of Leon Rappaport, Kenneth

Anbender, and Humberto Maturano have been profoundly stimulating and immeasurably valuable.

Finally, we thank Mary Good, our Dearborn editor, for her faith and artful guidance, and Marcia Connor for sending Mary our way.

INTRODUCTION

. . .

"Innovation occurs for many reasons, including greed,
ambition, conviction, happenstance, acts of nature, mistakes,
and desperation. But one force above all seems to facilitate
the process. The easier it is to communicate, the faster
change happens."

—JAMES BURKE, *CONNECTIONS* (1995 ED.)

What two chronic concerns plague most executives, managers, and employees the world over? In our work with more than 200,000 people around the world, we hear the same two things over and over: time and money. Those two concerns survive any change in the economy, remaining important in good times and bad. If you put time and money together you get the measure of success for this book: creating more economic value in less time. By *value*, we mean what customers and investors are willing to pay for, that employees are willing and able to provide. *The Communication Catalyst* focuses on the greatest leverage point a leader has for creating high-velocity value: conversation.

In our consulting practice, Conversant, our area of expertise is communication. More specifically, we work on how communication affects how people act. Much of our time has been spent in working with executives and managers to achieve business goals more quickly and effectively than the norm. Time-to-market, process improvement, product and service development, sales cycles, acquisition integration, and the time it takes for a new employee to be productive are common examples of such time-sensitive business goals. We have proven something both deceptively simple and very important: fast value for customers, investors, and employees begins and ends with changing how people interact.

Many executives and managers trivialize the power of conversation. They fall into a common speed trap: they think communication issues are "soft," unlike the supposedly more important "hard" issues of technology and measurement. This line of thinking is dangerous, costly, and wrong. The opening quote is from *Connections*, James Burke's book and PBS television program about the inventions that altered the course of history. Not only does Burke *not* trivialize communication, he calls it "one force above all."

A case in point: In 1995, we were contracted to assess the effectiveness of a product development methodology for a company that makes measurement instruments. They are successful, leading in most of the markets they target. However, a senior executive was convinced that there were unnecessary delays in getting new products to market. As part of our preliminary work, we held a meeting with about 40 senior engineers.

The purpose of the meeting was to solicit input on what they considered the main barriers to accelerating time-to-market. The engineers broke into groups and made lengthy lists. The walls were papered with flip charts when we asked them the following question: "What percentage of the barriers is technical and what percentage social?"

After reviewing all their charts and labeling barriers as "technical" or "social," they gave us these percentages: 19 percent technical and 81 percent social. One engineering manager said: "We're always trying to take waste out of our technical processes, but in the 22 years I've been here, we have never even looked at taking waste out of our interactions with people."

This technical community went to work on the waste in their interactions with each other and reduced an 18-month product development cycle to 9 months. The executive sponsor of the project said: "If we had done this five years ago we would have saved $50 million."

The engineering manager points to an amazingly unexamined asset: conversation. Very few managers consider the following:

- We live and work in a web of conversations.
- Those conversations affect perceptions, priorities, and action.
- For most leaders, conversational effect is accidental and slows achievement.
- It is possible to converse by design and accelerate achievement.

Conversational skill is particularly important whenever we need to coordinate the efforts of different people to produce value. Every executive, manager, or supervisor faces the coordination challenge. We talk about it in a variety of ways: teamwork, trust, and group productivity to name a few. Most of us are not aware of a reliable design for how conversation affects coordinated effort. If we were, there would not be nearly as many break-downs in teamwork, trust, and group productivity.

Have you ever seen conversations damage an organization and slow its success? How many problems are caused or aggravated by the quality of interaction? The Challenger disaster, the nuclear accident at Chernobyl, General Motors' expensively late response to Toyota, and the management meltdown at Xerox were all rooted in terrible communication. Consider breakdowns between CEO and COO, Board and CEO, senior leadership and the rank and file. Consider problems with important customers, allies, and investors. Review the challenges of acquisitions and mergers. These is-sues are largely social troubles that arise in the conversations people have with themselves and each other. Conversation, then, is the leverage point for meeting social challenges.

As a whole, executives and managers do not seem to be improving their conversational leadership. Otherwise, the rate at which they solve such so-cial problems would be improving. For example, statistics regarding suc-cessful mergers, acquisitions, and alliances have stayed the same for many years. Studies by many reputable firms, like Cap Gemini Ernst & Young, Mer-cer, Accenture, McKinsey, and PricewaterhouseCoopers all arrive at similar conclusions: most mergers and acquisitions fail. The consensus statistics are:

- 60 percent of merged companies have less net value five years after the merger than before.
- 30 percent have no increase in value.
- 10 percent meet or exceed their goals.

Merger statistics do not show improvement every year, and it is not for lack of effort. Billions have been spent on integrating enterprise software, getting common hardware systems, and installing new information man-agement systems, all in the interest of agile, integrated performance. While much of this expense has been worthwhile, hardly any of it has returned all the value expected. Why? Because we misunderstand a source of value that is as common, crucial, and taken for granted as the air we breathe: how we converse with one another. In conversation, we assign meaning and then take action. All the hardware and software systems in the world are impotent in-vestments, if people do not have meaningful relationships with those systems and the people involved. Because we do not understand how conversation affects meaning and action, the statistics on acquisitions and mergers do not improve.

Of course, the coordination challenge is not limited to mergers and acquisitions. Most attempts to collaborate across boundaries are equally vexing. Interactions between marketing, R&D, and manufacturing can be disappointing and wasteful. Connections with important allies, major customers, internal partners, and governmental authorities have similar challenges. Do you get substantially better at meeting these challenges year after year? If not, a probable cause is unintended conversational effect.

There are leaders, of course, who do respect the power of communication to accelerate value for customers, investors, and employees. As Greg Merten, vice president and general manager of Supplies Operations at Hewlett-Packard, has said: "Our investments in developing conversational skills have been extremely valuable. I can easily show hundreds of millions of dollars of additional profit directly attributable to our work on high-performance conversation."

Merten has sound business reasons for investing in valuable conversations. This investment does not require an infusion of capital, it raises productivity, it increases employee commitment, and it accelerates the achievement of goals.

That sounds great, but what exactly is high-performance conversation? High-performance conversation is not about being glib. It is not spin control. It is not limited to emotional intelligence, because conversational intelligence includes emotions and much more. *High-performance conversation is well-designed listening and speaking that creates high-velocity value.* Remember our definition of *value: What customers and investors are willing to pay for, that employees are willing and able to provide.* You can accelerate that kind of value if you:

- Understand a useful model for how conversations affect perceptions, priorities, and action.
- Apply the model to any current challenge that requires you to coordinate different interests.
- Measure the results.
- Use the model to debrief, learn, and adjust.

The Communication Catalyst provides a conversational model, which we call the cycle of value. The cycle of value promotes teamwork, creativity, planning, accountability, and learning; we also address how those same things break down. Use the cycle of value well, and you will accelerate achievement and prevent a multitude of mistakes.

The three-part cycle of value:

1. *Align* conversations create shared purpose, stimulate creativity, and ensure smart planning.
2. *Act* conversations clarify accountabilities and launch action.
3. *Adjust* conversations review performance and translate experience into improvement.

When these three related elements are effective, work is meaningful, satisfying, and fast. We infuse work with meaning, galvanize teams, and inflame loyalty among customers, employees, and investors. When these elements are ineffective, we decelerate our high-speed ambitions. We render work meaningless, destroy teamwork, and inflame discontent among customers, employees, and investors.

Consider the design of an automobile engine. If you understand the nature of an internal combustion engine and all its connected parts, you are less frightened by a breakdown than the rest of us. For many people, raising the hood is merely an alert to other drivers that a car is not moving. The ignorant among us confront that mass of sound and motion and are left to merely fret. Those of you who understand the design can diagnose problems and take action. The same is true if you understand the "design" of conversation.

If you take the time to understand and apply our conversational cycle of value, we promise you will see measurable results. The cycle includes aligning the interests of employees, customers, and investors, so conversational leadership will ultimately effect three measures:

1. Attraction and retention of valuable people (employees perceive value)
2. Profitable revenue (customers perceive value)
3. Investor return (shareowners perceive value)

You also can see the benefit in other measurable areas when you apply the architecture. Decreased time-to-market, increased customer loyalty, and increased earnings-per-share are examples.

If you are responsible for coordinating the efforts of others, you are a prime candidate for *The Communication Catalyst*. To find out for sure, answer "yes" or "no" to these six questions:

1. *Do you think it's important to increase the rate of achievement around you?*
2. *Are you unsure how to accelerate things to your satisfaction?*
3. *Are you interested in accelerating your learning curve by profiting from others' mistakes, victories, and lessons?*
4. *Are you frustrated by not getting others to adopt the attitudes and practices that you know would improve performance?*
5. *Do you believe that the conversations you have with stakeholders (e.g., customers, employees, executives, board members, allies, and shareowners) are important to value creation?*
6. *Are you willing to question your own habits and beliefs and explore new ones to speed business success?*

If you answered "yes" to four or more questions, *The Communication Catalyst* is well worth your time and money.

If you said "yes" to all six questions, it would be wise to make *The Communication Catalyst* an immediate priority.

If you answered "no" to most or all of the questions, then do not read *The Communication Catalyst.*

Much success and failure informs this book. The people of Conversant have had the good fortune to work with people from 18 countries, 400 companies, and 31 consulting practices. Our clients and colleagues have taught us a lot. Many of them are people who care greatly about how communication affects conduct: teachers, managers, executives, negotiators, therapists, television personalities, police, and process improvement consultants. Project managers, program managers, R&D professionals, advertising executives, and religious clergy have also contributed to our body of knowledge. We have combined their input with the credentials of our associates, which are substantial and diverse. We have backgrounds in process engineering, chemical engineering, social psychology, and criminology. We also have backgrounds in the hospitality industry, advertising, therapeutic intervention, and high-stakes negotiations. Most importantly, we have mutual love and respect for the power of communication to produce high-velocity accomplishment. We have learned a lot from our mistakes. There is no need for you to make the same ones. We think your mistakes should be original and interesting, not redundant. You will enjoy the efficiency of learning from ours.

The core group at Conversant is maturing. In our 40s and 50s, we no longer want our contribution to be limited by where our bodies are. We do not just want to sell our time until we drop dead. We want to leave behind the lessons of a career. *The Communication Catalyst* is an important part of that ambition. Here, we get to address a subject in the dead center of our hard-won expertise: the social side of speed.

It will be useful to know a little about the design of *The Communication Catalyst,* because it is actually two books in one. Each chapter will walk you through proven concepts and techniques. Although we are two authors, we occasionally use the first person to tell a story. Just know that it is one or the other of us talking to you. At the end of each chapter, we offer a quick summary of major points for easy reference. That isn't all, however.

Accompanying each chapter is an episode of a story. The story is fictional (though loosely based on a medley of real people and events) and demonstrates the practical power of the ideas behind *The Communication Catalyst.* The title of the parable within our book is Rev Lessons and stars Rev Baker, who owns a popular barbecue restaurant in Austin, Texas. Rev has a complex and mysterious past from which he has learned much about how communication affects action. Rev shares the lessons with a frequent customer, a frustrated manager from a high-tech company. Surprisingly, Rev's colorful past yields valuable insights that apply well to the business problems of today.

We recommend that you read both parts of *The Communication Catalyst.* The nonfiction prescriptions for action are too detailed to remember and apply easily. We provide the detail so that you can return to the book when facing specific challenges, using it much like a field manual. However, when you combine a general understanding of the principles with the fictional story, everything makes more sense and is far easier to retain.

Now, Rev Baker, our fictional star, gets his own introduction.

R E V   L E S S O N

▪ ▪ ▪

My name is Walker O'Reilly. Not long ago, I asked Rev Baker how to repay him for the remarkable difference he had made in my life. Rev said: "Share the wealth, Walker."

Most of my lessons started with Rev leaning his six-foot-four-inch, 225-pound frame on the granite counter at his restaurant. His face looked like the supple, wellworn leather of a baseball glove, one with years of service and much linseed oil lovingly applied. His mother was Mexican and his father African American, and it was easy to see the struggles and inequities of that combined lineage in Rev's large face. Amazingly, he ended up patient, compassionate, and wise rather than bitter. Few people estimated Rev appropriately, and he liked it that way. He told me once, "My way is to relax folks, not impress 'em. They're way easier to manage relaxed than they are impressed."

Rev and I first met in New Orleans when I was fresh out of Tulane University. I was at Jazz Fest, the annual spring festival that celebrated the music that stirred soulful people, not just jazz. Rev was standing tall at the gospel tent at the New Orleans fairgrounds, shouting out "No!" to the Dynamic Clark Sisters who were asking the musical question "Is my living in vain?"

I felt awestruck and out of place in the gospel tent. Stunned by the intense, rhythmic emotions, I felt like a voyeur participating in unearned pleasure. I attended no church, played no instrument, and stood out like a cotton ball in a coal bin. Rev watched me watching him and smiled his way over to me. "Son, you're lots more welcome than you think. If the music moves you, you belong here. Heck, they let a half-breed like me in here just to prove God loves us all."

Rev seemed safe even then, a big coffee-colored teddy bear of a man. His eyes burrowed into me, both welcoming and researching. The experience was of being smaller than Rev, physically and intellectually, all the while being relaxed by his disarming way. I did not yet know his shockingly formidable and serious sides. I also did not know that he would be very important in my future.

It was ten years later that I saw Rev again. I was a failing middle manager being crushed by the demand for world-class speed. We'll just call the company I worked for MightyTek, a large corporation in Austin, Texas. Rev, this expert at high-velocity achievement, was performing an apparently modest task. He was cooking barbecue at our annual all-manager gathering.

In previous years, we had gathered in grander style. This year, our all-expense-paid trip to a resort had been replaced by a picnic. Our financial results were below expectations, and expense cuts were common. As I approached the food area, I looked up at a large white banner with bright red letters:

Rev Baker's
Mighty Fine, Mighty Tasty
Beautiful Central Texas Hill Country Barbecue

My eyes jerked down, looking for a man whose face was a vivid memory. He was looking back.

"Well now, I believe we've met before." Rev spoke with a warm smile of recognition. "Jazz Fest, 10 years ago. I'm Walker O'Reilly."

"Walker, I remember. We had a fine time at Jazz Fest, didn't we? How are you doin', son? You seem 10 years older and 20 years tireder."

I was startled. The people I knew were not that direct, at least not without being insulting. "Oh, I'm fine, just a big workload at the moment."

Rev looked quietly into me. "Walker, if you drop by my restaurant for lunch, I'll buy you a barbecue sandwich. You let me know when you're comin'."

Rev handed me his business card. I said, "Sure, that will be great" without meaning it. I was too busy to hang out with a cook.

"Walker," Rev said, "unless you're absolutely sure about how to handle that workload, you come by."

Rev's comment haunted me, because I surely wasn't sure. I lunched at Rev's four days later. Good thing. He is a barbecue wizard with an interesting past. It's amazing what you can learn from a cook, especially one who has tested how communication affects conduct in situations with high stakes and mortal consequences.

Enjoy Rev's lessons. And pay attention. A man like Rev can teach you a lot.

PART / ONE

. . .

Uncommon Leadership, Uncommon Value

"When you do the common things in life in an uncommon way,
you will command the attention of the world."

GEORGE WASHINGTON CARVER

Unexamined resources hide unexpected value. Communication, the connective tissue of humanity, is woefully unexamined as an asset to business leadership. The power to lead may live simply in the ability to initiate a conversation that generates valuable action when you are not around. Much like the innocent atom holds astonishing, hidden power, so does conversation.

CHAPTER ONE

THE COMMUNICATION CASE FOR HIGH-VELOCITY VALUE

. . .

"Language exerts hidden power, like a moon on the tides."

RITA MAE BROWN, *STARTING FROM SCRATCH*

Communication is a risky topic. Offering insight into communication includes at least two major pitfalls.

Communication is an all-too-familiar topic. "I already know lots of things about communication. I am successful and I know how to get my point across. I do not use verbal crutches such as 'like' and 'you know' when I am making a presentation. I practice listening and speaking every day of my life. Really, what else is there to learn?"

Unless you have successfully handled every issue of coordination, cooperation, and misunderstanding in your life, communication is probably still worth pursuing. People tend to stop studying subjects that are familiar and common. Whoever continues to improve at a familiar, common practice has an enormous advantage over those who take it for granted.

Agnes de Mille, the great dancer and choreographer said: "As soon as I already know, I begin to die a little." In our consulting practice, Conversant, our biggest challenge is to learn more about how communication affects human conduct every day and never stop learning. We invite you to join us on the journey.

■ ■ ■

"It is what we think we know already that often prevents us from learning."

CLAUDE BERNARD, FRENCH PHYSIOLOGIST

Communication is not an "attractive" topic. Several years ago, *USA Today* published a survey on an interesting subject: the greatest fears of modern Americans. At Conversant, we have worked in many parts of the world, and the findings do not seem limited to Americans. The #1 fear was public speaking. The #2 fear was death. Shortly after the survey results appeared, comic Jerry Seinfeld commented: "This says that, at a funeral, you would rather be in the casket than delivering the eulogy."

Yes, it seems that communication is not a popular, comfortable subject to pursue. We are going after it anyway. You see, communication accelerates or decelerates the creation of value, and that attribute makes it very interesting. It is the foundation for all coordinated achievement, so it is not a trivial topic, just as the foundation under your house is not trivial.

Conversations are not neutral; they always affect the quality and pace of the outcome. There are profound implications to this statement; however, we will not engage in a rigorous philosophical investigation into the hidden power of language. Instead, we will check out the practical implications of how business conversations dictate business results. The profound implications we'll leave up to you.

Building Blocks for High-Velocity Value

To launch our investigation, let us define a few terms. These words will be building blocks for the rest of the book.

Value. We define *value* as *what customers and investors are willing to pay for, that employees are willing and able to provide.* In a public, for-profit enterprise, sustainable value requires all three groups. Value must be worthy to those paying and those providing, or it will not endure. When this mutual value is identified, delivered, and paid for faster than usual, we term it *high-velocity value.* This conspiracy of value, like all things mutual, involves communication.

Waste. *Waste* is any use of resources that does not create value for customers, investors, and employees.

Communication. A popular, and narrow, definition of *communication* is "the exchange of ideas, messages, or information" (*Webster's Dictionary*). In architecture, communication is the term for linking different spaces. A hallway, for instance, is a method of communication for the offices that open into it. In *The Communication Catalyst*, we say *communication is any action that links separate elements into a larger system.* Without communication, there is nothing in common: no teamwork, no mutual benefit, and no business value.

Conversation. *Conversation* is the uniquely human kind of communication. In the forms of *impression* (e.g., listening) and *expression* (e.g., speaking), conversation is how we learn about and influence the world and ourselves. *Conversation is a language cycle that causes perception, meaning, action, and learning.* Most business writing about conversation is trivial compared to its real nature and power. The education of any leader is incomplete without an accurate working knowledge of how conversation causes perception, meaning, action, and learning.

■ ■ ■

"I believe that words can help us move or keep us paralyzed, and that our choices of language and verbal tone have something—a great deal—to do with how we live our lives . . ."

ADRIENNE RICH

"Language is our meeting place, the sea we live in . . . it is the common ground of our humanity."

TOBY WOLFE, *VANITY FAIR* (SEPTEMBER 1985)

Catalyst. A *catalyst causes or accelerates activity between two or more persons or forces.* Communication is the primary catalyst for anything that requires the coordinated effort of people.

The terms we defined are building blocks for this statement: *Communication in any business environment, especially in the form of conversation, causes or accelerates value or waste.* Any attempt to accelerate business results without effective communication is doomed to create waste, not high-velocity value.

The False Promise of Speed Worship

Many leaders have begun to worship a modern golden calf: speed. We are doing business in a headlong rush of activity. The slow ones are road kill, so go fast, fast, fast. You may not have seen the following passage, but we're betting it feels familiar:

Every morning in Africa, a gazelle wakes up.
It knows it must run faster than the fastest lion or it will be killed.
Every morning a lion wakes up.
It knows it must outrun the slowest gazelle or it will starve to death.
It does not matter whether you are a lion or a gazelle:
When the sun comes up, you better be running.

Unknown

What is your reaction to this lion and gazelle dynamic? Is business only a well-dressed, rapid-fire fight for survival? We say it is not. Besides, it is too tiring to settle for running ever more quickly just to stay alive. The running needs to be valuable both to runners and to the people for whom they run. However, leaders often forget this reciprocity of value in their lust for speedy output. So, we burn up and burn out the source of value: the mutually beneficial contract between customers, investors, and employees. When disconnected hurry displaces communication, the burning out begins.

In the face of cutthroat competition, faster and faster time-to-market, rapid technology development, and wild-eyed change, speed matters. But, it's not even close to the whole story. Speed does not disguise stupidity and, in fact, may amplify it. Imagine driving down a street at 30 MPH. Perhaps you do something foolish, like look down to dial your mobile phone. A car backs out of a driveway up ahead of you, and the peripheral movement pulls your eyes back to the road. A desperate lunge at the brakes saves the day. In the gasping, grateful aftermath, you silently promise to not dial and drive again. Now, replay the scene at 60 MPH or 90 MPH. Your mistake has dramatically different consequences. You might not even be alive to learn from the mistake. There are similar stories in business where managers who are proud of their speedy decisions are sowing the seeds of their own destruction. Speed on its own is *not* a reliable path to success, much less a means to personal satisfaction.

■ ■ ■

"What is the use of running when we are not

on the right road?"

GERMAN PROVERB

"We make fast decisions, but we don't make smart decisions." This comment was made by a vice president in a technology company that had been losing market share for three years in a row. We interviewed him for one of our clients, because he let it be known he was interested in leaving his present company. "The new CEO made a big deal out of fast decisions. His staff all had pagers, cell phones, and wireless e-mail, so they could be reached quickly. He really thought just going faster helped. Do you know how we made faster decisions? We excluded the people who knew our customers and our technologies the best. People joked about going to marching-order meetings, because they knew there would be no discussion, only instructions. Our big improvement was getting to market faster with products that only sold if we discounted them so much we couldn't make our profit targets." This account is a painful description of a recipe for wasted time and money.

We have seen strangely similar events in a variety of businesses. Most new economy start-ups fail and do so while going very fast. Most acquisitions and mergers fall short of their intended economic value and not, for the most part, because they were slow. They fail mainly because of poor quality interactions among the people who are crucial to their success.

Static and Dynamic Business Situations

Valuable interactions are the key to the victory of high-velocity value over mere speed. The simple reason is that conversation is the field of play for coordinated action. Whether the venue is telephone, e-mail, staff meetings, project reviews, or casual discussion, it is still a conversational field of play. The interactions in static business conditions, however, are different from the interactions in dynamic conditions. It is very possible that you already possess the leadership and communication skills that meet the challenge of static conditions. They have been honed since the dawn of the Industrial Revolution. The dynamic skills are unusual, and developing them fully requires considerable personal interest. Map your own situation onto this section as you read. See if you are reminded of your own challenges, particularly in the dynamic section. If you see yourself in this part of the book, the rest will be a worthy personal investment.

Static conditions are based in predictable challenges. The crucial variables are known. Although no business condition is completely static and unchanging, some are definitely more static than dynamic. Most business-people long for the static situation, because it makes investing safer. Confident predictions of the future allow for capital investments and for potential long-term profit.

For example, if you operate a contract manufacturing company, your binding contracts with "A" credit clients allow you to invest in manufacturing lines. You know exactly what to manufacture, so you can develop exact processes for doing the same things over and over. Economies of scale become the primary source of economic value for customers, investors, and employees. The main risk factor is the accuracy of your predictions.

Take advantage of mainly static situations whenever they present themselves. These relatively stable situations are ripe for rigorous processes and standard protocols. World-class cost structures frequently emerge from these economy-of-scale opportunities. Contrary to popular business press claims of "permanent whitewater everywhere," such opportunities do exist.

There are useful guidelines for leading in a mainly static condition. The *static imperatives* are:

- *Invest in the quality of your predictions.* Can you confidently predict the commitments and capabilities of customers, investors, and employees? Can you predict the actions of important competitors? Are your predictions grounded in information you trust?
- *Create value through economies of scale.* Return capital investments through cost efficiencies, reliable profits, and a high volume of activity.
- *Communication culture is following instructions.* Processes are rigorous in a static environment, so you do not want much deviation. If you *know* what it takes to make a high-value product, then you do not want people making things up.
- *Preserve rigid roles.* In a static environment, you know how each role fits with the whole system. You want everyone to do a good job of doing his or her part. Do not get in each other's way.
- *Separate organizations.* This is the organizational equivalent of *rigid roles.* Share the information necessary for people to make their promised contribution and no more.

- *Experience and credentials grant credibility.* People trust you because you are in charge, you know how the system works, and you have proven yourself in similar situations.

However, not all business conditions are static. None, in fact, is completely static. Many times, you cannot safely predict the commitments, capabilities, and actions of customers, investors, employees, and competitors. In those times, leadership and communication must be more *dynamic* than static. The guiding principles for leaders are dramatically different.

Please answer the following question and trust your immediate, subjective guess:

- What percentage of the time are you working in conditions that are substantially unpredictable?

If you are confident in your answer, then skip the numbered exercise below (unless you are just curious). If you are not confident in your answer, here is a simple and revealing exercise. Take out a clean sheet of paper, and then:

1. Draw a small circle in the center of the page and label it with the name of any particular responsibility you hold. This could be a company name, a division name, a project you led, or any distinct accountability.
2. Ask yourself, "What events, forces, or situations are substantially affecting my area of responsibility?"
3. Write your answers (e.g., "Our biggest competitor is introducing a new product" or "Our company is restructuring") on the page anywhere in the white space between your accountability and the edge of the paper. Draw a circle around each answer. The page may get cluttered quickly.
4. For each answer, assess the size of the impact on your accountability on a scale of 1 to 10 (1 is little impact, 10 is enormous impact). Write the number in the appropriate circle.
5. Keep identifying, assessing, and scoring the various impacts for ten minutes.
6. Add up all your scores. The number is your *Estimated Gross Adjustment Demand Score* (fondly known as EGADS!).
7. Divide the EGADS score by the number of impact circles on the page. This number is your *Average Adjustment Demand.*

In our experience, either an Average Adjustment Demand of 5 or more, or a total EGADS score of 30 or more puts you in dynamic conditions. You do not have to believe our assertion. Trust your own judgment: Looking at the page, does your environment tend more toward static or dynamic?

In our consulting practice, we have asked many managers and leaders to do this simple analysis. Most of them say that there are a larger percentage of dynamic situations than static situations. The rest say the percentage is substantial if not in the majority.

In dynamic situations, the static imperatives cause damage and create waste rather than value. The *dynamic imperatives* are:

- *Invest in real-time learning and adjustment.* You cannot predict safely. Your risk factor is how quickly you learn and adjust rather than your ability to predict. People who learn slowly fear dynamic times. It is essential to be in open, responsive communication with customers, investors, and employees.

■ ■ ■

"I'm not afraid of storms, for I'm learning to sail my ship."

LOUISA MAY ALCOTT

- *Create value through rate of adjustment.* Many of us used to think there was no way to compete with someone who enjoyed vastly superior economies of scale. We were wrong. Agile response to customer, investor, and employee information is an extraordinary advantage. Komatsu exploded onto the heavy equipment scene with shocking success in the face of Caterpillar's economies of scale. Dell did the same to IBM as Canon did to Xerox, Toyota to General Motors, and Wal-Mart to Sears. All of these were victories of *rate of adjustment* over *economies of scale.*
- *Communication culture is valuable conversation.* In valuable conversations, we interact, learn, and immediately apply the lessons. There is no manual, no instructions to follow. Marching orders are grossly inadequate. Meetings need to clarify purpose and yield new insight and action, not simply report and instruct. This quote from baseball great Satchel Paige is especially apt in dynamic times: "None of us is as smart as all of us." Tapping into that intelligence requires unusual, though learnable, communication skills.
- *Preserve adaptive roles.* In dynamic conditions, few people should be doing exactly what they were doing last year at this time. Muhammad

Ali and Katherine Hepburn are good examples. Ali kept adjusting his strategies and tactics to befit his age, athleticism, and opponent. This flexibility marked his startling upset of George Foreman with the now-famous "rope-a-dope" tactic. His boxing was markedly different in winning different titles. Hepburn has gracefully occupied role after varied role in a career that has known no limit. From *Bringing Up Baby* to *On Golden Pond* and beyond, she chronically links her gifts to the opportunities at hand and has never stopped creating value. Their flexible artistry is a great lesson for us.

- *Connect organizations.* In dynamic conditions, let information flow freely, as blood flows through the organs of our bodies. The most valuable discoveries come from connecting the previously unconnected. Be generous with information, and let your constituents become creative cohorts. When we are afraid to share information, we are protecting what we already have. In dynamic times, what we already have is insufficient. The risk of exposing information is far less than the risk of limiting ourselves to what we already know. Compared to *separation*, free *connection* is a messy, stimulating, and necessary source of value.

■ ■ ■

"Experience after experience with innovations that fizzle after a bright start, be they new work systems or new products, shows that external relations are a critical factor: the connections, or lack of them, between the area initially producing the innovation and its neighborhood and beyond."

ROSABETH MOSS KANTER, *THE CHANGE MASTERS*

- *Visible learning and adjustment grant credibility.* Dynamic leaders are frank about mistakes and quick to learn and adjust. They waste no time deflecting new challenges or defending the past. Who has credibility in dynamic times? It is the women and men who are visibly learning and adapting, not the ones clinging desperately to failed plans and familiar habits.

The chart in Figure 1.1 summarizes the imperatives in a side-by-side comparison.

We are *not* saying that static is bad and dynamic is good. Economies of scale are always going to be valuable. In the right situation, rigorous

---

FIGURE 1.1 / Static and Dynamic Value Imperatives

Static Imperatives	Dynamic Imperatives
PREDICTION	LEARNING AND ADJUSTMENT
ECONOMIES OF SCALE	RATE OF ADJUSTMENT
FOLLOWING INSTRUCTIONS	VALUABLE CONVERSATIONS
RIGID ROLES	ADAPTIVE ROLES
SEPARATE ORGANIZATIONS	CONNECTED ORGANIZATIONS
EXPERIENCE AND CREDENTIALS	ABILITY TO LEARN AND ADJUST

---

standard practices create great value for customers, investors, and employees. We *are* saying that the conversational skills of dynamic leadership and communication are important to both static and dynamic value for two reasons:

1. Someone adept at the dynamic imperatives has the skills necessary to identify static opportunities; in our experience, the reverse is not so. The ability to recognize and respond to both static and dynamic opportunities is fundamental to high-velocity value. Valuable conversation, the core competence for leading in dynamic times, allows a leader to recognize and act on each of these occasions for value at the right time.
2. In the knowledge and service economies of today, the dynamics of conversation *are* the dynamics of high-velocity value.

In the Industrial Revolution, people were looked upon as tools for production of value. A frustrated Henry Ford is rumored to have complained, "I ask for a pair of hands and they come with a head attached!" In the service and knowledge economy, what is in those heads is the value. How do we access the extraordinary contribution of people to create high-velocity value for customers, investors, and employees? At Conversant, we have found the answer lies in the dynamic imperatives.

Waste Signals

These are the telltale signs that you are in dynamic times and using the static imperatives:

- Chronic complaints that stay unresolved
- Poor track record of executing agreements
- Conflicting charters (lack of shared purpose)
- Organizations withholding information from each other
- Wasteful explanations (an explanation of a problem that does not help solve it): "It's not my fault," "I'm right, they're wrong," "We're in a bad economy," etc.
- Relationships are deteriorating

If any of these warning signals apply, then the ratio of waste to value is unhealthy and demands attention.

To meet the challenge of dynamic leadership, read on. The first major key to high-velocity value comes next.

The Intersection: Launch Point for High-Velocity Value

Here are some dangerous, wasteful myths:
- The customer is always right.
- The sole purpose of a business is to make a profit.
- Nothing happens without employees, so take care of them first, last and always.

There is some truth in each statement. Greater truth, however, is at the place where the three statements intersect (see Figure 1.2).

This notion of an intersection is a fruitful source of high-velocity value. The wasteful norm: Promote my own agenda and protect myself from the intrusion of your agenda. A valuable change: Research your agenda and find out where mine intersects with yours. The intersection is about integration, not domination.

Contrast integrating the agenda of customers, investors, and employees with determining which of the three should dominate. You will find that integration produces more value with less time, money, and stress. The reason is simple: Customers, employees, and investors need each other. Their

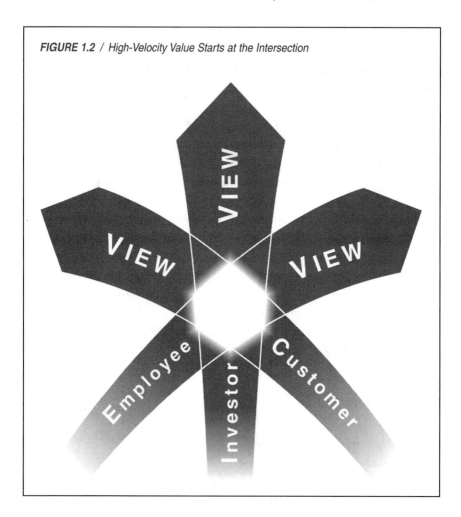

FIGURE 1.2 / High-Velocity Value Starts at the Intersection

purposes are reciprocal and interdependent. Like a pyramid of purpose, each requires the other two to stand at all. Anything produced at the intersection will be gratifying for all. A benefit for one at the expense of the other two is an investment in the demise of a business.

Meaningful work and long-lived relationships are rooted in the intersection. If we are not able to see shared value, we are left with manipulation and domination. Many leaders have damaged employees, customers, or investors, not because they wanted to, but because they saw no other course of action. Those of you who are willing to master the art of the intersection will not be so limited.

Many people have told us that it is liberating to be able to produce superior business results by researching and intersecting with other people's purposes. After considerable work on getting to the intersection quickly, a senior manager in a Fortune 100 company told us: "This is the first time in my 36-year work life that I see high performance and being completely honorable coexist without compromise. We're producing a lot better results than we thought we could, and I'm sleeping better than I ever have."

We heartily agree. Like him, we have found that meaningful work, ethical peace, high profits, and great customer satisfaction are *not* mutually exclusive. Also, we made a lot of mistakes on the way to that insight. As we said in the introduction, it is best for you to learn from our mistakes and then make fresh ones for yourself.

Employees, investors, and customers are groups with distinct purposes, concerns, and circumstances. High-velocity value is launched from where they intersect. The value of the intersection, however, extends way beyond these three groups. Anytime you benefit from the coordination, support, or collaboration of others, the intersection is a gold mine of value. If you care about value (i.e., the rate at which employees provide what customers and investors are happy to pay for), then get interested in intersections.

Intersection conversations are the essential foundation for high-velocity value. They call for:

- Researching the point of view of anyone whose support you desire or require
- Discovering where your view overlaps or intersects with theirs

For now, we define *view* as:

- *Purposes*—essential commitments I cannot abandon
- *Concerns*—things that might interfere with my purposes
- *Circumstances*—essential facts that I must account for

For example, I could have a *purpose* to assure my children a great education. I am *concerned* about the drug problem in schools. The school district in which we live is a *circumstance* to be taken into account. In Chapter 3, we will develop a more complete definition of *point of view*.

The Axioms of the Intersection

An *axiom* is a self-evident statement that is accepted as a basis for further conversation. We have found it highly productive to accept these three axioms:

1. All humans have purposes, concerns, and circumstances.
2. If someone perceives that you are unaware or disrespectful of his or her purposes, concerns, and circumstances, he or she will consider you a threat. And, he or she will actively avoid, resist, and undermine any significant threat. This creates waste.
3. If someone perceives that you are aware and respectful of his or her purposes, concerns, and circumstances, he or she will join you in conversation. He or she will share information, coinvent solutions, and move into action. This creates value.

■ ■ ■

"We put our energy into staking out the widest

common ground all can stand on without forcing

or compromising. Then, from that solid base

we spontaneously invent new forms of action . . ."

MARVIN WEISBORD, *DISCOVERING COMMON GROUND*

If you want to accelerate the trip to the intersection, then keep the axioms in mind. Read them ten times a day. Catch yourself respecting and violating the axioms and note the different outcomes. Virtually every impasse, argument, or upset you encounter can be explained in terms of the laws. The axioms also can explain virtually every inspired result and group victory.

Here is some active research you can do. For the next difference of opinion you encounter, we suggest that you research the following *before* you argue your point:

• What important purpose is at stake for them?
• What concerns do they have about achieving their purpose?
• What circumstances are affecting their purpose?

For example, imagine that you just heard of a new policy that lowers your expense authority. In the future, you will have to get approval for many expenses that had been left to your discretion. If you wish to have any

influence at all, answer the above three questions before you voice any objections. If the presentation of your view does not acknowledge those purposes, concerns, and circumstances, *you will not be heard.*

Review what you discover with the other party to make sure he or she
endorses your findings about his or her view. Now, say what you have to say.
You will notice he or she is listening to you carefully and that you naturally
express yourself in a way that includes his or her purposes, concerns, and
circumstances.

When we train and coach negotiators, we say the following:

- Negotiation is the art of discovering an intersection of mutual interest
  that the parties will mutually protect.
- Do not introduce a new point into the discussion until you have expressed the last speaker's point to his or her satisfaction.

This counsel to negotiators comes directly from the axioms of the
intersection.

In most business conversations, people note differences first and similarities second. This is especially true in the face of a problem. If any resolution is possible, it accelerates dramatically if you focus on intersections
first. Intersection conversations give us a place from which to deal with the
differences. Without an intersection, there is only argument and protection.
The resulting outcome is doomed to be a mere extension of the existing
positions, and no new value is produced.

Intersection conversations identify unforced opportunities for high-velocity
value. Anything at the intersection tends to happen fast and does not require much oversight. Getting to the intersection quickly is a function of
intention, skill, and practice. In Chapters 2 and 3, we will give you skill and
practice, including a model to tell you how you are doing and how to improve. You, of course, have to provide the intention.

Although intersection conversations are essential, they are only part of
the design of high-velocity value.

The Architecture of Conversation

Ordinarily, an architect is the designer and sometimes builder of a physical edifice. An architect of conversation is the designer and builder of
achievement of all sorts.

If you want to create quizzical looks and blank stares, spend a day asking people this question: "What is the design of a valuable conversation?" You probably will not get immediate, insightful answers. We spend countless hours listening and speaking, but the nature of those hours goes unexamined.

Part of our consulting practice is devoted to *process transformation*. The purpose is to radically increase the return on invested time and money in any business process. Fifty percent decreases in time are frequent. Unleashing the brilliance of a work community through valuable conversation adds an extraordinary new source of value to conventional process improvement.

We have learned a simple lesson regarding process transformation. The greatest results come from examining a system with two characteristics:

1. It is widely used by many people.
2. It has not been rigorously examined for a significant period of time.

An unexamined system in wide use is ripe for a value harvest. Waste has crept in over time and is now invisible and rampant. We really like these kinds of assignments, because we know we are going to achieve great gains. The point here is this: The process of business conversation is an unexamined system in wide use. It may be the most unexamined, widely used system of value creation in the world.

Most people *hope* conversations are valuable. However, hope is insufficient for high-velocity value. Hope is impotent without *awareness* and *purpose*. We need to deepen our awareness of how conversation generates perception, meaning, action, and learning. Add to awareness the genuine purpose to create value (instead of just hoping for value), and we can design a model for turning hope into reality.

Our exploration has two paths:

1. The architecture of conversation as a *cycle of value*
2. The architecture of conversation as a *cycle of waste*

There is a reliable design for conversations that produce a cycle of value and for those that produce a cycle of waste. If you appreciate both, you can catch waste early in the cycle and shift to value. In this chapter, we do a high-level overview of both. In Chapter 2, we give the keys to making an early shift from waste to value. In Part Two, we give thorough instructions for ensuring a cycle of value rather than waste.

The Cycle of Value

When conversation builds recurrent value, the cycle of align⇒act⇒adjust is at work (see Figure 1.3). Look at the three elements like thirds of a wheel. When all three are present, we are rolling. When any one of the three is missing, we experience a very bumpy trip.

Align. Align conversations unite people, time, and money to pursue a valuable opportunity. Problems of teamwork, creativity, and resource allocation are largely due to poor alignment. The ultimate test for alignment is execution. The interim test for alignment is the assignment of time, money, and key people. People who are genuinely connected to each other

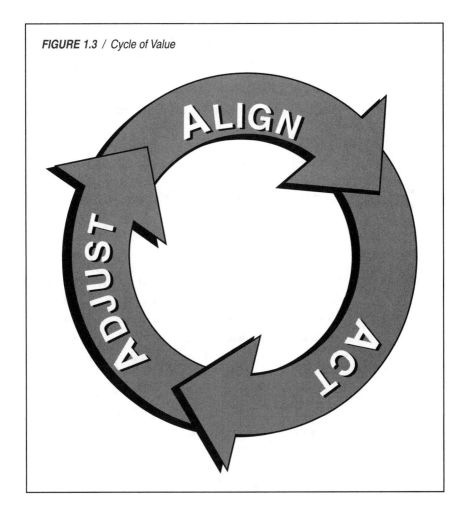

FIGURE 1.3 / *Cycle of Value*

in a worthy effort are resourceful and tenacious in the face of a challenge. As Leonardo da Vinci once said, one "turns not back who is bound to a star." If you have mediocre execution of strategies, then look first at the quality of alignment.

There are three elements of alignment: Intersect, Invent, and Invest. We discover shared purpose at the *intersection* of our individual purposes, *invent* ideas for achieving those purposes, and *invest* time, money, and key people in the ideas that advance our purposes. When all three are present, there is authentic alignment rather than cheap agreement. People often agree to things intellectually without thoroughly confronting the reality of their agreement. Such false agreement is impossible if you intersect, invent, and invest. In Part Two, you will find complete instructions for how to ensure authentic alignment rather than cheap agreement.

When alignment is strong, you have access to the commitment and intelligence of a community. Without it, you are betting on the self-serving talents of a disconnected group; we think that is a bad bet.

■ ■ ■

"Genius is the capacity for seeing relationships where

lesser (people) see none."

WILLIAM JAMES

"Talent wins games, but teamwork and intelligence

win championships."

MICHAEL JORDAN

Act. Act conversations make commitments explicit and launch action. Poor act conversations cause dangerous assumptions, failed expectations, and mistrust. The evidence for action is action, as simplistic as that sounds. If people spend more time *talking about* work (gossip, opinion, excuses, and blame) than actually *doing* work, there will be weak align conversations, weak act conversations, or both.

The three elements of action are *engage, clarify,* and *close.* We *engage* with those who must carry out action, connecting their best interests to the purpose at stake; we *clarify* precise expectations; we *close* the question of accountability by asking for explicit promises to deliver measurable value. Managing these conversations well frees all parties to make unique, specific contributions in a coordinated way.

■ ■ ■

"Action springs . . . from a readiness for responsibility."

DIETRICH BONHOEFFER, *LETTERS AND PAPERS FROM PRISON*

Adjust. Adjust conversations return the investment of action by translating experience into improvement. Through adjustment, we stay true to purpose. Virtually nothing of consequence happens as we imagine, so it is vital that we learn and adjust. Leaders who adjust well know foresight is inevitably imperfect. Dynamic leaders know that they are not prescient and that they do make mistakes. For those leaders, learning is acceleration of value rather than cause for embarrassment.

The two elements of adjustment are *review* and *renew*. Public, timely review of measures and results breeds accountability and accelerates achievement. We renew our efforts and our relationships with the lessons learned. Examples of timely occasions for adjustment are:

- When results are far better than expected, and you do not know why
- When results are worse than expected and not improving
- At obvious milestones (e.g., new leadership, new budget, major deadline)
- When key players are having major disagreements or losing interest

Performance evaluations, project debriefs, and process reviews are all occasions for valuable adjustment.

A well-done adjustment conversation accelerates value by discovering best practices, solving problems, eliminating waste, and deepening the alignment of the parties involved. In Chapter 6, you will find a proven seven-step method for high-velocity debriefing and adjustment.

■ ■ ■

"However beautiful your strategy, you should

occasionally look at the results."

WINSTON CHURCHILL

The three elements of the architecture—align, act, and adjust—work together to create a reliable cycle of increasing value. Every turn of the wheel escalates the quality of alignment, action, and adjustment. Relationships get stronger, trust and creativity increase, goals are met, and learning grows (see Figure 1.4).

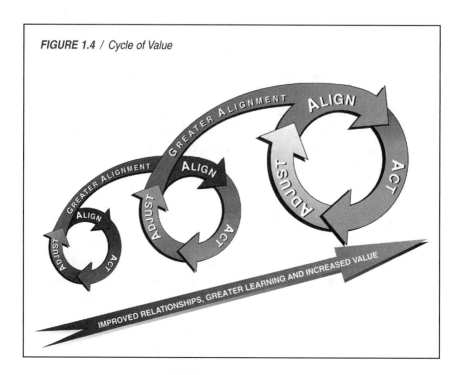

FIGURE 1.4 / *Cycle of Value*

Whenever these substantial increases *do not* happen, there has been a breakdown in one of the three areas of conversation. Ample insight into diagnosis and correction is on the way in the chapters to come.

Here comes the bad news. There is a competing cycle of action: the cycle of waste.

The Cycle of Waste

When value deteriorates the cycle of conversation is disagree⇒defend ⇒destroy. These three have a connected relationship, as do align, act, and adjust. In this cycle, though, waste increases instead of value (see Figure 1.5).

Disagree. Conversational waste starts most often in the presence of differences. The disagreement may or may not be obvious. The waste cycle does not care. If the disagreement is significant to what we are trying to accomplish together, waste escalates. Disagreements abound. The likelihood that anyone fully shares my agenda and is aligned automatically with my desires is small. If I am not intentionally searching for intersections, then differences proliferate as weeds do in an untended garden.

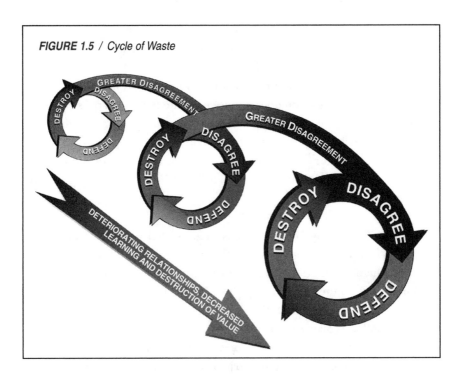

FIGURE 1.5 / Cycle of Waste

There are three elements in disagree conversations—and they are poor, disconnected relatives of intersect, invent, and invest: *separate, protect, and settle*. In the waste cycle, I *separate*, wittingly or unwittingly, from anyone who does not share my view. I do whatever I can to *protect* my viewpoint (cajole, convince, argue, persuade, and manipulate), and then *settle* on a course of action. The protecting and settling tends to be mightily influenced by who has more power and authority. If you have the authority, you can mandate a course of action and settle for (as in "put up with") whatever level of partnership you have. If you lack authority, you settle for the course of action whether or not you actually agree. Does any of this sound familiar?

■ ■ ■

"What we have here is a failure to communicate."

STROTHER MARTIN IN *COOL HAND LUKE*

An explanatory note: There is an aspect of human brain function that is prominent in the waste cycle. Our biological survival is being chronically attended to by a part of the brain called the amygdala. This ancient, almond-shaped bit of brain is constantly orchestrating an environmental scan for any possible threat to our well-being. The moment the amygdala senses anything that is *or might be* a threat, it commandeers our bodies to combat that threat. When the amygdala takes over, it wants a fast answer to this question: "Do I fight with it, flee from it, immobilize, or submit?" This "fight, flee, freeze, appease" response figures greatly into how we communicate in the face of difference. The brain does not discriminate between a physical threat and a social threat. In a meeting, a perceived insult triggers the same biological response as a physical assault. Sometimes this response is damaging to our most essential purposes. In Chapter 2, we will delve into *bioreaction*, the universal response to threat. We will fully explore how to manage bioreaction in our own best interests.

Defend. After disagreement comes defense. If I got what I wanted in the face of our differences, I now expect everyone involved to act exactly as I would. This is irrational. Those who lose the disagreement tend to be compliant, not committed. Nonetheless, I expect the losers to be committed, creative, and resourceful. When they are not, you can count on me to defend myself and blame them.

If I lost in the face of our differences, I defend my position by pointing out poor results. I am now longing to prove that we should never have done it your way.

The winners and losers wittingly and unwittingly defend their original position. Contrast this scenario with people standing together for a worthy purpose and coinventing multiple ways of succeeding. It is not a pretty comparison.

Destroy. Separated people with disconnected expectations of one another are usually not happy with the results. So, we have to explain the failure. Those explanations often destroy any possibility of recovering alignment.

If I am the dominant party, my faith in those I counted on is shaken. I am likely to find fault with the people who did not do as I would have done. I punish to get the poor performers in line. I consider finding better people.

If I am lower on the power ladder, gossip is my method of destruction. Hallway discussions with sympathizers are peppered with "I knew it wouldn't work." The powerful people being blamed are not around. I cannot (or will not) confront them; instead, I will quietly undermine them.

Either party can blame the circumstances and destroy any chance for learning and adjustment. Occasionally, I destroy my own contribution by wallowing in shame and guilt.

Destruction is a function of disconnected disappointment. The residue of our separated distress is greater disagreement. Relationships are destroyed, learning is lost, and organizational capability declines. The cycle of waste goes on.

■ ■ ■

"It's not whether you win or lose;

it's how you place the blame."

RALPH KINER, BASEBALL GREAT

What you do *not* see in the cycle of waste are mutually committed people putting their heads together to see what they can do to make a valuable difference. More likely are lost energy, increased worry, and little faith in turning the tide.

This vicious cycle of waste continues unless one or more of the following happens:

- A major emergency melts differences and resets the relationship.
- People come and go, and a new set of relationships is at work.
- An intentional shift is made to the cycle of value.

Conversation works as a cycle of value or a cycle of waste. The behaviors in the two cycles are rooted in conversations. If you do not alter the conversations, you will not alter the behavior. We all know we should be more patient, confront our disagreements honestly, and not give in to blame and gossip. Mandating those behavior changes does not work, because they are a function of conversation. Have the right conversations at the right time— *that* is how you alter behavior. We keep changing people (trying to fix them or replace them), when all we really have to do is change the conversation.

The cycle of waste is well embedded and requires little or no study and practice. The cycle of value is natural and gratifying. However, it will require study and practice. In *Time and the Art of Living*, Robert Grudin makes a comment that truly fits mastering the cycle of value: "Hard work crystallizes into pleasure as you grow in skill."

The rest of *The Communication Catalyst* is dedicated to the hard-won pleasure of valuable conversation. Remember, Rev Baker has a bit to say on the subject. We'll hear from Rev right after the chapter summary.

CHAPTER SUMMARY

The Heart of the Matter

Communication in any business environment, especially in the form of conversation, causes or accelerates value or waste; it is the foundation for all coordinated achievement.

In dynamic times, our rate of adjustment to changing conditions and purposes is the source of value. Every conversation we are in is an occasion for valuable adjustment. There is a conversational cycle of value: *align, act, adjust.* Apply the cycle of value to everyday business challenges and create substantially more value than waste.

Definition of Terms

- *Value:* What customers and investors are willing to pay for that employees are willing and able to provide.
- *High-velocity value:* Mutual value that is identified, delivered, and paid for faster than normal.
- *Waste:* Any use of resources that *does not* create value for customers, investors, and employees.

Static and Dynamic Business Environments

Value track: The ability to recognize and respond to static and dynamic opportunities is fundamental to producing high-velocity value.

Different conditions call for different approaches.

Static Imperatives	Dynamic Imperatives
Prediction	Learning and adjustment
Economies of scale	Rate of adjustment
Following instructions	Valuable conversations
Rigid roles	Adaptive roles
Separate organizations	Connected organizations
Experience and credentials	Ability to learn and adjust

Waste track signals:

- Chronic complaints that stay unresolved
- Poor track record of executing agreements
- Conflicting charters (lack of shared purpose)
- Organizations withholding information from each other
- Wasteful explanations
- Relationships deteriorating

The Intersection: The Source of High-Velocity Value

Value track: Intersection conversations are about integration, not domination. Integrating the agendas of customers, investors, and employees produces more value with less time, money, and stress.

The Axioms of the Intersection

1. All humans have purposes, concerns, and circumstances.
2. If someone perceives that you are unaware or disrespectful of his or her purposes, concerns, and circumstances, he or she will consider you a threat. And, he or she will actively avoid, resist, and undermine any significant threat. This creates waste.

3. If someone perceives that you are aware and respectful of his or her purposes, concerns, and circumstances, he or she will join you in conversation. He or she will share information, coinvent solutions, and move into action. This creates value.

The Architecture of Conversation: An Introduction

There is a reliable design for conversations that produce value and for those that produce waste. Learn and adhere to the design to accelerate value.

The Cycle of Value

Conversation builds. Relationships get stronger, learning occurs, trust and creativity increase. Value accelerates value.

Elements of the cycle of value:

- *Align* conversations unite people, time, and money.
  - *–Intersect* separate purposes to reveal shared purpose.
  - *–Invent* ideas for achieving shared purpose.
  - *–Invest* time, money, and key people in ideas that advance shared purpose.
- *Act* conversations make commitments explicit and launch action.
  - *–Engage* with those who must carry out action, connecting their best interests to the purpose that is at stake.

–Clarify precise expectations and measures of success.

–Close the question of accountability, requesting explicit promises.

- *Adjust* conversations translate experience into improvement.

–Review measures and results.

–Renew efforts and relationships.

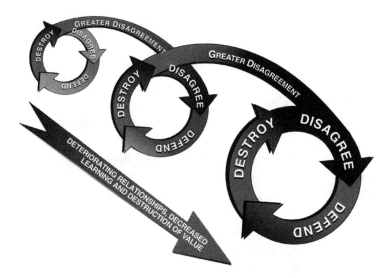

The Cycle of Waste

Value deteriorates; waste accelerates. Relationships are lost, organizational capability and creativity decline.

Elements of the cycle of waste:

- *Disagree* conversations accelerate waste by focusing on differences.
- *Defend* conversations focus on defending individual agendas and original positions.
- *Destroy* conversations blame, justify, and gossip away any possibility of recovering alignment.

Action to take: If elements of the waste cycle are present, an intentional shift to the cycle of value is called for. If you do not alter the conversation, you will not alter the behavior.

REV LESSON

■ ■ ■

The Fishin' Blues

"Here's a little tip I would like to relate: Many fish bites if you got good bait."

TAJ MAHAL, *FISHIN' BLUES*

"Walker, is there** anything else you want to say about the situation?" Rev looked at me across the granite counter. I paused, glanced at my wrist, and took a deep breath. I'd been talking for quite a while.

"No, Rev. I think I've said enough. I'm sure you're bored enough with my problems anyway."

Rev smiled slightly. "You know, Walker, a person can be sure *and* wrong. I'm not bored at all."

That was far from the last time that Rev made a quiet, disturbing statement to me. I thought back over my story, wondering where I might be both sure and wrong.

I'd entered Rev Baker's Beautiful Central Texas Hill Country Barbecue Café about an hour earlier. Rev saw me and started singing *Walk right in, sit right down,* a line from a '60s pop song. Rev enjoyed music. He had an old jukebox, one of those with bubbles running through neon-lit tubes, right in the middle of the café. You didn't even have to put money in it. Sometimes he'd walk over and play a song to punctuate a point he was making.

After polite greetings, I tried to sound confident and casual. "Rev, you promised me a barbecue sandwich, so here I am. I'm not one to pass up a free meal."

"Walker, I invited you for a conversation. The sandwich was just bait. You seemed all beaten down and I thought we should talk." Rev kept his eyes on me until I spoke.

"Well, I'm just busy and tired, no big deal."

"Walker, busy and tired do not necessarily go together. You can be busy and winnin' and not be tired at all. Now, if you're busy and losin' that'll make you tired . . . real tired."

I thought, What am I doing here? I'm going to tell a cook my complex business problems? Not very likely. I'm getting ready to quit, anyway. Soon they'll be someone else's problems. I formulated my response.

"Rev," I said, "MightyTek is struggling with a bad economy. All the high-tech companies are. Hardly anyone is winning at the moment."

"Someone is winnin'. They either have better conditions or they are playing the game better or they made up a better game. Maybe all three. My grandpa was a merchant marine, Walker. He used to say, 'Smooth water never made a great sailor.' It sounds to me like you've given up on being a great sailor, son. I'll bet you've got Resume Writer 9.0 on your C-drive right now."

I flinched. How did he know that? And since when did a guy running a barbecue joint talk about software and C-drives?

"Walker, if talking to me doesn't fit for you, then don't force it," Rev said. "I'll give you that sandwich and you think on it for a bit. Do you want your brisket sliced or shredded?"

I told Rev my choice (shredded) and watched him deftly assemble my sandwich. He poured a glass of iced tea for me. Before the tea glass touched the counter, Rev spun a square napkin in the air. The napkin slid into place neatly under the glass just in time. Then Rev told me he was going to go visit customers. That made sense, since it looked like all the tables in Rev Baker's barbecue café were full. He walked away as I stewed in my unhappy thoughts.

At MightyTek, I was leading two major product development efforts. They were both far behind schedule. The income they were supposed to provide was late and I was on the hot seat. I did not think it was my fault, because I was laboring in impossible conditions.

I had inherited a research and development team filled with cynical engineers. Two of them thought they should have my job and were resentful, unproductive partners. My boss came from the sales side of the house and did not understand anything about product development. She thought she did, and that was a big problem. We called her "Shotgun Sharon," because she made big, impulsive commitments to upper management without even knowing if they were reasonable. The only time my staff felt like a team was when we were complaining about Sharon Scott. Our latest complaints were about her cutting our budget without changing any promises to the higher-ups. Also, Shotgun Sharon reacted to input like she was allergic to it. What a mess. The situation was impossible and getting worse. I wanted out, but the job market was not great.

I sighed and picked up my glass of tea. As I sipped, I noticed some words printed at the bottom of the napkin. Below the wet ring that blurred the café name I read:

There are more things in Heaven and Earth, Horatio,
Than are dreamt of in your philosophy.
William Shakespeare, *Hamlet, Act 1 Scene 5*

I thought, "This is one strange barbecue joint. Who *is* this Rev Baker guy?" The implications of the Shakespeare quote rattled me a little. Then a gray blur entered my peripheral vision.

"Hello."

I looked up to see a face I knew, though only through newspapers and television. Sara McGregor was the founder and CEO of the most successful venture capital fund in Texas. The current media adulation was about how she and the fund somehow emerged from the dot-com crash in strong financial condition. "Sara Mac," as she was known, made millions as one of the early executives in Austin's famous computer company. Those millions launched The McGregor Fund.

I shook the offered hand as she introduced herself. I said, "I know who you are, most everyone does. I'm Walker O'Reilly." I looked under my stool to see if she had left some personal item earlier.

"May I offer some advice, Walker O'Reilly?"

I looked at this impeccably tailored icon and stumbled through, "Of course." It is not that easy to talk while in opened-mouth awe.

"I overheard some of your conversation with Rev. Confide in him and then listen. I know people who would pay thousands of dollars for the advice he is prepared to give you for free." This wildly successful, widely respected executive looked directly into my eyes. She flashed a smile, nodded slightly, and walked toward the café door.

"Bye, Mac!" Rev's voice boomed across the café.

"See you soon, Rev," Sara Mac boomed right back. I watched her go, listening to her shoes hit the gravel parking lot. Then I think I closed my mouth.

Rev Baker was obviously a man superior to my first impression. When he returned, I spilled my sorry tale into his lap. Then he asked me again if I had anything else to say.

"Rev, I can't think of anything else right now."

"Fine, Walker, fine. I have a question for you. Do you want help or pity?"

"What? I don't want pity. Of course I want help." I was offended by the implication.

"OK, Walker, I'll take you at your word and give you your first lesson in world-class problem solving."

That got my attention. I leaned forward.

Rev's large, dark face leaned a little closer to mine. "You talk like someone who is proving doom, not reporting facts. Here's the lesson: *If you want to solve really big problems, first you've got to stop proving that you can't.*"

Rev walked away and tended to his café. All of my "yeah, but" reactions were sticking in my throat. When he came back I said, "Alright, Rev, you got me. I want help and I'll stop getting in the way of your helping me."

"Walker, let's make a deal. I'll show you some things to think through and do differently *only* if you promise you'll take one new action by the end of the day tomorrow. If you get value out of the action, come back. You don't get value, we stop."

I agreed. Rev grabbed one of those square napkins and started to sketch out a design. He called it a "conversational cycle of value." Thus began the first of my "bevnap" lessons (that's what Rev called the napkins, which was I think short for beverage napkin). Over time, my collection of bevnap insights became more valuable than my MBA.

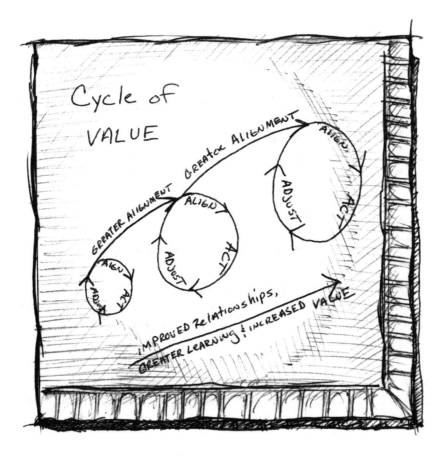

Rev said that:

- I needed to look at my two projects as networks of conversation rather than hierarchies of authority.
- Anyone who really knows how conversation affects behavior can lead high-performance teams through difficult times.

- Any shared achievement (for example, the projects I was leading) requires three conversations. The first is the launchpad for the second and third.
  1. *Align:* get together.
     –Locate a point of common interest and translate it into a shared purpose (Rev calls that "intersect").
     –Give the new "mutual purpose group" chances to brainstorm new ideas and sort them for value to the shared purpose (Rev calls that "invent").
     –Allocate time, money, and key people to the valuable ideas so the shared purpose group knows what they are *really* doing to support the purpose (Rev calls that "invest").
  2. *Act:* produce results together.
     –Clarify accountabilities.
     –Secure genuine commitments from specific people.
     –Move into action to fulfill the promises.
  3. *Adjust:* learn and adjust together.
     –Summarize results early and often.
     –Note which conversations (align, act, adjust) are strong or weak; try changing the *conversations* before you decide to change the *people* involved (as in fix them or fire them).
     –Appreciate and acknowledge valuable contributions.
     –Translate failure into actionable lessons.
     –Share lessons and improvements with the shared purpose group.

Rev drew a wheel divided into align, act, and adjust sections. He said they work together like a value cycle, one with its own source of fuel. Rev also said I should only claim value for what MightyTek employees provide that customers and share-owners pay for.

"Walker," Rev said, "the value is at the intersection, not in your disconnected opinion. In a business, people tell you what they value in a real plain way: how they spend time and money. It's a bad fisherman who thinks he is doing a great job fishing but the fish just won't bite. Fish bite when you got something that interests them."

Rev made a lot of sense, so I took a lot of notes.

"This is a lot to swallow, Walker. If we keep gettin' together, I'll explain how all these conversations work. For now, let's move on to what new action you're gonna take. Tell me, Walker, who are you having the most trouble working with?"

"My boss, Shotgun Sharon."

Right then, one of the cooks walked by and said, smiling at me, "Now you listen up when Doctor Baker is talking. He only does it after an awful lot of listening."

I looked at Rev and said, "So, are you a doctor *and* a minister? Pills and prayers from the same man?" I thought I was being clever. Rev ignored my questions and went back to the subject of my boss.

"Do you want some coaching, Walker?" I nodded yes.

"Here's my coaching, son, in three pieces. First, stop calling Sharon Scott Shotgun Sharon. Don't call her anything she would not want to answer to, even when you're talking to yourself. You got that?"

I nodded again. I could tell that would make more sense than I'd fully understood yet.

"Next," Rev continued, "make three lists regarding Ms. Scott. First, any *purposes* she has that you can respect. Second, any *concerns* she might have that you can respect. Y'know, things that might get in the way of her purposes. Third, any important *circumstances* you know she has to deal with.

"Last, write a description of Ms. Scott using only the words on your three lists. This is important: No words other than the ones on your three lists. Read your description right before you hook up with her next and see if it helps any. If it does, you call me and we'll have another sandwich. If not, we won't."

I thanked Rev for his time and promised to take the three-part coaching to heart.

"That's good, taking it to heart . . . if that means you take it to action, too," Rev said.

"Walker," he went on, "you are a good man, a valuable man. The only reason you suffer so much is because you have big purposes that truly matter to you. The sufferin' is just nature's way to remind you of what matters. If you didn't have purposes that matter, you wouldn't care so darn much about how things are going.

"It's time to shift your attention from the sufferin' back to the purposes you suffer about. Otherwise, you've got your attention on the very things you don't want. Then you can give yourself another chance. I've found that it's best if I don't give up too quick on something that matters enough to suffer over."

I felt my mouth open and my eyes widen just barely. I was seeing something important, and it had not come into full focus yet.

"Oh, and Walker, you have a really fast trigger 'bout what things mean. We'll talk about that next time, if there is one. You see, the name 'Rev' has got nothing to do with ministry, and my doctorate is in social psychology, not medicine."

Rev winked at me and straightened up from leaning on the granite counter. He waved as he turned to go into the kitchen. I watched him through the opening as he put on a white apron over his denim shirt. I pushed my stool back and he looked up. A smile split his dark, leathery face. His eyes were bright, clear, and relaxed.

As I left I could hear Rev singing. Someone in the kitchen joined in:

"Here's a little tip that I would like to relate,
Many fish bites if you got good bait,
I'm a goin' fishin', yes I'm goin' fishin',
And my baby's goin' fishin' too."

I left Rev Baker's barbecue café that day more confused than when I entered. Somehow I was more hopeful, though. It seemed strange for both confusion and hope to get bigger at the same time. Interesting lunch, that's for sure.

CHAPTER TWO

VALUABLE PERCEPTION
The Leader's Edge

■ ■ ■

"Not to mince words, Mr. Epstein, we don't like your boys'
sound. Groups of guitarists are on the way out."

DECCA RECORDS EXECUTIVE, REJECTING THE BEATLES IN 1962
BRIAN EPSTEIN, *A CELLARFUL OF NOISE*

The value of action is dictated by the value of perception, and yet few people cultivate their perceptive talent. Perception makes all the difference, however. Shift your perception habits from *ordinary* to *high value,* and you will produce more benefit in less time than you ever have before. You will be a *communication catalyst.*

Consider two people in a similar situation: Both are walking their dogs in the woods, and both are wearing corduroy pants as they brush past vegetation on the walk. They exit the woods, say goodbye, and head for their respective homes.

Person #1 enters her garage and notices that her corduroy pants are covered in burrs, and so is the dog. The burrs, small round bundles of tiny thorns, are hard to remove, and she pricks her hand when trying to pull them from the pants. She thinks, "This is annoying! These pants are ruined." I'll just cut off the legs and make shorts. The dog will have to be shaved.

Person #2 enters a similar garage and notices burrs all over his pant legs and his dog. The thorny burrs are hard to remove and prick his hand as he pulls on them. Person #2 thinks, "This is fascinating! I barely brushed against these burrs, and they *really* stick to the corduroy. Hmmm, I wonder if I could design a fastener that worked like this?" Person #2 is George de Mestral, the Swiss inventor of Velcro. His curiosity led him to examine the burrs under a microscope. De Mestral's observations became the basic design for the hook and loop fasteners now in use throughout the world.

Similar circumstances + different perceptions = different outcomes. If we compare the perceptions in terms of what they provide that customers and shareowners would be willing to buy, a single pair of shorts loses to a revolutionary new fastener. High-value perception is a craft worth cultivating.

Learning a craft is distinct from having talent. *Talent* is the special natural ability with which a person is blessed. *Craft* is the collected concepts and skills that are fundamental to success in a particular area of achievement. You can cultivate a talent by mastering a craft.

A talented singer, for instance, may be blessed with a clear, melodious voice but be weak at the craft of singing. She may not know how to use her voice in a way that protects the health of her vocal cords. She may not know the exercises and drills that will help her expand her vocal range. She may not know the difference between straight tones and vibrato and so cannot provide either when asked. Craft is the accumulated wisdom of many people over many years in a particular arena, in this case singing. Talent is the unique ability of one.

Some people are blessed with natural perceptive talent. They see what others do not, and they hear what others miss completely. They naturally connect things in valuable ways and see possibilities where others see none. Then there are the rest of us, the more normally gifted. Whether brilliant or normal, none of us has to settle for our current perceptive ability. We can abandon the popular view of perception as mere biological reaction beyond our personal control. Instead, we can treat perception as a noble craft worth cultivating.

■ ■ ■

"One of life's most fulfilling moments occurs in that split second when the familiar is suddenly transformed into the dazzling aura of the profoundly new. These breakthroughs are too infrequent . . . and we are mired most of the time in the mundane and trivial. The shocker: what seems mundane and trivial is the very stuff that discovery is made of. The only difference is our perspective, our readiness to put the

pieces together in an entirely new way and to see patterns
where only shadows appeared just a moment before."

EDWARD LINDAMAN, *THINKING IN FUTURE TENSE*

Mastery of any craft includes at least:

- *Awareness* of how the craft works
- *Methods* for practice and skill building
- *Personal stakes* that make personal change worthwhile

Awareness of How the Craft of Perception Works

The craft of perception is challenging mainly because of the popular belief that we have no control over what we perceive. The normal view is that
sight, hearing, touch, taste, and smell operate independent of creativity. Supposedly, our senses just report what is "there," and *then* we assert our free will.
At Conversant, we have found that we can assert our free will in how we perceive information as well as in how we respond to it. This is very good news.
Tennis, baseball, squash, and racquetball all share the aim of hitting the ball
in order to win the game. In each, great hitters are adept at "picking up" the
ball early. Steffi Graf's match-winning tennis shots did not start when she
struck the ball. They started with her visual awareness of the ball coming at
her. Barry Bonds's home runs in baseball do not begin when the bat connects with the ball; they begin when his eyes connect with it. These athletes'
greatness lives first in how they receive information and second in what they
do with the information. This is a perfect parallel with how communication
creates value.

Think of a time you said something valuable. Perhaps you were in a meeting and voiced a comment that solved a problem or revealed an opportunity.
Maybe it was in a one-on-one conversation, and you said something especially
insightful. In either case, value did not begin in the moment of speaking; that
insightful comment began in how you listened. Valuable perception is the
source of valuable speaking. Value begins with the quality of impression (e.g.,
listening), not the quality of expression (e.g., speaking). Very few people work
on improving the quality of perception. It is an improvable craft, however.

At Conversant, we sort perception into two categories: *ordinary* and *high
value*.

Ordinary Perception: Value by Accident

Ordinary perception is governed by unconscious biological reactions. These biological responses occur without our personal permission. They are not chosen; they happen to us. We cannot eradicate them and would not want to even if we could. We do need to understand ordinary perception as deeply as high-value perception, however. Only then can we note when it does damage and switch to high value.

Answer, if you will, the following two questions about ordinary perception:

1. *What is the speed of an opinion?* Does it take hours to form an opinion? Seconds? How long does it take for you to agree or disagree, like or not like, approve or disapprove?
2. *How long does it take someone to understand your purposes and concerns?* Does genuine understanding take less or more time than forming opinions?

We have asked thousands of people those two questions. The overwhelming majority says that the speed of an opinion is faster than the speed of understanding. This opinion-understanding gap explains a lot of miscommunication and frustration. How do we access the intelligence of a group when people have opinions *prior* to understanding one another? Why do rational humans allow this opinion-understanding gap to exist? What does this have to do with seeing Velcro where others only see shorts? Let us look at some relevant factors.

Perception is more a filter than a camera. The perceiver always affects the perceived. It is impossible for you to see, hear, taste, touch, or smell anything without habit, history, belief, biology, and culture coloring your perception. What you see may not be so. For instance, when you look down a railroad track, off in the distance the tracks come together in a single line. Do they really? When someone's suggestion occurs to you as stupid, is it really? As C.S. Lewis said, "What you see and hear depends a good deal on where you are standing."

■ ■ ■

"Logic is in the eye of the logician."

GLORIA STEINEM

Perception filters can be *automatic* or *proactive*. Proactive filters are central to high-value perception. Automatic filters are imposed on us and are based on forces not of our making. They do, however, greatly impact our perceptions. Consider the following profile:

- Male
- Born in 1950
- Lifelong citizen of the United States
- Grew up in Texas and Louisiana
- Only language is American English

All of these biological and social influences automatically filter this man's perceptions. The most indefensible claim he could make might well be, "I am unbiased and completely open to what you have to say." He is not alone. Every one of us shares his dilemma.

If perception is inexact, then proving a perception right is impossible. The various filters that color our view make a pure, unbiased perception impossible. Opinions are based on perceptions, so we can never rationally be sure our opinions are *the* truth. No matter how much evidence we gather, we will not achieve absolute proof of a perception.

■ ■ ■

"Sebastian said, 'Truth is the bottom of a bottomless well.'"

KATHERINE HEPBURN, IN *SUDDENLY LAST SUMMER*

Instant opinions are often a biological response to threat rather than a thoughtful deduction.

The portion of the brain known as the amygdala, as mentioned in Chapter 1, is at the heart of every human's danger-detecting system. When a threat arises, the amygdala wants a *fast* answer to this question: "Do I fight, flee, freeze, or appease?" A fast selection is very good for surviving physical danger. In fact, the people who reacted too slowly are not our ancestors; they did not last long enough to procreate.

■ ■ ■

"All animals have to protect themselves from dangerous

situations in order to survive, and there are only a limited

number of strategies that animals can call upon to deal with

danger. Isaac Marks, who has written extensively on fear,

summarizes these as withdrawal (avoiding the danger

or escape from it), immobility (freezing), defensive

aggression (appearing to be dangerous or fighting back),

or submission (appeasement)."

JOSEPH LEDOUX, *THE EMOTIONAL BRAIN* (PARAPHRASING AND EXPLAINING

COMMENTS FROM ISAAC MARKS, *FEARS, PHOBIAS AND RITUALS*)

A hyperfast response to threat is not always helpful. Unfortunately, the brain is not able to differentiate between physical threat and social threat. Anything that differs from your purposes, concerns, and circumstances can trigger the amygdala. Precisely then, the amygdala bypasses the cerebral cortex and you fight, flee, freeze, or appease. In this moment, instant opinions make their appearance. Think of the last time you were involved in a serious difference of opinion. Recall your reactions: Were any of them fight, flee, freeze, or appease responses? Do not bother being embarrassed or defensive. Bioreaction is not a personal flaw. Fighting, fleeing, freezing, and appeasing are reactions that happen to us all.

The amygdala favors fast assessments. Rapid opinions allow for rapid reactions to threat, and that is good for biological survival. The amygdala, given its lust for speedy assessment, automatically connects what is happening now with what has been experienced before. At Conversant, we call this phenomenon *fast past matching*. Quickly matching what is happening now with something from the past can be useful. Knowing the way home is a function of matching, as is pattern recognition in general. It is not always good for creative perception, however. In the words of T.S. Eliot, sometimes "knowledge imposes a pattern and falsifies."

Thoughtless, rapid reactions occur in ordinary conversation. Here is a brief experiment you can do. Think of the last time someone said or did something that occurred to you as rude or insulting. If you can, put yourself back in that moment. Which of these reactions is closer to your actual thoughts at the time?

1. "That was rude!"
2. "That seemed rude. I wonder if I misinterpreted him."

Most people tell us the first, not the second. When thoughtless fast past matching is running the show, we have irrational confidence in our first perception. We give ourselves no chance to differentiate valuable pattern recognition from careless, wasteful opinions.

As soon as I can explain my perceptions, I assume they are correct and defend them. People tend to settle for a perception as soon as it makes sense to them. For example, I will tend to stop exploring what you say to me as soon as I make sense of what you said. The fastest available explanation comes from my memory, because understanding your actual intention takes longer than a fast past match. The result: I am far more likely to relate to you in terms of what you remind me of than in terms of your unique communication.

Then, the defense begins. I must defend a perception I believe is true, because I will *always* defend reality. What if the perception has only negative implications for my important purposes? For example: "My most important employee is impossible to manage." "No customer will buy our old products." "My boss is close-minded." "Those two suppliers will not work together." "I cannot get through to my 16-year-old child." Each of these, if it occurs to me as *true*, must be defended and thrusts me into a cycle of waste. Polluted instant perceptions masquerading as truth have great destructive power.

Ordinary perception is a reliable chain of events. A stimulus causes an instant perception, fast action and a cascade of effects ensue, and I automatically defend it all. This chain is an asset when my reactions are coincidentally helpful to my purposes. However, it can be a serious liability when my reactions damage my own important purposes.

- *Stimulus.* Something interferes with getting what I want. The spectrum of concerns ranges from inconvenience to mild apprehension all the way to terror.
- *Perceived threat.* I perceive a stimulus as a threat. Threat thoughts include "disagree," "disapprove," "unfair," "stupid," "wrong," and "Oh, no!"
- *Rash action.* Avoiding the threat leads to a cascade of effects that issue from and reinforce the threat perception. I fight, flee, freeze, or appease, and launch the cycle of waste mentioned in Chapter 1 (disagree, defend, and destroy).
- *Defense of the action.* You are now an unconscious magnet for evidence that defends your perceptions and actions. Being right occurs to the

amygdala as safety, so I defend my perceptions even when they hurt my creativity and resourcefulness. The automatic filter for all post-perception input is a question: "What proves me right?"

People rarely notice that their impassioned explanations for a rash action usually come to mind *after* the action. Here is an example of ordinary perception cascading into a cycle of waste. After you read this episode, we recommend that you lay the book down and find a story of your own. As we all have discovered, reality is a terrific accelerant for learning.

Several years ago, we became involved in a messy dispute. A billion-dollar company had acquired a $50 million company. The owners of the smaller enterprise were preparing to sue the larger company and its CEO for fraud. The acquiring CEO was hiring attorneys and preparing for the fight. Simultaneously, he was requesting that Conversant consult with him regarding cultural integration of the disrupted and confused workforce of the smaller company.

We made a recommendation to the CEO: Give us a chance to reconcile the dispute. We were confident that cultural integration would be a lot easier without legal combat. The CEO was not thinking in terms of reconciliation at that time; it seemed impossible. After all, he had talked to both owners and they were unreasonable. The problem, the CEO told us, was that "these are not sophisticated businesspeople, and they have unrealistic expectations." We asked for a two-day chance to reconcile and he agreed. "It will look good in court if we give it a try," he said.

We spent a day interviewing all the parties. The facts we uncovered kept leading to more conversations, until we arrived at the following chronology:

1. The parties had signed a letter of intent for the purchase, although either party could still exit the deal.
2. A major potential customer told the CEO they were not going to sign a multiyear contract, because the CEO lacked certain capabilities in his supply chain (stimulus). The CEO thought that he needed this contract to achieve promised revenue goals, and that the missing capability was a deal killer (perceived threat).
3. The CEO told the customer that he was acquiring that capability (the new acquisition had the missing competence). The major customer, thus assured, signed the multiyear purchase agreement (rash action: *appease*).

4. As the closing date of the acquisition approached, the sellers began to have second thoughts about going through with the deal. The alarmed CEO made promises he did not have resources to fund (rash action: *appease*) in order to close the transaction.
5. The promises made to the acquired parties were still unfulfilled one year later. When they raised the issue with the CEO, he defended his lack of performance with an attack on their competence as executives (defense: *fight*). Both parties hired lawyers.

Fortunately, we were able to resolve the dispute using the methods we will cover in Chapter 3. Here we simply point to the cycle of waste that comes from ordinary responses to social threats. The cost of the attorneys, our fees, and the lost productivity of many people are real, measurable waste. There are few creative options available once the amygdala commandeers brain function. There are ways, thank goodness, to get the cortex to regain control. It is best to have the whole brain at work in the face of differences and disappointments.

Crucial skill: Observe your own bioreactions. Start looking for bioreactions at work and at home. They will tend to erupt when you are thwarted, embarrassed, angry, disappointed, or inconvenienced. A bioreaction can result from someone cutting you off in traffic, your child saying "no," or someone at work interrupting an important phone call. Notice the rash behaviors that follow: Are they simply fighting (e.g., argument), fleeing (e.g., leaving the scene), freezing (e.g., ignoring the problem), or appeasing (e.g., false agreement)? You cannot correct what you do not observe. The next section shows how to switch to high-value perception. By noticing what most people fail to notice (bioreaction to perceived threat), you set the stage for value.

High-Value Perception: Value on Purpose

A valuable difference can be made by using the perception apparatus to achieve our most important purposes. Such value demands a tidal change from conventional thought. Perception is not a camera; it is a filter that can serve or destroy our purposes. For the extraordinary person functioning as a communication catalyst, purpose governs perception. For the ordinary person, purpose is the unwitting victim of automatic perception. Next, we look at how we turn perception from ordinary to high-value.

■ ■ ■

"The important thing is not the camera but the eye."

ALFRED EISENSTAEDT

Filters are not only automatic; I can proactively place filters between the world and me by asking *valuable questions.* The valuable question is a great ally in steering my own perceptions and, in turn, my own life. To show the power of a valuable question, we focus on a particular form of perception: *listening.*

Start upgrading the value of your listening with this thought: *listening is not neutral.* Listening is biased, and you can turn that fact to your advantage with a valuable question. Changing the question a listener asks radically alters what is heard.

Consider this scenario: A subordinate named John leaves a voice mail asking to talk with you about an important work issue. You are out of the country and in an inconvenient time zone, so you ask him to describe the problem in another voice mail. John calls back and leaves a lengthy message. Later you listen to it four different times. In each case, you focus intensely on a different question you want to research: two bioreactive questions and two valuable questions. Notice how different your findings may be:

- Question #1: "How can I get out of dealing with this problem?"
- Question #2: "What's wrong with John *this* time?"
- Question #3: "What important lesson does this issue teach us?"
- Question #4: "What valuable contribution is John making to me and our business?"

The words in John's message would not change, yet you would hear very different things. Each question filters the speaking through that question and predisposes the findings. Answers that fit the question register very strongly. Answers that do not fit the question register weakly or not at all. The quality of the question dictates the quality of the answer.

■ ■ ■

"Which questions guide our lives? Which questions do we

make our own? Which questions deserve our undivided and

full personal commitment? Finding the right questions

is crucial to finding the right answers."

HENRI NOUWEN

Proactive questioning allows you to be the author of what you hear. Rarely do we examine the questions we find ourselves asking, so we are stuck with ordinary perception. We are stuck with whatever question occurs to us, and we are stuck with the answers that follow. *What you ask gives you your life, so take care with the questions you ask.*

Have you ever been preoccupied with questions that created no value? Most of us could find examples if we looked. When we train and develop people to lead communication courses at Conversant, we upgrade the quality of the questions the new leader asks. For instance, "Do they like me?" is an impotent question compared to "Do they see new, valuable actions to take?" Impotent questions can sneak into a career or a life and steal away years.

There is a *master question* that is the dominating focus for ordinary listening: "What proves me right?" This thoughtless query keeps us bound up in proving positions that have no value. There is also a master question for valuable listening: "What value will I create?" These two questions are the launch points for radically different perceptions. "Am I right?" and "Am I valuable?" are two very different questions in which to dwell.

When history, habit, and biology support my addiction to being right, asking the question "What value will I create?" is a courageous act of will. Shortly, we will cover some methods for shifting from "right" to "value," but those methods will be useless if you are not an agent of value.

Agency may be the most profound choice available to a human being. It may also be the greatest challenge. To be an agent of value means to generate value when it is absent, no matter what the circumstances. Without agency, my life is out of my control, and if it turns out well, it is a happy accident. With agency, my eyes are open and looking for opportunity.

If you are a parent, you know what it means to be an authentic agent. You have given yourself wholeheartedly to the welfare of your children. You are an agent of their welfare, not a hopeful spectator. Agency exacts a price: you have to give up excuses and blame and trade them in for responsibility and creativity. Responsibility and creativity require each other like the concave part of an eyeglass lens requires the convex. They are inseparable aspects of one thing: value. Agency for value is the difference between reading *The Communication Catalyst* and being a communication catalyst.

There is an easy way to tell if you are an *agent of value* or a *critic of value.* (Those do seem to be the two alternatives.) We all care about value, and that care is expressed in one of two ways: causing value or criticizing value. We all have moments when a challenge outstrips what we already know. In those moments, our first response to the question, "What should I do now?"

is often "I don't know." In such a time, what happens after we utter the words "I don't know"? For the critic of value, "I don't know" stops inquiry and creative action (no valuable questions) and stimulates criticism and inactivity. For the agent of value, "I don't know" stimulates inquiry (valuable questions) and creative action. If value is missing and "I don't know" stops you in your tracks, you are not being an agent of value. If "I don't know" launches valuable questions, you are being an agent.

All of us question. The critic is stuck with the first automatic question that comes to mind. The agent can consider various questions and delve into the most valuable. The difference between the critic of value and the agent of value is the difference between "rash" and "intelligent." If you research the etymology of the word *intelligent,* you will find that it means, "to choose among." If I cannot pose a variety of questions about a problem and choose the one with the most potential value, I lack intelligence. Intelligent questioners choose questions that help them achieve their purposes. Rash questioners stick with their first thoughtless question, whether or not it produces value.

It is impossible to oblige anyone to be an authentic agent of value. Just raising the subject with someone can seem presumptuous and arrogant. It is always and only a personal choice, because choice is the essence of agency. That choice is the source of power that enables the upcoming methods to make a valuable difference. As an analogy, consider the relationship of electricity and toasters. The methods of valuable perception are like a toaster, and your agency is like electricity. You bring the electricity. Here comes the toaster.

■ ■ ■

"All means prove to be blunt instruments
if they lack a living spirit."

ALBERT EINSTEIN

Methods for Practicing High-Value Perception

Conversant's perception methods are focused on listening. We have found that listening affords lots of chances to practice, and improvements in listening improve perception overall. As you will see, we care most about how we listen when people differ, because the fate of any work community lives in its capacity to deal with difference.

Valuable listening is a muscle that needs exercise to develop. The exercise involves:

- Climbing the ladder of listening
- Flipping the brain switch

Climbing the Ladder of Listening

Use the ladder of listening as a method of observation and adjustment (see Figure 2.1). We will take you through the ladder one rung at a time, but first some short definitions:

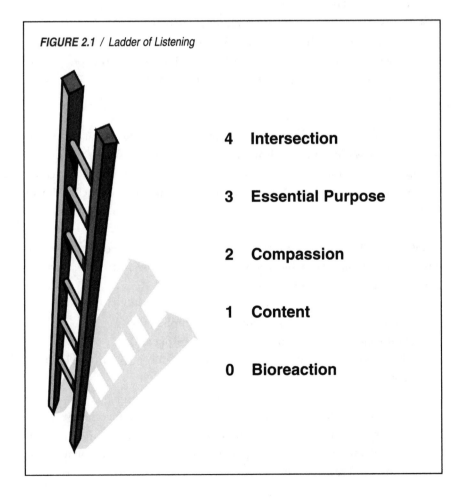

FIGURE 2.1 / *Ladder of Listening*

4   Intersection

3   Essential Purpose

2   Compassion

1   Content

0   Bioreaction

0. *Bioreaction.* Listen through the filter of a threat response. The focus is on your preferences and their transgressions. No value points.

1. *Content.* Focus on what has actually been said. This is conversational hygiene: separate the words that have actually been spoken from what those words might mean. One value point.

2. *Compassion.* Listen to appreciate the speaker's personal emotional relationship to what he is saying without trying to change anything. Compassionate listening allows the speaker to vent safely and recover his or her poise. Two value points.

3. *Essential purpose.* Listen to appreciate the most important purpose at stake for the speaker. This kind of listening is rare, because most people are already responding before they could possibly have grasped the essential purpose of the speaker (political debates are a perfect example). Three value points.

4. *Intersection.* Listen for mutual value, particularly in the face of differences. I focus on how your purposes, concerns, and circumstances intersect with mine. Patterns of potential value emerge as I connect the previously unconnected. This kind of listening is very rare. Four value points.

As you climb the ladder, each rung includes competence at the rungs below. For example, if you are listening with compassion you get two points, because it also includes content, the previous rung, and the ability to catch bioreaction and correct it. Now, more detail on the skills of the ladder of listening.

Bioreaction. The basic bioreaction skill is "catch and correct." Get interested in catching your bioreactions. They will be easy to find, because they occur any time you experience being:

- Dominated (someone is forcing your compliance)
- Diminished (you are embarrassed or disrespected)
- Disrupted (anyone interferes with your preferences, no matter how petty)

Catching bioreaction takes practice, because bioreaction comes wrapped in an explanation that justifies it. Some of the explanations are attractive and self-justifying; they just do not produce any value. Julie Naster, a senior member of our firm, calls those justifications "well-dressed bioreactions."

Action to take: Research your unique fight, flee, freeze, and appease reactions.

- What are your habitual ways of reacting when things are not going your way?
- Make a list and sort your reactions under fight, flee, freeze, or appease.
- Look for a theme that connects your bioreactive habits and label it (e.g., "irritated," "dominating," "confused," "superior," "hurried," or "victimized").
- Research what happens right before you react and you will have an early warning signal. Your signal could be as simple "my jaw clenches."

Catching bioreaction is honorable work, because valuable communication is an art of correction, not perfection. Our bioreactive fits are dishonorable only when we catch them and refuse to correct. The correction allows you to move up the ladder.

Content. Accurately understanding what was said is far superior to an ignorant bioreaction. Sometimes you will find yourself *really* disconnected and relating to the other person as an annoying enemy. In those moments, catching the impending waste and asking, "Could you please say that again?" are heroic moves. The second time through, note exactly what is said and separate the words from what they *might* mean.

The shift from bioreaction to content is significant. It is in this shift that listening goes from bioreaction to learning. Listening to learn is the bedrock of valuable discovery.

■ ■ ■

"Every person I work with knows something better than me.

My job is to listen long enough to find it and use it."

JACK NICHOLS

Action to take: Make learning your listening test. Do you have new information, ideas, or insights after you listen? When you make learning the test for listening, you set the stage for the shift from bioreaction to content. Practice separating verbal content from meaning; it is the first step in listening to learn rather than listening to justify. You will be miles ahead of people who make the test for listening, "Can I explain what they said to my satisfaction?"

Action to take: Interview someone you know who has a strong opinion about a controversial issue.

- Ask: "How did you come to this point of view? What events or situations have you gone through that have brought you to this position?"
- Separate what she actually says from the meaning you attach to the words. Draw a line down the middle of a blank page. Label the left column "What was actually said" and the right column "My explanations of the words." Take notes in the appropriate column as she speaks.
- Catch your bioreactions when she says things that trigger your opinions and return to accurately understanding how she came to this position.

Compassion. Compassionate listening requires that I suspend my own feelings and judgments in order to appreciate yours. I am not trying to "fix" you or solve your problem. I am not agreeing or disagreeing. My opinion is immaterial when you need to be heard; instead, I am giving you a chance to vent while learning about your emotional relationship to the situation.

Action to take: Practice compassionate listening the next three times someone important to you is upset (angry, annoyed, disappointed, etc.).

- Give him your undivided attention.
- Ask him to explain what it was that upset him; focus on understanding his explanations and noticing how you might feel similarly if you had his viewpoint.
- Do not interrupt. Let him talk until he stops on his own. Ask, "Anything else?" when he does stop to make sure there is nothing left unsaid.
- When the venting is complete ask, "What do you think should happen now?"

Many of us discount the value of compassion. It can seem like nothing valuable is happening, but this is not the case. Compassionate listening saves significant time by allowing the upset party to recover his poise and responsibility. His experience of being worthy of your time and respect gives him a place to stand to relook at the problem. Often, he starts to see new actions and generates his own valuable response to the issues at hand.

■ ■ ■

"One of the easiest human acts is also

the most healing. Listening to someone.

Simply listening. Not advising or coaching,

but silently and fully listening."

MARGARET WHEATLEY, *TURNING TO ONE ANOTHER*

 Actions not *to take:* These are waste traps, classic mistakes that displace compassion and lengthen the conversation.

- *Impatient interruption.* If you interrupt an upset person, she will talk even longer to make up for the interruption.
- *Giving advice when she has not asked for it.* If she is not requesting your advice, she is unlikely to hear it and even less likely to act on it. If you have a suggestion, give it only after she is done talking. First ask, "May I make a suggestion?" Do not give the advice unless she says "yes." Remember: What the other person *hears* dictates the value created.
- Asking "Why are you upset?" instead of "What happened that has upset you?" The question "What happened?" evokes the real events and circumstances that prompted the upset. "Why?" evokes justifications of bioreaction.

Essential purpose. If you develop an opinion before you appreciate essential purpose, you are adding time to an interaction without adding value. Most of the time, people react so quickly to what is said that their responses are disconnected from the essential reason the talker is talking. Notice how many times you hear a response to your words that is unrelated to your purpose for talking (pretty frequent, isn't it?).

Consider the difficulty of controlling the flow of the Mississippi River as it pours into the Gulf of Mexico versus controlling it from its source. The closer you are to the source of an issue, the easier it is to address it valuably. At the root of every issue is essential purpose. In general, the reason anything occurs to us as a problem is because an important purpose has been impeded.

For versus against. My purpose is what I am *for*, and my concerns are what I am *against*. In the face of differences, guess where the focus normally goes? Right, it goes to what I am against. This is wasteful, because now I am focused on the very thing I do not want. Listening *for* someone's purpose allows me to connect with what he is committed to rather than what he does not like. *For* is much more efficient than *against*.

Here is an illustration: Lyle, a talented young football player, gets injured. He has been the starting running back on his high school team until a shoulder separation puts him on the sidelines for a month. When Lyle returns to play, he is "not the same running back." He is running for shorter yardage and being tackled sooner. Lyle's teammates are worried that the injury is still a problem, because he is not as fast as he used to be.

Coach Brown is intrigued. He cannot see how a shoulder injury explains running more slowly. Coach Brown invites Lyle to come and look at game films from before and after the injury. Lyle and the coach look at hours of film comparing success and failure and looking for lessons. Lyle grows despondent as he sees himself tackled repeatedly. The coach sees something remarkable, however.

"Lyle, I'm going to play a couple of these back, and I want you to notice what you are looking at. Your eyes are looking at one thing before the injury and another thing afterward. Tell me what you see." After a while, Lyle sits up straight and says, "I see it, Coach! I see the problem!"

"What do you see, Lyle?"

Lyle is excited and relieved. "Before the injury I was looking for open space to run through; after the injury I'm looking for tacklers to avoid. There is nothing wrong with my speed. I'm just adding a split second to every move, that's why I'm slower and that's why I'm tackled so fast!"

Coach Brown smiles broadly. "That's great, Lyle. Go back out there and focus on what *you want,* which is open space, instead of what you don't want, which is tacklers." The next game, Lyle focused on open space and his preinjury performance returned.

Focusing on purpose accelerates value for two reasons:

1. It orients the conversation around what you are *for* rather than what you are *against.*
2. It builds trust and respect.

Every human's moment-to-moment test for trust and respect is "Am I heard?" Focus on what is essential and important to someone. Penetrate bioreactions with a laserlike focus on essential purpose, and that person's experience of trust and respect will soar.

Action to take: The next meeting you attend, keep a note in front of you that says, "What is essential to him?" or "What is important to her?" When anyone speaks, look and listen for his or her most important purpose. This is especially valuable when your first thought is, "I disagree." Here are some tips to help you research purpose.

Once you know the subject being discussed (e.g., a new product launch), ask the other, "For you, what is important about *(subject)?*" This question usually evokes a statement related to purpose.

As the other speaks, sort his preferences into three categories: *purpose, method,* and *specific result.* For example, you might have a purpose to strengthen an area of competence that is important to your major customers; the method you prefer is hiring people who already have the competence; the specific result you prefer is to hire five people with a certain competence in the next three months.

Purpose is the essential driving force. *Method* is the process I choose to forward my purpose. And *specific result is* a particular outcome that serves my purpose. The most important of these is purpose (see Figure 2.2). Many disagreements are conflicts over method or result, not purpose. If you understand purpose, you will be agile and inventive in the conversation.

If you do not understand purpose, you are working in the dark. It is fine to take the first few steps in the dark if you are searching for purpose. As you discover the other's purpose, the lights come on and you can see your way around barriers. Most people do not see another's purpose simply because they do not look for it. They never ask the purpose question and are stuck as soon as they disagree with a result or method. The other person is

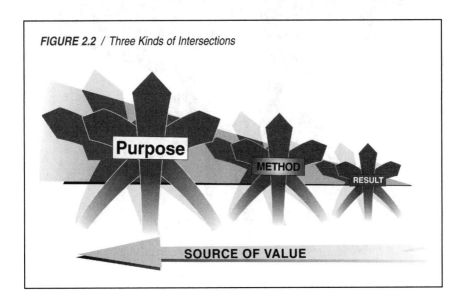

FIGURE 2.2 / *Three Kinds of Intersections*

threatened by the disagreement. Fighting, fleeing, freezing, and appeasing take over and catalyze the cycle of waste. Conversely, when your words emerge from awareness of the other's purpose, you are much better received.

The intersection. In Chapter 1, we spoke of the intersection of employee, customer, and investor viewpoints. Now, we add another factor: mutually observable facts. Four arrows get cluttered (the intersection looks like a big asterisk), so we will use a generic image of an intersection from now on. The intersection is always at least three lanes: my point of view, your point of view, and mutually observable relevant facts (see Figure 2.3).

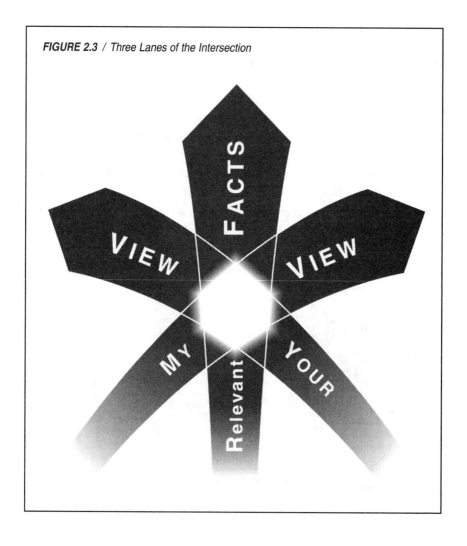

FIGURE 2.3 / Three Lanes of the Intersection

The intersection is *not:*

- Convincing the other to think what I think
- Attacking the flaws in the other's position
- Manipulating the other to get what I want

The intersection *is:*

- An unforced area of mutual interest; that is, common ground where the other's purposes cross mine and relevant circumstances. Ask yourself, "Where do our paths cross?"
- A point of valuable collaboration on which we can build
- A search for themes, patterns, and hidden connections

By relating the normally unrelated, you will reveal previously invisible possibilities (like Velcro). We consider the intersection so important that the entire next chapter focuses on how you find the intersection fast. For now, bother yourself with these thoughts:

- Most folks see differences and pieces, not intersections and patterns.
- People who see intersections create more value with less time and money than people who see differences.
- The moment an intersection is revealed, the other party moves from guarding against your input to interest in your input.

Here is a real example: Shortly after the September 11, 2001, terrorist bombings, we worked with a group of insurance industry sales executives. They felt completely thwarted by the underwriters who were focused on new, unforeseen liabilities in new policies. Salespeople reported clients all over the United States who were ready to buy insurance, but underwriters would not approve policies. One executive said, "Where I live we have a brand new 30-story building that tenants cannot move into because no one will underwrite the insurance." Many of the executives believed there was no common ground. We recommended that the sales executives research the facts and the view of the underwriters to see an intersection of purpose:

- *Sales executives.* They had purposes to serve clients and achieve sales and personal income goals; they were concerned about clients being severely damaged by lack of insurance coverage; they were concerned about current and future income prospects.

- *Facts.* Unanticipated claims of billions of dollars coming from the September 11th disaster; insurance companies reviewing underwriting procedures; sales goals widely reported as below plan; some clients ready to buy; some sales executives reported highly motivated employees with time on their hands as they waited for firm new underwriting guidelines.

- *Underwriters.* They had a purpose to charge appropriately for risks involved, to ensure that their companies remained solvent and successful, and to serve clients that represented a risk acceptable to ownership; they were concerned about making mistakes with huge consequences.

- *The Intersection.* The sales executives offered personnel, data, and client contacts to the underwriters to accelerate the review of underwriting processes and guidelines.

By making their offer to serve the efforts of the underwriters, the sales executives were no longer a threat. Information that was being withheld began to be shared. Large customers began to help, instead of wait on, the review. The review was completed in approximately 25 percent of the time expected. Salespeople know the new conditions now and are adjusting sales efforts accordingly. The building that stood unoccupied is now nearly full of tenants, although the developer is paying sharply higher premiums. It is still a challenging situation, but people are back in valuable action.

Being able to climb the listening ladder to purpose is your place to stand from which you can see high-value intersections and patterns. The next section will tell you what to do when you fall off the ladder.

Flipping the Brain Switch

Flipping the brain switch involves a method you can use to solve this important problem: When the amygdala bypasses the cortex how do you reconnect? In our brains, any perceived threat generates information that is sent to both the thalamus and the cortex. The thalamus is mainly a router of sensory input and does not provide much analysis. The cortex contains most of the master controls of the body, conducts sophisticated analysis, and stimulates creativity. Both the thalamus and the cortex have connections to the amygdala, but the thalamic path that goes directly to the amygdala is twice as fast as the cortical path. The thalamus warns the amygdala of possible danger *before* the cortex analyzes the danger. Imagine getting up in the middle of the night to get a glass of water and hearing a sudden, unfamiliar sound. What happens to your body in about zero seconds? Prior to any analysis, your body tenses, and adrenaline flows to prepare you to fight, flee, freeze, or appease. The amygdala is sending instructions to the rest of your body, completely bypassing the cortex.

Imagine you are in a meeting. Also in the meeting are several people important to your career, including your boss's boss. You make a presentation to the group, in the middle of which your boss's boss stands up and says, "I've got more important things to do than listen to this nonsense" and leaves the room. The exact same amygdala bypass of the cortex occurs, and your body gets lightning-fast instructions to fight, flee, freeze, or appease. Here you are in a moment important to your career, and the cortex is on vacation. Your responses are being dictated by a part of the brain that conducts analysis no more complex than, "Should I kill him, run from the room, faint, or turn over on my back and expose my belly like a scared, small dog?" Many people have done and said things they regret in similar moments. They look back and think, "How stupid! I cannot believe I did that!" The reason the actions are so obviously stupid in retrospect is because the cortex has reentered the conversation.

We need to recover the cortex in the moment of being challenged, not later. The walkout of your boss's boss certainly deserves the attention of your whole brain. Flipping the brain switch so that the cortex reassumes control is a two-step process:

1. Notice that you are having a threat response.
2. Ask a question the amygdala cannot answer.

The amygdala has a short list of subjects it can engage with: fighting, fleeing, freezing, and appeasing. Noticing the threat response awakens the cortex, and valuable questions allow it to reassume control. Suddenly, you begin to see valuable actions rather than impulsive reactions.

Perfect "brain switch" questions are:

- What purpose am I here for? For example: Am I here
  to accelerate time-to-market,
  to raise revenues this quarter, or
  to retain our best software engineers?

- What valuable difference can I make?
- *Who* needs *what* from me now?
- What purpose(s) are they here for?
- How do I turn this into customer and shareowner value?
- *Accurately*, what just happened?

Make up your own brain switch questions. They should be questions related to purposes that matter to you, even when you are afraid.

Action to take: Practice switching back and forth between bioreactive listening and valuable listening (content, purpose, and intersection). It may feel strange to do these exercises, because they involve modeling bioreaction on purpose. When you do something on purpose that you normally do impulsively, you become more vigilant and able to catch and correct. You need a willing partner for these exercises. Ask someone with whom you can be uninhibited.

Exercise: Destroy and build. You and your partner each select an interesting, attractive, or exciting possibility you want to pursue (possible new project, idea for the business, a vacation scheme, etc.). One of you speaks first, and the other focuses on listening.

Listening to destroy (a fight response): Do the following for two minutes and then switch roles.

Speaker: Tell your partner about the possibility that interests you.

Listener: Focus completely on finding flaws in the proposal. Give all of your attention to destroying your partner's interest in this idea. Do not worry about what to say. If you listen destructively, destructive words will spill easily from your mouth.

After the four-minute role-play, stop and both answer this question: What adjectives describe what it was like for you as a speaker to speak into "fight" listening? List as many adjectives as you can in thirty seconds.

Now, switch your focus from destroying to discovering value and building on it.

Listening to build (valuable listening): Do the following for two minutes and then switch.

Speaker: Return to your proposal and again share it with your partner.

Listener: Focus completely on "What value can I build on?"

Afterwards: What adjectives describe what it is like speaking into "build" listening? List and compare with the "destroy" adjectives. Which list accelerates value?

You can do "switching fear to value" exercises using the other bioreactions, too:

- *Flee.* Pick a contentious issue and discuss it. Focus first on listening to change the subject, then switch your focus to "What facts matter to us both?"
- *Freeze.* Using the same issue, focus first on ignoring the issue and then on "What happened and why does it matter to me?"
- *Appease.* Using the same issue, focus first on placate, flatter, and agree and then on "What purpose can I not abandon?"

We strongly recommend that you do some of these exercises, even though they are unusual activities for mature, sophisticated women and men. Reading about them is a weak substitute for actually experiencing them.

■　■　■

"Learning music by reading about it is
like making love by mail."

LUCIANO PAVAROTTI

Personal Stakes That Make Personal Change Worthwhile

In our consulting practice, we have made a repetitive discovery: learning accelerates in the presence of purpose. If you wish to accelerate your personal value, then explore the craft of perception in light of your most important purposes. We have found the following exercise to be highly productive.

Set aside 15 private minutes. List your current most important, meaningful purposes. Write whatever comes to mind for five minutes with no editing. Then, look through the list for themes that run through your purposes. Which theme is the most important to you? That theme is your *senior purpose.* What methods and specific results are you focused on to achieve your senior purpose? *How can the craft of perception accelerate your success?* Pick an insight you found valuable and go to work on it relative to your senior purpose.

It is usually a waste of time to try to remember and apply a lot of new information everywhere at once. Focus on one important aspect of your work and improve your perceptive power there. You will find the benefit spills over into the rest of life. Learning a craft requires practice, which can be disruptive and inconvenient. Make the disruption worthwhile by focusing on an important purpose. Make practicing the craft of perception convenient by linking it to work you already have to do. For the busy person, practice must help, not displace, current priorities. Improving perception, no matter how expert you already are, will help.

Resourcefulness and creativity all start with impression, not expression. John F. Kennedy was a graceful, confident, and powerful speaker. Ted Williams was one of the best hitters in the history of baseball. They had something in common: they were great at taking things *in,* which is why they were so brilliant at putting things *out.* They were masters of the craft of perception.

Rev Baker is about to give Walker O'Reilly a few lessons in valuable perception. Rev does have a unique way of explaining this perception business, and his perception lessons follow the chapter summary.

CHAPTER SUMMARY

The Heart of the Matter

As leaders, we cultivate our perceptive talent so that we can increase value in conversation. The value of action is dictated by the value of perception. Similar circumstances + different perceptions = different outcomes.

Perception does not have to be automatic and choiceless. Valuable perception is a creative craft in which you can excel.

Understanding the Craft of Perception

There are two categories of perception: ordinary and high value.

Ordinary perception is governed by unobserved biological reactions to perceived threat (bioreactions) that launch us into a cycle of waste. If value occurs, it is by accident. Ordinary perception occurs like this:

- *Stimulus.* Something interferes with me getting what I want.
- *Perceived threat.* I perceive the stimulus as a threat. The amygdala does not differentiate between a physical threat and a social threat; anything that differs from my purposes, concerns, and circumstances can trigger a fear response.

- *Rash action.* I rapidly react to the threat by fighting, fleeing, freezing, or appeasing.
- *Defense of the action.* I assume that my perceptions are "the truth" and collect evidence for what proves me right. Polluted perceptions masquerading as the truth have great destructive power.

Perception is more like a filter than a camera. It can serve or destroy our purposes.

- Our filters make a pure, unbiased perception impossible. "Instant opinions" are often a biological response to threat rather than a thoughtful deduction. We can never be sure our opinions are "the truth."
- Perception filters can be automatic or proactive.
  Automatic filters are imposed on us. They are biological and social influences: our habits, history, beliefs, biology, and culture.
  Proactive filters are central to high-value perception. We impose valuable filters by asking valuable questions.

High-value perception is governed by valuable purpose.

- In place of automatic filters, we put proactive filters in place. We ask valuable questions, because the quality of the question dictates the quality of the answer. Instead of "What proves me right?" we ask, "What value will I create?"
- Be an *agent* of value, not a *critic* of value. Let "I don't know" stimulate inquiry rather than despair.

Methods for Practicing High-Value Perception

Climb the Ladder of Listening

Use the ladder as a way to see where you are and adjust to a more valuable place.

0. *Bioreaction.* In response to what happens or is said you are dominated, diminished, or disrupted and then justify and defend your thoughtless bioreactions.

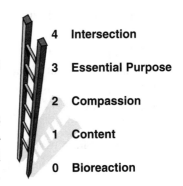

4 **Intersection**

3 **Essential Purpose**

2 **Compassion**

1 **Content**

0 **Bioreaction**

1. *Content.* Focus on what is actually being said and separate the words from what they might mean. Learning is your test for listening, so you will have new information, ideas, or insights after you listen.

2. *Compassion.* Listen to appreciate the speaker's personal emotional relationship to what he is saying without trying to change anything. Ask, "What happened that has you feel this way?" Avoid impatient interruption and advice giving. Have him experience being worthy of your time and respect.

3. *Essential purpose.* Listen to the root of a speaker's issue to understand what her essential purpose is. Focusing on purpose orients the conversation around what she is *for;* her concerns represent what she is *against.* If you understand and can state what is essential to her, you are well on the way to being agile and inventive in conversation.

4. *Intersection.* Listen for mutual value, particularly in the face of differences. Discover common ground by looking for how your purposes, concerns, and circumstances intersect with mine. As you search for themes, patterns, and connections, you will reveal previously invisible possibilities.

Flipping the Brain Switch

Quickly reengage the cortex after the amygdala takes control. This will shift you from bioreactive listening (fight, flee, freeze, and appease) to valuable listening.

Flipping the brain switch is a two-step process:

1. Notice that you are having a threat response.
2. Ask a question the amygdala cannot answer.

Sample brain switch questions are:

- What purpose am I here for?
- What valuable difference can I make?
- What purpose are they here for?
- How do I turn this into customer and investor value?

Personal stakes make personal change worthwhile. Learning accelerates in the presence of purpose. Take time to uncover what themes or purposes are important to you and identify your *senior purpose.* Examine how high-value perception might accelerate your success. Practice valuable perception by linking it to work you already have to do.

R E V   L E S S O N

■ ■ ■

Resistance, Research, Mail, and Sandwiches

When your heart's on fire,

You must realize,

Smoke gets in your eyes.

"SMOKE GETS IN YOUR EYES"

(WORDS BY OTTO HARBACH, MUSIC BY JEROME KERN)

"Listening is not like the mail, Walker. What you receive is not necessarily what got sent."

Rev and I were taking a walk from the café down to the lakefront. The restaurant is at the top of a gentle slope that leads, some 50 yards away, to Lake Austin. We were passing three magnolia trees in full bloom. "Breathe it in, Walker," Rev said. "That magnolia air does a fine job of gettin' the traffic and such out of your lungs." The lush bouquet competed for my attention with the hearty aromas of Rev's barbecue.

"What do you mean, Rev? I sure know what I heard."

"Yes, Walker you do. That doesn't mean you know what she said or what she meant by sayin' it."

"Rev, I really don't know what you're talking about." I had that look that my dog gets, my head tilted slightly sideways to express my confusion. I found confusion annoying back then. If someone said something to me that I did not understand, I was sure I was dealing with an idiot. I would have understood if they had made any sense, right? The problem was I knew Rev was no idiot, and that fact played havoc with my theory.

It was some time later that Rev gave me his take on confusion. He said if I never felt confused, I was jamming everything I heard inside of what I already knew. He said most people are more comfortable that way, but they don't get smarter that way. He told me, "Confusion's the evidence that you've run into a thought you haven't thought before. Nothin' wrong with that. Every confusion you work through makes you smarter. Then you're ready to be confused by things you weren't smart enough to be confused by before."

I was poised to get smarter, because I definitely had run into a thought I had not thought before? Come again? I know what I heard but not what she said?

"Let's go through the meeting," Rev started, "word by word as best you can."

We sat in wrought-iron chairs rooted in the ground several feet from the water's edge, and I gave Rev the details of my last meeting with Sharon Scott, my boss. Rev mostly listened, occasionally inserting "What exactly happened that has you say that, Walker?" I finished with my lament that, though things went well for a while, they sure did not end well.

Rev laughed out loud when I was done. I was a little offended.

Still smiling, Rev said, "Walker, you miss a lot . . . and a lot of what you catch isn't worth keepin'."

"What's so funny, Rev?" I was doing my best not to express my irritation.

"Now, Walker, don't get all offended. I'm on your side. C'mon, I want to show you something."

I was quiet on our walk back to the kitchen. We went in through the back screen door and it banged shut behind us, punctuating our arrival. Rev walked over to a big pot rack above a six-foot stainless steel table and pulled down three utensils. They were full of holes.

"Walker, these are strainers." Rev waved me over as he set the strainers on the table. "Take a look. What's the difference between the three?"

I looked over the nickel-colored kitchen tools. Two were obviously older than the third and had duller finishes and more scratches. The holes, though, were the real difference. "Rev, they have different-sized holes."

"Yeah, they do. What difference does that difference make? What happens that's different when you use one rather than the others?"

"I guess different things get through the strainer depending on how big the holes are," I said.

"That's a fact, Walker. Each strainer catches some things and lets other things go by. Different strainers catch different things. Listening filters operate the same way. In your meeting with Sharon Scott, you caught some things and other stuff went right by you. Like most folks, you're an accidental listener. You got no control over what you hear and what passes by. An accidental listener is like a driver who never puts his hands on the steerin' wheel and then wonders why he gets in so many wrecks."

"Hold on, Rev," I said. "I may not be the most perceptive person on the planet, but I'm not that bad. You make me sound like an idiot."

Rev smiled and said, "Do you know what language the word *idiot* comes from?"

"No." I did not know where he was going with this either.

"It's a Greek word and it means 'separate.' All it takes to be an idiot is to think you're separate from things you're really connected to. You're separating from Ms. Scott because you don't see the connections. That's idiotic all right, but it's not your personal flaw. You're pretty normal. Normal's just not good enough to do the big things you're tryin' to do, Walker."

I took a deep breath. "OK, Rev, it sounds like you caught some things that I missed when I told you about my meeting with Sharon Scott. What did you hear?"

"I'll tell you only if you'll work on how you do it for yourself." I agreed to go to work, and Rev pulled up a stool, shoved another one across the tile floor in my direction, and went back through my report point by point. Of course, you readers are going to hear about my problems, and they may not be the same as yours. I hope you follow along, though, and look hard for anything that might apply to you, too:

- My purpose was for Sharon Scott to include my recommendations in her next update to the division Strategy Council.
- Our meeting was scheduled for 30 minutes and lasted for one hour and 15 minutes; this was our longest one-on-one meeting to date.
- Ms. Scott took notes, which she had not done previously.
- She said my revenue projections for the two products were outdated and asked for new projections based on current market conditions.
- She asked me to compute the "cost of a day" in terms of revenue to MightyTek. She wanted to know how much revenue was delayed for every day we were not in the marketplace.
- She said she was more interested in redesigning our development process to speed introduction than she was in giving me more resources.
- She said she wanted me to attend the next Strategy Council update.
- She asked me to schedule a development process review that she could attend and then ended the meeting.
- I said she was obviously setting me up as the problem by questioning our process and refusing to provide more resources.

"Walker, you're listenin' through a 'what could possibly be wrong now?' filter. You're catching things that could go wrong and everything else passes by. The biggest problem is that you think your first explanation is all that happened. It's the most popular kind of arrogance in the world, son, havin' your first thought on a matter be your last one.

"I see this a bit differently. Ms. Scott stayed in the discussion longer and took notes 'cause she was gettin' more value than she expected. You did what you set out to do, which was to influence the next Strategy Council meeting. Last week, you said that she's never taken time to understand your work, and now she wants to study your most important process. She didn't refuse more resources; she said she would rather see if you could use what you have more effectively before adding resources; and, she offered to help. Ms. Scott asked a question about cost of a day that shows her interest in your contribution to the company. You've triggered two new chances to spend time with her and build a valuable relationship: the process review and the Strategy Council. All in all, this was a valuable interaction."

I was stunned. Rev's analysis reached back in time and completely changed the tone of the meeting. "Rev, how did you get all that and I missed it?" I needed to know.

"Simple, Walker. I was lookin' for it and you weren't."

Then I had a disturbing thought. "Rev, how do you know you are right and I'm wrong about his meeting? What if she is setting me up for a fall?"

"If she is settin' you up, what do you do next, Walker?"

"Just be careful not to give her ammunition and gather information about the things that have hurt our ability to deliver but are not our fault."

"If you go with my version, what do you do next?" Rev looked very interested.

"Well . . ." I had to think about what to do because it was not immediately obvious to me. After a minute, I saw some things. "I guess I'd get the information we talked about together and schedule the process review. I'd see if the new revenue forecasts and cost-of-a-day information justify spending more money to get out faster. Also, I'd meet with my staff to design the process review."

"Walker, do you remember when I said you can only claim value for what Mighty-Tek employees provide that customers and investors are willing to pay for?" I nodded.

"Well, which action plan has a better chance of being valuable for MightyTek employees, customers, and investors?"

After brief reflection I said, "The second one, although it does not protect *me* much."

Rev's face was suddenly serious. "If you won't bet with your career that doing the best thing for employees, customers, and investors is the best thing for you, then you're not cut out to be a business leader. You need to place your bet, Walker. Are you betting your career on being valuable or on something else, like provin' that you're not to blame?"

I told Rev I was going to take a walk and think things over. He nodded, stood up, and walked into the bar. Seconds later, he was back with a long-neck bottle of Rowdy Root Beer. He said, "A walk to the dock with a bottle of Rowdy Root Beer is a fine recipe for makin' sense of things. I'll see you in a while."

I passed the magnolias and two other trees, just the right distance apart to hold Rev's hammock, and then stepped out onto the dock. At the end of Rev's dock is a built-in bench, which I headed for. When I sat down, I noticed a drink holder extending from the armrest, perfectly sized for my root beer. I took a sip, dropped the bottle in place, and reflected on the last week.

I'd taken Rev's coaching and prepared for the meeting with Sharon by writing down purposes, worries, and circumstances of hers that I can respect. It was challenging to only use those words to describe her, but I did it. Before I sent her my meeting agenda, I rewrote it using details about her purposes, worries, and circumstances. When we started the meeting, I used the same vocabulary. She seemed more approachable than normal and more interested. Things went well for a while, but I got very tense when she questioned my revenue assumptions and my use of resources. After that, it all went downhill. Everything pointed toward a blame fest with me as the guest of honor. Rev saw some things I did not and I still did not see how; I thought he was just more perceptive than me. I also wasn't sure I could trust Sharon enough to presume her goodwill.

Still, there was something to Rev's comment about betting my career on creating value rather than avoiding blame and covering my butt. It seemed as if Rev and I were playing two different games on the same field. He was playing the "value game," and I was playing the "blame game." Mine wasn't working out too well, so I became interested in his. I thought that maybe I was scared to presume Sharon's good intent was because I was not confident in my ability to play the game for value. I started to relax some. I really had taken some ground with Sharon Scott, but I wanted Rev's help to hold the ground and build on it. My solo learning curve looked too slow.

I took another sip of root beer, stood up, and stretched. I looked up and down Lake Austin, my eyes lingering for a moment on Mount Bonnell. Funny, I'd been down at the lakefront twice already today, and its beauty had escaped me both times. I went to find Rev.

I walked into the café dining room. Rev was sitting at a table doing paperwork and singing along with the jukebox to Dinah Washington's version of "Smoke Gets In Your Eyes." He looked up, stopped singing, and said, "Welcome back, Walker. What kind of sense have you been makin' of things?"

I shared my dockside reflections with Rev, and he nodded approvingly along the way. I got to my request for more coaching, and he walked to the bar, picked up a

couple of bevnaps, and returned to the table. This napkin lesson was about listening. Rev said ordinary listeners take their first impressions as final. Valuable listeners know they can't be sure their impressions are the absolute, final truth, so
they work on something else: finding a valuable action to take. That starts, he went
on to say, by "taking charge of your ears."

"Walker, the questions you ask change what you see and hear. Take charge of
your questions to take charge of your ears." Rev noted my confused-dog look.

"Walker, look over there where I'm pointin'." I followed Rev's outstretched arm
to a corner of the room. I could see a wooden service station with full shelves
against a wall under a light fixture. "What am I pointin' at?" Rev said.

"Something in that corner."

"OK, what am I pointin' at that's plastic?"

Quickly, I noticed some gray plastic bins for putting dishes in. "The bus tubs."

"Now, what am I pointin' at that's liquid?

"The coffee in the pots."

"Fine, what am I pointin' at that's wooden?"

"The bus stand or the picture frame."

"Perfect, Walker. What you saw changed with each question. Things you hadn't
noticed came into focus with a new question. You think you see what is 'there,' but
you don't. You see what you're set up to look for. For instance, we're set up to look
for things in our memories. The older we get, the more we tend to see different ver-
sions of the same things over and over again. We've got a 'familiar filter' that lets
new stuff slide on by. You can change the filter, though. Just ask your own questions instead of questions that come up like a burp."

I laughed. "I think I've been burping a lot, Rev."

"Well, let's settle your stomach." We both laughed and Rev started writing on a
napkin about the ladder of listening. He drew a ladder with five rungs, lowest to
highest: (0) bioreaction, (1) accuracy, (2) compassion, (3) essential purpose, and
(4) the intersection. He said that bioreaction was hyperfast reaction that comes
from human survival instincts and is triggered any time things aren't going our way.
The problem is that bioreactions can damage our own purposes.

"Walker, when Ms. Scott asked about revenue and the efficiency of your
process, how did your body react?"

I scanned my body as I thought back. "My jaw, neck, shoulders, and chest got
very tight, similar to how a clenched fist feels."

"If you couldn't control your reactions, what would have happened next?"

"I think I would have pounded the table and yelled something like 'How dare you
blame *me* for this mess!' I didn't, though. I just agreed to everything to get the
meeting over with."

"That," Rev said, "is bioreaction. Fight, flee, freeze, and appease. Fight came first, but it looked like a bad bet so the amygdala switched you to appease. None of that was helping your purposes any, Walker. When your fast reactions hurt your own purposes, you might call that a 'bioreactive fit.'

"You see, Walker, when somebody's a real threat to you, the last thing your body wants to do is listen to him. When the amygdala's in charge, listenin' looks like losin'. You got to ask a question that stumps the amygdala, so it sends the question over to the rest of the brain. That old amygdala is real suspicious, and it doesn't think much about any purpose except physical survival. The cortex cares about *all* your purposes. When you think up smart questions instead of burpin' up fight, flee, freeze, and appease questions, you've got charge of your ears.

"The bioreactive questions have a particular flavor to 'em, Walker. They all have something to do with provin' my first reaction was a right one. Problem is, my fast reactions are only good when my whole self is connected to things, not just the 'threat brain.' The smart questions get all of me involved."

I thought this ladder of listening was fascinating. We posed different questions about my meeting, and I saw new things and came up with one very good idea I was eager to try out. Maybe most importantly, Rev told me, "When you get resistance, do research!" He said when things weren't going my way, ask content, compassion, and purpose questions and work my way up to the intersection. I liked his advice, because I can sure tell when I'm running into resistance, and that will remind me to do the research.

I thanked Rev for all his insights. He waved me into the kitchen, saying I needed to work for my lunch. He threw a bunch of shrimp in one of the strainers and asked me to go wash them "real well," so they could go in the Saturday shrimp gumbo. I went dutifully to the sink, turned on the water, and started to laugh.

"Very funny, Rev." When I turned around, he was smiling.

"Rev, you know darn well the holes are too small. The dirt and grit are staying in the bowl with the shrimp." I walked over to the prep table and got the right strainer.

"Yep, Walker, if you don't have the right strainer, garbage and food get all mixed up, kind of like bioreaction and purpose. And, if we put that garbage in our pot, we're gonna have garbage for gumbo. I promise you, you can't get anything *out of* your relationship with Ms. Scott that you don't listen *into* it."

"Strainers and the questions I listen with are related, Rev. I get the point."

Rev is a creative teacher. He'll use whatever is at hand to make a point. His final lesson of the day came over lunch. I was eating the Mighty Fine, Mighty Tasty Barbecue Sandwich as we talked about how fear can shut down listening.

"Walker, this morning I said listenin' is not like the mail, you remember?" I nodded. "Well, listenin' is not at all like that barbecue sandwich, either."

"How is that, Rev?"

Rev asked me if he could have the remaining half of my sandwich. I politely and reluctantly said yes. He reached over and took it, placing it in front of him.

"If you give me your sandwich, then I have it and you don't. If you give me your listenin', we both get something good out of it."

I stopped to make a bevnap note and then said, "Great point. May I have my sandwich back, oh wise one?" He smirked and gave it back. I happily finished eating it.

About 15 minutes later, I was shaking Rev's large hand on my way out when I heard the slight squeak of the screen door opening. I turned to see Sara Mac walk in carrying two golf clubs. She was outfitted in an Old Head Ireland golf hat and long linen shorts, looking nothing like her newspaper photos.

"Hello, Ms. McGregor," I nodded respectfully in her direction.

"Hi, Walker O'Reilly. Call me Sara or Mac." She held the clubs in one hand and offered me the other. As we shook hands, she asked, "How are the lessons going?"

"Well. Very well, I think." I wondered what she knew about my situation.

"I hope ours goes as well as yours, then. Rev, are you ready for me to help you with that mediocre short game of yours?" She pointed a club at Rev, smiling.

"I'm ready, Mac, I'm ready." He wiped his hands on a bar towel, dropped it in an unseen linen bag, and headed for the door. "Call me next week sometime, Walker, will you? I'd like to hear about your adventures." He turned to Sara Mac and said, "He is mighty entertaining, Mac."

I headed for my car and the two of them headed for an open patch of grass. I noticed a slight bioreaction to the "entertaining" remark. I wondered if it was a test. Regardless, I was off to try a new idea I'd written on the bevnap.

P A R T / *T W O*

...

The Cycle of Value: A Conversational Architecture

"When principles are well understood,
their application is less embarrassing."

THOMAS JEFFERSON

"Luck is the residue of design."

BRANCH RICKEY

There is a basic design to high-value conversation, as reliable and important as the design of a skyscraper or a suspension bridge. Waste decreases and value increases the more we adhere to the design.

Align conversations launch the cycle of value. Just as most of the energy required for a mission to the moon is expended at launch, the align conversations are where most of the energy is expended in the cycle of value. We devote one chapter each to the three elements of alignment.

- Chapter 3: Align: *Intersect*
- Chapter 4: Align: *Invent*
- Chapter 5: Align: *Invest*

Act conversations clarify expectations, roles, and goals.

- Chapter 6: Act: *Engage, Clarify, and Close*

Adjust conversations transform experience into improvement and strengthen alignment.

- Chapter 7: Adjust: *Review and Renew*

CHAPTER THREE

ALIGN
Intersect

. . .

"Wit is the sudden marriage of ideas which, before their
marriage, were not perceived to have any relationship."

MARK TWAIN

The average person sees objects. The communication catalyst sees connections between objects, both actual and potential connections. The syner-
gistic quality of those linkages makes the whole greater than the sum of the
parts. Synergy, one of those attractive notions that is discussed often and accomplished rarely, is the product of intersecting well.

Can you imagine your home without hallways or any other common areas? How about without doorways between rooms? Having all those rooms together on one lot is not very useful if they do not connect. The same is true of any group of people who are at work together. Intersect conversations are the human equivalent of hallways and doors; they reveal valuable connections that are the foundation for high-velocity value.

In the language of architecture, rooms communicate when they share a common passage, like a hallway. The common passages are what turn rooms into a house. A skilled architect designs the openings to serve the purpose of the space. The placement of doors is not accidental or haphazard. An architect of conversation disdains accidental, haphazard relationships. For this architect, relationships are a purposeful creation, not a happy accident. An architect of conversation builds valuable relationships out of intersections.

Enduring relationships are marked by an experience of mutual value. The reciprocity of a valuable relationship builds on itself, producing benefit beyond expectation. Bill Hewlett with Dave Packard, Ginger Rogers with Fred Astaire, Martha Graham with Aaron Copland, and Lorne Michaels with a legion of *Saturday Night Live* repertory players are all examples of such reciprocal magic. The intersecting contributions of these people have produced unprecedented benefit. Such marvelous alliances do not have to be happy accidents. If you learn and practice intersection conversations, you will produce strong, resilient relationships that in turn produce extraordinary value.

In Chapter 1, we asserted that high-velocity value is at the intersection of the interests of customers, investors, and employees. This notion of a valuable intersection applies any time two or more people need to coordinate. In Chapter 2, we enriched the intersection model by introducing the critical element of *relevant facts.*

Correlating your view, my view, and the facts reveals an unforced occasion for coordinated value. Whatever you find in that intersection is ripe and ready for achievement—and not because the parties are fond of each other.

Intersect conversations are valuable whether I like, trust, agree with, or approve of the other. If I need you in any way, I must have an intersection between your situation and mine to meet that need. *Coordinated value is the issue, not affection or approval.* In any goal-driven organization, respect and affection often show up in the wake of coordinated value, but they are not prerequisite. Rather, they are fortunate residue of producing value together.

For example, you may well have heard that politics makes strange bedfellows. Many times politicians who are foes on one issue are partners on another. The intersection is not a complete reconciliation of differences; it is simply an illumination of common stakes. When common stakes are clearly revealed, even enemies become allies. Whether or not we generally agree with the other party, anything at the intersection happens faster and easier than anything outside of the intersection. Often, when we achieve that mutual benefit, our relationship evolves to include previously unthinkable possibilities. It all starts with an intersection today. What you intersect with is a *point of view*.

What Exactly *Is* a Point of View?

You do not intersect with a person, you intersect with a conversation the person is having with themselves and/or others. A point of view is a conversation comprising purposes and explanations of fact (see Figure 3.1):

- A *purpose* is a willful intent. It is a direction of achievement I am proactively *for* rather than something I am *against.* In *The Communication Catalyst,* for example, our essential purpose is to accelerate business success through valuable conversations. *Explanations* assign meaning to facts. Explanations can be expressed as concerns (as we said in Chapter 2), opinions, and possibilities. Any meaning attached to a set of facts is an explanation. Bioreactive explanations assign meaning quickly and thoughtlessly to protect my body, not my purposes; they can accidentally shift my attention from what I am for to what I am against. Regarding *The Communication Catalyst,* a bioreactive explanation could be, "We don't have enough time to write a decent book." In contrast, valuable explanations account for facts to forward your purpose rather than distract from it (e.g., "Writing this book is an opportunity to examine all the ways we use our time and eliminate waste.").

Where points of view and relevant facts intersect, people create value together. Valuable intersections must not be left to chance. What follows is a model for causing intersections rather than just hoping for them.

■ ■ ■

"Valuable relationships are like home-grown tomatoes. You can't shop for 'em, you've got to grow 'em yourself."

REV BAKER

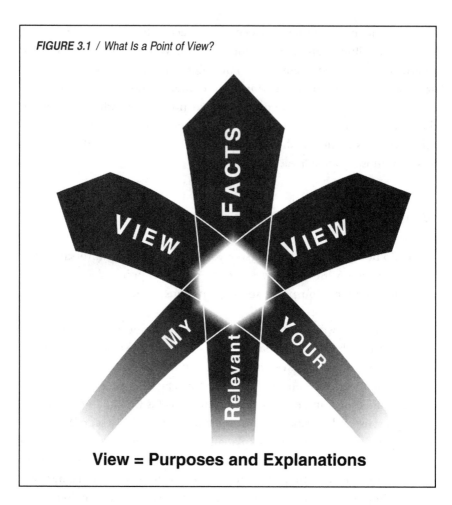

FIGURE 3.1 / What Is a Point of View?

FACTS

VIEW

VIEW

MY

Relevant

YOUR

View = Purposes and Explanations

The Conversation Meter

To accelerate a trip to any place, you need to know where you are going, where you are, and how to increase your speed. The conversation meter will help you get to the intersection by seeing where you are now and how to accelerate (see Figure 3.2).

Here are some quick definitions:

- *Pretense* is lying, evading, and withholding information.
- *Sincerity* is honest, untested opinion masquerading as reality.
- *Accuracy* separates observable facts from explanations (interpretations and opinions) and then compares the explanations to find actionable value.

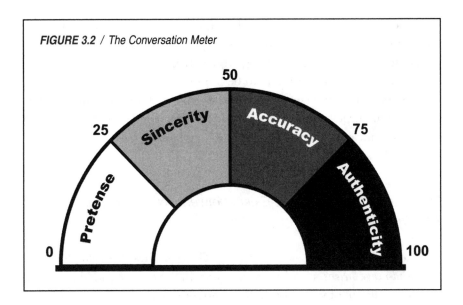

FIGURE 3.2 / The Conversation Meter

- *Authenticity* reveals previously hidden value at the intersection of someone else's view and your own.

As we explain how the meter works, notice that most of what we covered in Chapters 1 and 2 fits within the meter.

The value of conversation increases as you move from 0 to 100 on the value speedometer: The closer to 0 you are, the slower your trip to the intersection will be. As you move closer to 100, you will intersect and add value more quickly:

- The farther to the left of the meter (pretense and sincerity), the more polluted your perception of people and events. The farther to the right (accuracy and authenticity), the more genuine is your connection to the others' purposes so your responses are more valuable.
- The farther to the left, the more difficult it is to get your point across. The farther to the right, the more easily you will be received.
- The farther to the left, the more effort, stress, and time per unit of result you will experience. The farther to the right, the less effort, stress, and time per unit of result.
- The farther to the left, the slower you discover new, mutually important possibilities. The farther to the right, the more quickly you discover new, mutually important possibilities.

We begin our explanation of the four quadrants with a warning: You are the operator of the meter. For the meter to produce value, be an agent of the intersection, not an inspector. An agent searches with the conviction that an intersection exists and is waiting to be found. An inspector merely reports whether or not an intersection is obvious. Agents find many more intersections than inspectors do. Agents do make mistakes. However, they know that communication is an art of correction, not perfection. To hone the art of correction, look for personal examples as we explain each quadrant.

Pretense: *A Direct Conflict Exists between What You Truly Think and What You Are Saying or Doing*

- *Low pretense (0–8) is intentional lying.* These are lies we decide to tell.
- *Mid-range pretense (9–17) is reactive lying.* In the face of a sudden threat, a lie falls out of your mouth. It was not selected; it was a provoked fear reaction (flee or appease). You can recognize this moment easily: you realize you are lying in the middle of the lie.
- *High pretense (18–25) is withholding what you honestly have to say* when others are counting on you to tell the truth. This is the prevailing form of pretense. Here, you actually want to express yourself, but you do not because you are afraid the consequences do not merit the risk.

In our work around the world, we have found pretense to be the home of much business conversation. There are many examples. We explicitly or implicitly endorse strategies in a formal meeting, and then later, in hallways and parking lots, we attack their lack of merit. We make agreements and minutes later dishonor them. We harbor concerns that go unannounced, and yet we expect resolution. We gossip about someone we will not talk to directly. Sometimes we just lie. We explain all of this in terms of the terrible things that will happen if we actually tell the truth. Those are after-the-pretense explanations, though, and have little to do with what happened.

The cause of pretense is mainly bioreaction to threat; said another way, it is fear that I cannot cope with the consequences of honesty. The focus of the communicator who is stuck in pretense is *avoiding difficulty*.

■ ■ ■

"The origin of all conflict between me and my fellow-men is

that I do not say what I mean, and that I do not do what

I say. For this confuses and poisons . . . the situation

between myself and the other. By our contradiction,

our lie, we foster conflict-situations and give them

power over us until they enslave us."

MARTIN BUBER, *THE WAY OF MAN*

At Conversant, we are convinced that the harm pretense causes far outweighs the imagined damage of candor. Pretense bets that deception, suppression, and manipulation are more effective strategies than open, straightforward discourse. It is a bad bet. Consider this: Suppression begets violence. Withheld opinion rears its head in quietly violent ways like gossip, character assassination, listless work, and other forms of waste.

Not all silence is withheld information. It might be wasteful and untimely to say something now that is best said another time. It might be wasteful and damaging to announce a thoughtless bioreaction. We are not suggesting that you always say everything that crosses your mind. We do suggest that if you lie or withhold relevant information, you are decelerating the trip to the intersection. When you catch yourself in pretense, ask, "Does this pretense help or hurt my most important purposes?"

■ ■ ■

". . . what is most important to me must be spoken,

made verbal and shared, even at the risk of having it

bruised and misunderstood. The speaking profits me,

beyond any other effect."

AUDRE LORDE

Sincerity: An Honest Report Accompanied by the Conviction That What I Believe to Be True Is True

When we honestly mean what we say, we are in a state of sincerity. However, it is possible to be honest and inaccurate. Think about it: How many times in your life has a person honestly thought something about you that was inaccurate? More than a few, we bet. That person can sincerely believe things about you without thoughtful consideration of your purposes and relevant facts. None of us is capable of unfiltered, immaculate perception. Still, we often treat our perceptions as perfect reflections of reality. Sincerity, although flawed, gets more points than pretense because finding an intersection is faster with honesty than deception. It takes courage to leap beyond pretense into the unknown consequences of sincerity.

■ ■ ■

"Sincerity makes the very least person to be of more value

than the most talented hypocrite."

CHARLES H. SPURGEON, ENGLISH THEOLOGIAN (1834-1892)

- *Low-end sincerity (26–33) is unedited eruption of honest reactions and opinions.* Some of you have probably been in meetings where participants said whatever was on their mind without regard to the agenda. Sincerity spreads, and at the end of the meeting you are left with conversational rubble and no real value.
- *Mid-range sincerity (34–42) is saying my honest, firm opinion regarding the subject at hand.* Although more disciplined, this level is still not open to competing views.
- *High sincerity (43–50) includes soliciting other views while automatically rejecting those that do not fit with my beliefs.* This level can occur as dishonest to anyone who has given input. "Why did he bother to ask for my opinion if he was going to do what he wanted anyway?" It is probably more prejudice than dishonesty.

Sincere reactions tend to provoke equally sincere reactions from others, with everyone defending their reactions vigorously. When there are substantial differences, sincerity often deepens those differences. In the extreme, sincerity causes tragedy as "right and righter" do battle with no exploration of the other's view. We sacrifice learning and relationship on the altar of being right. The only way for sincerity to resolve difference is if the parties refuse to give up, sticking with the conversation until something valuable happens. Sincerity plus tenacity will produce value, although at the cost of increased stress, fatigue, and time. Sincerity *does* accomplish one important thing: What was covertly steering conversation is now "on the table."

■ ■ ■

"For the great enemy of the truth is very often not the lie—

deliberate, contrived, and dishonest—but the myth—

persistent, persuasive, and unrealistic. Too often we hold fast

to the clichés of our forebears. We subject all facts to a

prefabricated set of interpretations. We enjoy the comfort of

opinions without the discomfort of thought."

JOHN F. KENNEDY, COMMENCEMENT ADDRESS AT YALE UNIVERSITY,

JUNE 11, 1962

The basic focus of someone limited to sincerity is "be honest and defend my honest position." Sometimes, fed up with suppression, we blurt out judgments and complaints that have simmered in resentment and disapproval for a long time. When the resentment and disapproval evoke a response in kind, we think we gave communication a chance and communication failed. Now, there is even *more* evidence that pretense is unavoidable, and we slide backward on the meter. Other times, we may speak sincerely and passionately out of a sense of honor. If our sincere beliefs discount competing views, opposition heats up and arguments ensue. It is critical, then, to have choices other than pretense and sincerity.

■ ■ ■

"There is nothing in the world more dangerous

than sincere ignorance."

MARTIN LUTHER KING, JR.

The big shift: Bioreactive protection to valuable discovery. To go beyond pretense and sincerity, I must break from bioreaction and shift to valuable conversation. Valuable conversations (accuracy and authenticity) dramatically quicken the trip to the intersection, because they represent a major shift from *protection* to *discovery*. In the domain of bioreaction, I collect evidence to prove my view. In the domain of value, I shift my focus to researching views held by people with whom I interact. Imagine that I am a trapeze artist in the circus and I must let go of my trapeze for you to catch me. When I let go of the bar, where should my attention be, on you or me? My safety and success are served by attending to *you*. The same is true of any moment of coordinated action.

When pressed for time, researching the view of others seems wasteful. For managers, there is a powerful temptation to accelerate action by demanding compliance. They should just do it! Forced compliance will ultimately backfire, however. In the face of domination, fighting, fleeing, freezing, and appeasing run wild.

■ ■ ■

"Coercion begets violence."

ROBERT GREENLEAF

Accuracy: *Separating Facts from Explanations and Comparing the Explanations for Value*

The discipline of separating observation and explanation resolves "sincere ignorance." This is challenging because:

- Most people live as though their explanations (interpretations and opinions) *are* facts. Nearly all tragic conflict is rife with explanations masquerading as facts.
- It takes courage to move from avoiding harm and protecting opinion to researching new opportunities for high-velocity value.

Do you ever find yourself defending your point of view when it is wasteful or even stupid to do so? Sometimes, we hold strongly to the false security of a familiar position, though it is insufficient for our purposes. The shift from bioreaction (pretense and sincerity) to value (accuracy and authenticity) is the shift from protecting what we already have to discovery of new value. It can be frightening to let go of what we already know to explore value with no guarantee. Accurate conversations are fundamentally about learning, not protection, however. A leader who operates as a communication catalyst knows that he is safer learning than he is protecting.

■ ■ ■

"Security is mostly a superstition. It does not exist in nature, nor do the children of men as a whole experience it. Avoiding danger is no safer in the long run than outright exposure. Life is either a daring adventure or nothing."

HELEN KELLER

"You can't steal second without taking your foot off of first."

BOB CONNOLLY, MINOR LEAGUE BASEBALL PLAYER

An accurate conversation starts with mutually observable facts and finishes with valuable explanation. A connection forms as facts emerge because we share a view of reality. On that foundation, we can discuss explanations of the data, assessing them in terms of the value they add. Trying to go fast without accuracy is common and foolish. Hysterical speed worshipers fail to note how quickly and sincerely plowing through differences is a prelude to rework and surprising breakdowns.

■ ■ ■

"Fast is fine, but accuracy is everything."

WYATT EARP

- *Low-end accuracy (51–58) is reliably separating mutual facts from explanations of those facts.* A fact is something that is mutually or commonly observable. An explanation is a way to account for those facts. Suggestion: The next time you are upset by some event, get a sheet of paper and draw a line down the center. Title the left column "facts" and the right "explanations." Then, answer the question "What happened?" Only put undeniable facts in the fact column, and everything else under explanation. Notice how your emotions settle as you begin to explore accurately.
- *Mid-range accuracy (59–66) is communicating facts first and explanations second.* If you lead with explanation (your interpretations and opinions), the only people who are listening to the facts are the ones who already agree with you. Treating the facts as primary communicates your trust in the discourse, a triumph of learning and adjustment over safeguarded opinion. Others begin to disclose their explanations, and as you learn from each other common ground begins to form.
- *High accuracy (67–75) is facts first, explanations second, and comparing explanations for value.* If you are communicating in high accuracy, your bias is for value, not authorship. You do not care *whose* explanation wins; you care for the explanations that stimulate valuable action.

Accuracy benefits:

- You intersect more quickly with views you accurately understand.
- As soon as you learn from another, she begins to learn from you.
- Common facts provide unforced common ground, clear up groundless misconceptions, and calm emotional upset.

- Listing accurate observations chronologically (a summary of events) tends to revitalize interest, turning people from spectators to participants.
- The discipline of comparing explanations and selecting the most valuable accelerates coordinated achievement.

Once I was mediating a dispute scheduled to go into court the next day. About two hours into the morning, one of the participants said, "I want a new mediator." Because I was the mediator, I asked what had happened that led to the request. I was told, "You are entirely too arrogant to work with."

"Arrogant" is an explanation. An explanation without facts is almost impossible to act on, so I needed more information. I purposely did not argue with or even question his belief in my arrogance. Instead, I asked, "Could you tell me what exactly I did or didn't do that had you realize I was arrogant?" His response was that I had interrupted him the last three times he spoke. Accurately, I talked before he was finished talking. To him that meant "arrogant" and to me it meant "hurried." Bioreactively, I wanted to straighten him out and defend myself. Bioreaction would not have served the senior purpose of the day, however.

I said, "I apologize for interrupting you. I should not have done that. Would you give me 45 more minutes to make sure your points are made clearly and completely to your satisfaction? If you still want a new mediator after that, I'll do whatever it takes to find one." He agreed. Later, over lunch, he complimented me on how quickly I got my arrogance under control. The parties reached an agreement by the end of the day.

Earlier in my career, I would have spent time disproving his explanation, which would have worsened the problem. It is unlikely we would have resolved the dispute that day. It took a few failures to learn that arguing about explanations is a waste, because all explanations are valid. The important thing is to serve the purpose at hand. Accepting his explanations and responding to the facts served the purpose, even though I wrestled with a "fight" reaction for a few seconds.

The conversational focus for accuracy is *separating facts from explanations and comparing the explanations for value.* Accuracy reduces bioreactive upset, renews interest, restores faith in conversation, and establishes common ground.

Here is a celestial image that may help explain accuracy: Consider groups of stars and constellations as equivalent to facts and explanations. Virtually all of us would agree that there are stars visible in the night sky. Different peoples in the world explain the stars differently, resulting in different constellations. Is that *really* a bear up there? Is it *really* a woman in a chair? If you see a bear or a chair, it is a function of how you explain the stars.

Accuracy is not just a concept, however. It is also a skill. Here are some ways to practice:

- Debrief a recent event that did not go as well as you wished. Draw a line down the middle of a page and note all the major facts in the fact column in chronological order. Get an objective person to check your fact column for explanations disguised as facts. Then, write at least three explanations for each major fact. After logging all your explanations, rank them for value from lowest to highest. Generating various explanations for the same event is important practice. If you cannot entertain multiple explanations for a single event, you lack the conversational dexterity necessary for leading high-velocity value.
- Program your screen saver to float this question across your screen: "I know I *believe* it, but is it *accurate?*"
- Once a day for one week, audit your "explanation return on investment." Consider every explanation you uttered that day as an investment of your time, attention, and commitment. Ask yourself, "Do I really want to invest in *that?*"
- Make this sign and post it above your desk or someplace else that you frequent (see Figure 3.3).

FIGURE 3.3 / *Sign to Post above Your Desk*

EXPLANATION ROI

When I explain facts and behavior am I:

A RECKLESS SPENDER?
- RASH JUDGMENT (the myth of immaculate perception)
- VINDICATION
- INFLUENCE BY ACCIDENT

A SMART INVESTOR?
- INTELLIGENT JUDGMENT (compare explanations and choose)
- VALUE
- INFLUENCE ON PURPOSE

WHAT HAVE I INVESTED IN TODAY?

Authenticity: *Exploring Where Points of View Intersect with Each Other and Circumstances to Reveal Valuable, Unforced Occasions for Action*

Authenticity requires accuracy as a foundation. Accurate conversations turn relevant facts into a "center of gravity," creating a stable reference point and truing mechanism for the interaction. On that accurate foundation, authenticity marries multiple points of view, researching where they intersect for new insight and opportunity. The offspring of that marriage is high-velocity value. We use the term *authenticity* because each person's view is subjectively genuine, and yet no individual view is ever the whole story. Authenticity assumes that there is more truth at the intersection of relevant facts, your view and mine than in either of those three alone.

- *Low-range authenticity (76–84) is appreciating the essential purposes of others* even when you disagree with methods they use and results they produce. Few people inquire into purpose once they disagree with method and outcome, and potential value remains dormant. Fitting questions are:
  –What purpose does he have that I can respect?
  –What essential principle is at risk?
  –What is important for him about this issue?
- *Mid-range authenticity (85–92) is discovering actionable opportunity at the intersection of differing views.* Mid-range questions are:
  –How do our purposes connect?
  –What do we have to give to one another?
  –What actionable idea makes us interdependent?
  –What actionable issue is important to us all?
- *High authenticity (93–100) is the startling discovery of unimagined possibilities at the intersection of previously disconnected views.* Good questions are:
  –What essential contribution of theirs have I overlooked?
  –What unique lesson is here for me to learn?
  –What unique opportunities do the current circumstances support?
  –What value is available in this situation with these people and nowhere else?
  –What valuable picture emerges when I assemble their view, relevant facts, and my view?

Authentic conversations have a distinct character. They value inclusion over exclusion, curiosity over prejudice, commonality over difference, and inquiry over domination. Authenticity is *not* compromise. It *is* expanding your field of vision to include a larger system of relationships, so you can see how your purposes fit in that system.

If you want to discover surprising new sources of value, *legitimize the other by appreciating the purposes behind their methods and results*. If you have substantial differences, suspend disapproval while you search for purpose and contribution. Authentic intersections yield unexpected value as reciprocal contributions reveal previously hidden possibilities.

Reciprocity can be a startling engine of value creation. In 1943, Aaron Copland was invited by Martha Graham, the dancer and choreographer, to write the score for a new ballet. Graham and Copland were both highly accomplished and some predicted a difficult collaboration. Graham presented Copland with a rural American scenario she had in mind. Copland invented his music by intersecting with Martha's scenario (his working title was *Ballet for Martha*) and a factual constraint. The piece was commissioned by the Coolidge Foundation and was to premiere in the Coolidge Auditorium at the Library of Congress, a performance space that could only accommodate 13 instruments. So, Copland scored the piece for 13 instruments. A rural American scene, a logistical constraint, and a gifted composer came together to produce music that evoked images of America's heartland. Martha Graham choreographed the ballet inspired by the music that had been, in part, inspired by her vision. All these elements came together to create *Appalachian Spring*, so named by Graham on the day of the premiere. The dance and music were seamless elements of an extraordinary image of American hope and strength. *Appalachian Spring* won the Pulitzer Prize and remains a highlight in the history of American music and ballet. This was not Copland's *separate* achievement, nor Graham's, nor the Coolidge Foundation's. *Appalachian Spring* is a timeless creation that arose at the intersection.

One caveat: This intersection image seems productive, but what if it is not? What if all your collaborators want is to damage you? In our experience with many thousands of people, we have found that the majority of the time there is a purpose you can respect if only you look for it. However, any authentic intersection must account for relevant facts. Repeated action that damages mutual value may be cause for canceling the association. Just do not think that you are going to produce high-velocity value with anyone without intersecting with one or more of their purposes.

■　■　■

"We can turn away, or we can turn toward. Those are the
only two choices we have."

MARGARET WHEATLEY, *TURNING TO ONE ANOTHER*

Waste trap: *Sometimes managers aggrandize themselves with tough talk about what is wrong with other people.* These managers are unable to learn from anyone with whom they disagree. They voice their disapproval to people they think will agree with them and rarely to the persons being criticized. To their risk-free audience, they identify who they disdain and how exactly those people are flawed. Such righteous superiority fails to produce high-velocity value. The woman or man strong enough to research purpose in the face of difference will outperform a bioreactive braggart every day of the week.

■ ■ ■

"But when it comes to human beings, the only type of cause that matters is the final cause, the purpose. Once you know what people really want, you can't hate them anymore. You can fear them, but you can't hate them, because you can always find the same desires in your own heart."

ORSON SCOTT CARD, *SPEAKER FOR THE DEAD*

Tips for Finding an Authentic Intersection

Tip #1: Do not confuse purpose with method or result. Purposes are intentions that guide action; methods are means, processes, or tools; and results are specific outcomes that I think serve my purpose.

Consider this scenario: You have a *purpose* to grow your business in a way that creates barriers to competition. The *method* you prefer is acquiring companies that have unique, hard-to-imitate competencies valued by your customers. The *result* you are pursuing is acquiring XYZ Corporation by the end of the fiscal year. Which of these three is *least* flexible? If you are smart, it is purpose. When you disagree with a result or method, back up and research purpose before you argue about the other two.

Tip #2: If you cannot identify an essential purpose, do not fret. There are two that are *always* present for everyone. Every human being has two essential purposes that are always ripe intersection opportunities:

1. *I want to be heard.* If you want to build an instant intersection, then get someone's point. We live in a world of point givers who are all long-

ing for point getters. The moment you understand any point at all, they open up and you can look for other, more specific purposes.

2. *I want to be valuable.* No one we have ever worked with would want the following epitaph: "Lived longer than necessary and did not particularly matter." When we create value, we feel both safe and satisfied. To disarm fear and create trust, learn from them and acknowledge their contribution.

Tip #3: Use "upstream" alignment to accelerate the trip to the intersection. Look at purpose, method, and outcome as a river of alignment. The source of the river is purpose, the mouth of the river is results, and methods are the flow of the river between source and mouth. If you have an impasse about a specific result, look upstream to method. If you still have an impasse at method, look upstream to shared purpose. If you have an impasse at shared purpose, research the intersection until you find one. Remember, if you need each other there is a shared purpose in there *somewhere.*

For example, you may disagree with someone about investing unbudgeted resources to get a product to market faster than is predicted (a result impasse). Is there a preexisting process or method in place for making decisions regarding unbudgeted operational expenses? If so, you have a method intersection you can employ to make the result decision. If there is not a relevant method intersection, is there a preexisting shared purpose that can direct you in making the decision? For instance, "We have a purpose to only increase current spending on projects if we can do it in a way that still ensures long-term performance." What, then, does that purpose tell the two of you to do? If you lack a specific shared purpose, have an intersection conversation to discover one.

Have intersection conversations to discover shared purposes. Shared purpose is then senior to and governs the design of shared methods. Shared methods are then senior to and govern related result decisions (see Figure 3.4).

Tip #4: Prepare for the challenging interactions. When you know you are headed into an interaction that is not a sure success, follow these five steps to prepare. This works best if you answer the questions on a large whiteboard or on flip-chart paper that you can post and look at:

1. *What is your initial purpose?* It might alter as you interact, so be ready for new insights.

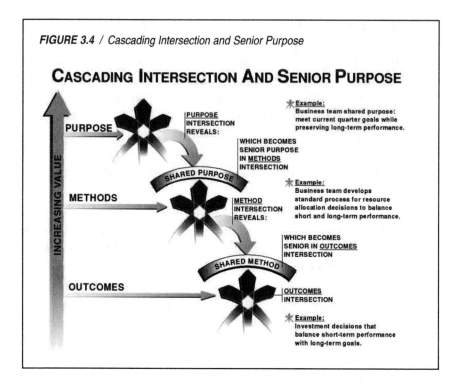

FIGURE 3.4 / Cascading Intersection and Senior Purpose

CASCADING INTERSECTION AND SENIOR PURPOSE

PURPOSE

INCREASING VALUE

PURPOSE INTERSECTION REVEALS:

✳ Example:
Business team shared purpose: meet current quarter goals while preserving long-term performance.

WHICH BECOMES SENIOR PURPOSE IN METHODS INTERSECTION

SHARED PURPOSE

METHODS

METHOD INTERSECTION REVEALS:

✳ Example:
Business team develops standard process for resource allocation decisions to balance short and long-term performance.

WHICH BECOMES SENIOR IN OUTCOMES INTERSECTION

SHARED METHOD

OUTCOMES

OUTCOMES INTERSECTION

✳ Example:
Investment decisions that balance short-term performance with long-term goals.

2. *Who is crucial to your purpose?* What purposes, facts, and explanations are important to them? Write them down for each person. If you know little, find someone who knows more or ask the crucial parties directly.

3. *What other facts are relevant?*

4. *What themes do you see across all those purposes, facts, and explanations?* Stand back from the lists and look for patterns.

5. *Name the intersection.* Survey the themes, asking yourself this question: What is the name of a meeting we would all be eager to attend? When you have titled a magnetic meeting, you have an intersection.

This is very smart prep, and it will set you up to be a poised participant. It is not the end. In the actual interaction, you will likely bioreact, correct, and then discover new possibilities.

■ ■ ■

"A relationship has a momentum; it must change and develop and will tend to move toward the point of greatest commitment."

CAROLYN HEILBRUN, U.S. WRITER AND EDUCATOR

Tip #5: Be grateful for sincerity and hold yourself accountable for accuracy and authenticity. If the other is sincere, it is easy to convert him to accuracy by just giving him a chance to tell his story. If you want to improve a conversation, you must be at least one state above the people you are trying to influence. If they are pretentious, you must at least be sincere. If sincere, you must at least be accurate. Our recommendation is you just practice accuracy and authenticity so much that valuable conversation becomes your "home," and then you are above both pretense and sincerity.

Here are some valuable exercises:

- Dissect a TV series episode or movie.
  Pick a movie or television program you like and watch it with a copy of the meter in front of you. Check off examples of the conversations on the meter as you see and hear them.
- Dissect a newscast.
  Have the meter in front of you and pay close attention to facts and explanations masquerading as facts.
- Teach the model.
  Explain the model to a coworker, your spouse, or another willing person. Focus on creating value for their important purposes.
- Make a dial and monitor a call.
  Draw the meter on paper. Use a paperclip as the dial and monitor your conversation on a telephone call. Keep moving the dial to where you are, and then see if you can upgrade the conversation.

If you get the image of the conversation model seared in your brain, you will find intersections faster than most people will. You will train yourself to see patterns where others see only pieces. You will establish a work community marked by experiences of inclusion, reciprocal contribution, and high achievement. You will establish enduring relationships that produce creativity and innovation, which is the subject of Chapter 4. All this value accrues because you are strong enough to keep your sights set on mutuality when most people are riveted on differences.

After the summary, it is time to check in with Walker and Rev Baker. Walker had a "new idea" at the end of Chapter 2. Wonder what it was and how it turned out? And Rev, of course, has a bit to say about how intersections produce surprisingly valuable relationships.

CHAPTER SUMMARY

The Heart of the Matter

To launch the cycle of value, focus on the intersection of relevant points of view and relevant facts. The intersection forms the foundation of valuable relationships necessary for high-value achievement. Use the conversation meter to manage interactions, and you will get to the intersection quickly.

The Intersection

High-velocity value is at the intersection of relevant facts and relevant points of view. Achievement slows when we focus on differences and accelerates when we focus on intersections.

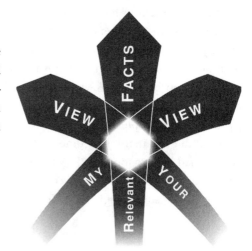

The Conversation Meter

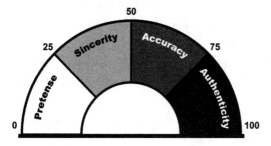

Pretense: 0–25

- A direct conflict exists between what you think and what you are saying and doing. Characterized by lying, evading, and withholding information.
- Focus: Avoid difficulty.
- Waste track: Bioreactive conversation. No value is being generated.

Sincerity: 26–50

- An honest report accompanied by the conviction that what I *believe* to be true *is* true. Honest, untested opinion masquerading as reality.
- Focus: Be honest and defend my honest position.
- Waste track: Bioreactive conversation. Little value is generated. Learning and relationship are sacrificed at the expense of defending personal views and "being right."

Accuracy: 51–75

- Separating facts from explanations and comparing the explanations for value.
  - *–Low-end accuracy:* Reliably separating facts (something that is mutually or commonly observable) from explanations (interpretations and opinions) of those facts.
  - *–Mid-range accuracy:* Communicating *facts first* and *explanations second.*
  - *–High accuracy:* Facts first, explanations second, then compare explanations for value. Your bias is value, not authorship.
- Focus: Reveal the facts and compare the explanations for value.
- Value track: Accuracy accelerates value as you start with mutually observable facts and finish with valuable explanations and a shared reality.

Authenticity: 76–100

- Exploring where points of view intersect with each other and circumstances to reveal valuable, unforced occasions for action.
  –*Low-end authenticity:* Appreciating the essential purposes of others even when you disagree with the methods they use and results they produce.
  –*Mid-range authenticity:* Discovering actionable opportunity at the intersection of differing views.
  –*High authenticity:* Startling discovery of unimagined possibilities at the intersection of previously disconnected views.
- Focus: Clarify shared purpose and reveal intersections for action.
- Value track: High-velocity value occurs as new insights and opportunities emerge.

Action to take: Notice where you are on the meter; determine where you wish to be and move there by asking valuable questions.

Tips for Finding the Intersection

1. Do not confuse purpose with method or result: purposes are directions of intent; methods are means, processes, or tools; results are specific outcomes. Purpose is the source of methods and results.
2. There are two essential purposes present for everyone: *I want to be heard* and *I want to contribute value.*
3. Use "upstream" alignment to accelerate the trip to the intersection. Intersection conversations reveal shared purpose; shared purpose is then senior to and governs the design of shared methods; shared methods are then senior to and govern related result decisions.
4. Prepare for challenging interactions by asking yourself:
   - What is my initial purpose?
   - Who is crucial to my purpose? What purposes, facts, and explanations are important to them?
   - What other facts are relevant?
   - Identify themes you see.
   Name a valuable, magnetic intersection. Be grateful for sincerity from others while holding yourself accountable for accuracy and authenticity.

R E V   L E S S O N

▪ ▪ ▪

You Can't Have a Band
without a Song

"You can't always get what you want

But if you try sometimes, you might find

You get what you need."

MICK JAGGER AND KEITH RICHARDS,

"YOU CAN'T ALWAYS GET WHAT YOU WANT"

"Thass the trouble** with wimmen. They'll steal yer money every time!"

He was loud, drunk, and out of place. His manic bias did not fit Rev Baker's barbecue café, like hearing an ugly scream in the middle of a pleasant ballad. Later Rev told me that it happens occasionally. A boat pulls up to the dock filled with heavy drinkers, and one or more of them stumble up to the café. This was one of those times.

I was sitting at the granite bar that doubled as a dining surface for people who liked to eat at a counter. Most of the time, as in my case, the counter diners came in by themselves. I was enjoying my mixed platter (sausage, brisket, and ribs with fresh slaw and mighty fine, mighty tasty potato salad) and waiting for Rev when the bellowing began. Rev arrived at the booth quickly, moving fast but without a lot of effort. It startled me how swiftly Rev, as big as he is, was standing in front of the screaming inebriate.

"Excuse me." Rev's voice was a quiet command and the man stopped in mid-yell, spinning unsteadily to face Rev. The young couple he was verbally assaulting looked up at Rev, too.

"What do *you* want, cook?" The man thrust his beer bottle at Rev, a glass finger pointing out the new object of his rage. Rev's white-clothed body looked relaxed in the face of the blistering inquiry.

The man and woman were sitting on the same side of a booth and had a platter-for-two in the middle of their table. They were looking at a checkbook next to the platter. I imagine the money association triggered the drunk's prejudicial outburst. Now, as the couple focused on Rev, I could see their faces move from shock to hope.

"I'm here to serve and to protect," said Rev. He looked directly into the man's eyes. "How can I serve you?"

"Yeah, well serve this!" The right hand of the shouting drunk flashed forward and a beer bottle headed toward Rev's face. In movement that was more like a ballet than a fight, Rev turned inside the blow and kept turning until he was behind the man. In a split second, Rev was walking the offender back into the kitchen, holding both of his arms behind his back, the beer bottle now resting safely between his shoulder blades. As they walked by me, I heard Rev softly say, "I've got some fresh coffee in the kitchen, plenty for both of us." The now-neutralized combatant looked confused, unsure of how he came to be in this position. As they disappeared into the kitchen, I heard an outbreak of applause from the dining room. The couple in the booth shook their heads and looked at each other as if to say, "What was *that* about?" After a momentary buzz the diners settled back down to eating.

Rev arranged for the man to be picked up by his family and his boat to be secured for the night. Once the sobering offender left, I asked Rev to show me how he subdued the attacker so easily. He patiently demonstrated how he simply got inside the blow and went in the direction of the force until he could find a safe place to stop.

"The key, Walker, is to go *with* the force until you can find a way to make good use of it. That way they're helping you. Most folks resist the attack instead of goin' with it. If I resist, someone usually gets hurt. If I flow with it, I can usually find somethin' valuable to do with the force of the blow. It's not really different from an argument. You can either go with the flow of an argument till you see an intersection, or you can resist it and get in a fight. There's less mess and it goes faster if you stay with it 'til you see an intersection."

"Rev, that fits with what you said about perception filters and questions last week. One kind of question sets up a 'fight' filter, and another sets up an 'intersection' filter. In fact, that's related to my 'great idea' I told you about."

"Walker, I would sure like to hear about your great idea. What was it and how'd it go?"

"And I'd sure like to tell you, Rev," I said. We sat down at the table next to the jukebox in the middle of the dining room, and I relayed the genesis of my idea and the results.

During last week's Rev Lesson, I formulated an experiment. After everything Rev said, it struck me that he was conducting a tutorial in relationship, and my hardest relationships came to mind. Louis Evans and Ray Garza were the engineering managers who had applied for my current job. Older than me, both had been at the company longer and had legitimate claims to the position. Since then, it seemed our relationship had been marked by combat half the time and covert disapproval the rest of the time. The relationship was not a source of high-velocity value, by any means. As I've reported, my interactions with Sharon Scott were no better. So all three were ripe targets for relational improvement.

My idea was this: In all my interactions with Louis, Bob, and Sharon for one week I would focus on one question: "What can I learn from you right now?" I was prepared to catch my bioreactions to their words and actions and shift to researching their contributions. I told myself I could continue proving they were dishonorable and incompetent again in seven days. For one week, I'd focus everything on "What can I learn from you right now?" in our e-mails, voice mails, and in-person conversations. I thought that if Rev was right, I should see things I'd never seen before because I set up a valuable perception filter.

It proved to be an amazing week.

When I reported on the promises I'd made to Sharon Scott regarding a process review, Ray objected loudly. I caught myself wanting to hit him with a brick and shifted my focus to "the question." These words fell out of my mouth: "Ray, I do not want to go on until I understand what you see that I don't. Tell me what you think we should do." I did not know I was going to say that until I did. So Ray got up and went to a flip chart and drew the flow of our Product Development Process. He then drew some business processes that intersect with our PDP, like purchasing, finance, forecasting, and marketing reviews, and said, "These crossroads are the parts of our processes we don't review. Everything in our PDP is being reviewed daily, weekly, and monthly. There may be some waste in there, but it won't be enough to speed us up much.

"The waste is in how we hook up with the business processes. That is where we get surprise demands and problems. We don't review this stuff because we don't own it, but it affects us every day. How are we going to get purchasing, forecasting, and marketing involved? *That's* where the waste is."

Ray's comments made a lot of sense. The real process that affects our time-to-market is bigger than the one we are formally accountable for. If the result was to accelerate time-to-market, we had to construct a different review than just the PDP. Then Louis jumped in.

"They won't come to any review. They'll just think we're trying to blame our missed deadlines on them," Louis said. I thought about how Sharon's review request first hit me, then realized Louis was probably right and told him so. I asked Louis and Ray about people they knew in the business processes who would not be suspicious of our motives. We each came up with some names. We decided to contact them informally and get their suggestions for how to get the right people involved in our process reviews. Each of us took names of people to contact and then scheduled a time to reconvene. It was the first time the three of us were freely and completely up to something together.

I reported to Sharon what we were doing and she said, "This is smart, but let's not wait to have our first process walk-through. Let's start with the business process leaders who *do* want to be involved, make the best process maps we can, then figure next steps from there." As Sharon spoke, I realized how often I waited for the "right" conditions to launch anything new. She was focused on extracting value from the people available now and building from there. All three of my problem people seemed to be getting smarter. Our attention seemed to be off of guarding against each other and on to what we were doing together. I told Rev that I considered my question experiment a success: We were relating to each other in a far more valuable way.

"Walker, that's a mighty fine experiment. You picked a terrific question to filter things through, and you've made a good start."

"Only a start?" I said. "It seems like things are really going to be different now."

"Walker, once you open somethin' up, you've got to shore it up."

Rev went on to say that every two years, letting water out of Tom Miller Dam into Town Lake lowers Lake Austin quite a bit. Lowering the lake lets people clean up the shoreline and work on docks and boat slips. It also gets rid of the duckweed, a thick vegetation that fills the lake and entangles swimmers, skiers, anglers, and sailors.

"Walker, I built my boat slip and boat hoist a few years ago. It was the second time I had to do it."

"What happened the first time?" I asked.

Rev smiled and shook his head slowly. "Well, I did a lot of work for not much benefit, I can tell you that for sure."

Rev said he had a friend with a tractor help him dig out the canal that was to become the boat slip. "I remember standing on the lawn when the digging was done and feeling pleased about the big difference we made. We had ourselves a fine canal. For a bit, anyway."

He recounted getting an unexpected call and having to leave town ("government work" is all he said). He was gone longer than he had planned. By the time Rev returned, the lake had come back up, the canal was full of water, and the sides of the canal were collapsing.

"Yep," Rev said, "the shoreline was quite a mess for quite a while. We dug out a nice opening for a boat slip, but we didn't shore it up with timbers for support. After a while, the whole thing just collapsed. It was real ugly and no use at all as a boat slip. Now, two years later we got it right."

"Rev, it sounds like you think I just dug out a big opening with Sharon, Ray, and Louis but I've got no timbers in place."

"I believe that's true, Walker. The timbers are that whole cycle of value we talked about a couple of weeks back. The first timber you need is an intersection with some staying power. You might call it a senior purpose."

"Can you say more, Rev?"

"Sure, Walker. You see, right now *you* are the intersection. The way you're listenin' makes room for folks to come together. But that only works when you're around. Next step is to find something important that all of you care about, and you need each other to pull off. It's as if you found some good musicians; y'all think each other are good players, but you have no song to play. You need music to keep a band together."

"But Rev, we already have things to do together. We've got this process review, and we've got to get these products out."

"That's true, Walker, *and* it's not an authentic intersection."

Often, just when I'm getting used to Rev's down-home delivery, he throws out a phrase that reminds me I'm dealing with a skilled, rigorous mind. Authentic intersection?

"What is an authentic intersection?" I asked.

Rev got that bright-eyed, focused look that drives his big points home. "It's a shared purpose that everyone would work on, even if they didn't have to. It's not watered down; it's not something so general that you can't say 'no' to it. It's a purpose that rings true to folks, something they say a loud 'yes' to. It's a shared intention people stay true to even when it's hard. You don't have to start out with an authentic purpose. You can work your way to it."

"Rev, I sense a bevnap lesson coming." Rev smiled and pulled out his pen.

Rev drew something that looked like a speedometer divided into four sections. He put 0 on one end and 100 at the other. He said the authentic intersection was up around 90. He labeled the four sections and said that just about everything we'd discussed so far could be found in this meter.

"Walker, some folks think I should just hand out this meter, but I don't find it helps much if we haven't gone pretty deep into perception and listenin' first. Once you've gone deep, the meter helps you hold on to the lessons. You and I have gone pretty deep, so it's time.

"I want you to know something, Walker. This conversation meter will look simple. Most good things are. Just don't get simple and trivial mixed up. It comes from the work of a lot of smart, brave people. All I did was write it down. If I show you this, I want you to practice, cause it's the way to honor those folks. You keep it in front of you 'til you just think it naturally. Will you do that?"

Rev was the most immediately trustworthy person I'd ever known. If he said it mattered that much, it was easy to have it matter to me. "Yes, sir, I'll practice with it until it's natural for me."

I asked Rev who the brave and smart people were and how he knew them. After he answered I said, "You're so full of surprises, you're like a mystery novel I'll never finish reading."

"Walker, that's a great way to respect people. Keep 'em as a mystery and don't ever finish gettin' to know them. It insults people to finish knowin' who they are."

That was wise advice and easy to follow where Rev was concerned. I found out his "smart and brave" associates were hostage negotiators, treaty negotiators, detectives, and prominent educators. Rev said they all had to find real intersections fast to do their work, and the measures of failure were harsh and obvious. His respect for them was loud.

"Walker, the best of them believe in their bones that there's always an intersection, even between enemies. Their only question is, Can we find it fast enough? The meter helps predict how fast you'll find a genuine intersection and what to do to speed the trip."

Here's Rev's meter:

0–25 *Pretense:* outright lying and avoiding telling the truth; very slow to the intersection because it is hard to go fast in the dark.

26–50 *Sincerity:* saying what I honestly think. My perceptions are right and competing perceptions are wrong. Still slow because the focus is on protecting what we already think rather than learning, discovery, and moving forward.

51–75 *Accuracy:* separating observable facts from explanations of the facts; researching competing views and comparing explanations for value. The trip is faster because we have common ground to run on and valuable explanations to fuel progress.

76–100 *Authenticity:* connecting different views to build a real intersection of purpose that inspires creativity, tenacity, and coordinated action. The trip is very fast because we have a common goal to run toward.

"Authenticity, Walker, that's where the song comes together. You know how you can hear a song and you start movin' with it? It's like a piece of you is in that music and you can't help hummin' along. That's a real intersection.

"You've had a real good start with your listenin' question. Keep it up and build an intersection with what you learn from each other. Start with promises you've already made, add in facts that you all need to pay attention to, and check out each of your explanations. Those explanations are a window to purposes that matter. You just need to fit those purposes together like pieces of a puzzle and you'll have your song. You'll know because folks walk around hummin' it."

"Rev," I said, "obligation doesn't make much of a song, does it? I think that's about all Sharon, Ray, Louis, and I have had in common."

Rev Baker's leathery face moved from side to side. "No, even though sometimes it's all you've got. People will work together for a bit because they have to, but they'll be lookin' for greener pastures. Constant obligation leads to anarchy, revolution, or despair, not authenticity."

"Do you mean obligation leads everyone to just do what they want?"

"Yeah, if it's anarchy. Anarchy is independence without community; authenticity is independence in service to a community. If you have a real intersection, you can trust folks to take independent action 'cause they have a song in common. They won't get too far off track before they notice the music is gettin' ugly. They'll start listenin' to the other players and find their way back to the song."

In that moment, I started to think of myself as a composer. The four of us are playing notes and I needed to hear the song. Then Fred Astaire came to mind, because he could turn anything into a dance. Hat racks, chairs, people . . . it didn't matter. He could find a dance in there somewhere. That's what I was going after this week: a song we could dance to. I know it's in there somewhere.

"Rev, next week I'm coming back with a song—not just my song, but also a song that's good for MightyTek customers, investors, and employees. My test will be if Sharon, Ray, Louis, and I trust each other to take independent action. Maybe we won't have so many meetings everyone feels like they have to attend."

Rev gave me his 1,000-watt smile. "That's just grand, Walker. It might not be easy, 'cause people tend to start off protecting what they want. You just keep 'em talkin' and learnin' from each other, and they're liable to run into what they really need.

"How about a piece of apple pie, Walker? Rolled out the crust myself, got some gorgeous apples. It's mighty fine and mighty tasty."

I said I'd love to eat some of Rev Baker's apple pie. When we got up to go to the kitchen, Rev lingered a moment at the jukebox to punch in a song. We ate our pie to the sounds of the Rolling Stones. Of course, we sang along:

"You can't always get what you want,
You can't always get what you want,
But if you try sometimes, you just might find
You get what you need."

ALIGN
Invent

■ ■ ■

"You can't do it if you can't imagine it."

GEORGE LUCAS

Invent conversations are stage two of alignment. The focus of conversation shifts from discovering intersections to generating possibilities. The mood of the relationship shifts, too, from thoughtful investigation of common ground to free, imaginative speculation.

To invent is the essential act of human freedom. Through invention, we make ourselves senior to circumstance and wage creative war on the limits of the past. An inventor is the opposite of a victim, transforming constraints into building blocks and barriers into launch points. When my purposes, circumstances, and explanations intersect with other purposes, circumstances, and explanations, the inventing begins.

Think of the last time you connected strongly with someone else. It is likely that two things happened:

1. You discovered you valued many of the same things, whether common ideas, pursuits, values, or ambitions.
2. You began to speculate about the possibilities for doing something together.

Whether it was a first business meeting or a first date, the same two things occur when people genuinely intersect. However, that natural interest in a common future needs to be cultivated or it will dissipate into fond, unfulfilled memories. In *The Communication Catalyst,* we are not trying to exhaust what there is to say about creativity. We are focusing on how to ensure sufficient invention to achieve your shared purposes. We call the key ingredients *the invention cascade.*

■ ■ ■

"When I examine myself and my methods of thought, I come

close to the conclusion that the gift of fantasy has meant

more to me than my talent for absorbing absolute knowledge."

ALBERT EINSTEIN

The Invention Cascade

The flow of invention we see in creative organizations is fourfold:

1. *Correlate.* Build relationships, identify resources, and forage through facts, constraints, and assumptions.
2. *Concentrate.* Focus everything you have on purpose, pattern, and possibility.
3. *Explode.* Host a chain-reaction inquiry and not a critical interrogation.
4. *Sort.* Compare the ideas and rank for contribution to stakeholders (i.e., customers, shareowners, and investors).

1. Correlate (Focus: Gathering Support, *Like Gathering Wood to Make a Fire*)

Invention is far more a communal act than a solitary one. Ideas are stimulated more than they are made up from nothing. The stronger the correlation between my purposes and concerns and those of others I work with, the freer I am to invent. The stronger the correlation with conditions, the more feasible those inventions become. The shared purpose from the intersect conversation is our foundation for inventing. Now we expand the intersection to include other purposes, explanations, and facts.

Take care of the relationships (focus: *vigilance*). Have you ever tried to brainstorm new ideas with people you do not trust? It is difficult to invent freely when you are guarding against harm. Those brainstorming sessions tend to devolve into defending and attacking ideas the participants had before they came to the meeting. Conversely, when the interests of a community are at stake, your thinking expands. Personal habit and history become less of a force than being counted on by a network of people. You focus on what must be done more than on the barriers. The previous chapters on valuable perception and intersection conversations are sources of information for taking care of relationships.

Keep the conversation meter from Chapter 3 in front of you. In any interaction with a stakeholder, assess where you are on the meter. Catch pretense and sincerity and upgrade to accuracy and authenticity. Every time you upgrade the conversation, you are upgrading the relationship.

Invention calls for courage; so does being a soldier. S.L.A. Marshall was an American troop commander in World War I. By World War II, he was a general charged with answering an important question: What makes soldiers brave and effective in the face of death? His research culminated in the remarkable book, *Men Against Fire*. After exhaustive studies and interviews, he reached the conclusion that there is "an inherent unwillingness of the soldier to risk danger on behalf of men with whom he has no social identity." General Marshall concluded that the soldiers' courage came from their relationships.

Identify resources (focus: *contribution and partnership*). The intersection also comes into play as the network of people who you can connect with to stimulate ideas. The next time you take on a major new purpose, try this: Get together with the core group you know is working on this purpose with you. Post the question, Who benefits if we succeed at (the purpose)? Then brainstorm answers to the question. Asking Who benefits? will bring to mind many people that you would otherwise not think of as resources. Whether they know it or not, they have a stake in your success. You can make requests of these people. Some of them would be great "invent" partners, bringing fresh and stimulating perspectives and their own network of resources.

Forage (focus: *fascination and exploration*). Give you and your team some time to collect and intersect with lots of related information. This is like eating well before running an important race. Connect, inquire, and wonder about:

- What *senior purposes* must we honor? These are strategic imperatives or other major commitments that our purpose is inside of and our inventing must respect.
- Are there any other "givens" in the equation that should be included; these might be decisions already made, promised delivery dates, etc.
- What is at stake? What happens if we are successful? What happens if we fail?
- What purposes, explanations, and facts are important to us?
- What purposes, explanations, and facts are important to other crucial stakeholders? How will they assess our success?
- Who has succeeded at similar challenges? What do they have to contribute?
- What assumptions limit us? Which ones are unnecessary?

Keep the answers to your foraging in front of you, preferably on a big space like a wall covered with chart paper or Post-it notes. Post your list of who benefits and forage through it from time to time. As you forage, let your imagination run free.

■ ■ ■

"Creativity arises out of the tension between spontaneity

and limitations, the latter (like the river banks)

forcing the spontaneity into the various forms

which are essential to the work . . . "

ROLLO MAY, *THE COURAGE TO CREATE* (1975)

2. Concentrate (Focus: Faith in Purpose and Self)

Canvassing all the commitments and conditions is not enough. There always comes a time when you must surrender to the purpose. This is a deep shift in mindset or, as some would say, being. Concentrate all of your faculties on the purpose and let the patterns of possibility emerge.

The shift to concentration can occur seamlessly and be unnoticed. Without it, though, the mind entertains distractions that sap invention. Some writers have described this as "giving yourself no alternative." We do not endorse that description, because it pits you *against* something (alternatives) rather than *for* something (purpose). Instead, focus on a singular future: your purpose. It is not that you avoid other choices; it is that you are entertaining only one choice: successful purpose. If patterns of possibility and vital ideas do not emerge, then check in with yourself: Are you fully given to the purpose? What is distracting you? Can you fully shift your attention to the purpose? Inventors have an indispensable trust in insight. It is natural to trust yourself to invent the only future you entertain.

In the movie *For the Love of the Game,* there is an interesting depiction of how concentration works. The aging baseball pitcher (played by Kevin Costner) has a discipline for moving into a state of concentration. We suggest that you see the movie and pay attention to the visual image. As he focuses in on his purpose, everything else goes out of focus. His intention gets sharp and clear and everything around it softens and moves into the background. Imagine yourself honing in on a purpose in the same way, letting all else move out of focus.

■　■　■

"To believe in something not yet proved and to underwrite it with our lives; it is the only way to leave the future open."

LILLIAN SMITH

Trust invention to someone who has faith in the purpose and herself. To the faithless, evidence of failure is as attractive as evidence of success. People with misgivings can certainly contribute as long as there is at least one heroine or hero with faith.

Ask people you are counting on for invention these questions:

* For you, what is important about our purpose?
  Can you hear a strong personal connection to the purpose in their response?

- On a 0 to 100 scale, what is your level of confidence that we can be inventive enough to achieve the purpose?
- What explains your rating?
  If their explanations are *only* circumstantial (because of certain conditions, etc.), they will not inspire invention. If their reasons are about commitment, abilities, and the value of the purpose, they will sponsor a geyser of ideas.

3. Explode (Focus: Free Inquiry)

The time it takes to move from correlation through concentration into an explosion of ideas can be seconds for people enthused about their purpose. Whether it takes seconds, minutes, or days to get there, invention needs unconstrained speculation. To serve this free, creative explosion, host an energetic *inquiry,* not a critical *interrogation.*

■ ■ ■

"They never raised a statue to a critic."

MARTHA GRAHAM

"If I were to wish for anything, I should not wish for wealth

and power, but for the passionate sense of the potential, for

the eye which, ever young and ardent, sees the possible."

SOREN KIERKEGAARD, *DIAPSALMATA, VOLUME I, EITHER/OR*

"Explode" is a chain reaction of ideas. If you attack each idea as it is uttered, you will break the chain. When you are asking for new ideas, tell all involved you want a specific period of time for unedited and unattacked brainstorming.

Let the conversation roll until the agreed time to stop the idea explosion. Ed may say something that strikes most of us bizarre, which triggers Susan to say something outlandish, which triggers Mary to trigger Fred to trigger Sue to voice a brilliant, feasible possibility that would have come to mind no other way. Interrogating each speaker about the quality of his or her idea will destroy this free and fertile inquiry.

These are the six conditions for an idea explosion:

1. Post the purpose for which you are inventing.
2. Pose the purpose as a question for which you are brainstorming answers.

3. Post the "Who benefits?" list.

4. Agree on a start and stop time for the brainstorming.

5. Announce a mood of creative inquiry and contrast it with critical in-terrogation. Secure an agreement to let ideas roll and step in and correct when people forget. Listen to discover and build on possibil-ities rather than to find flaws.

6. Capture the ideas on big spaces (e.g., paper-covered walls or big whiteboards). Relative to working on small spaces (computer screen or notepad), big spaces open and broaden thinking.

4. Sort (Focus: Valuable Leverage)

An idea explosion will usually leave you with more ideas than you can apply. The sorting of ideas brings the notion of value back into focus: What will your customers and investors be willing to pay for what you will be will-ing to provide? Look for the ideas that make the highest leverage contri-bution. A leveraged contribution is one that serves multiple purposes of multiple stakeholders. To catalyze sorting, have the inventing group make three different lists by answering these questions:

1. Which ideas make the highest leverage contribution to our shared purpose? These serve multiple purposes of multiple stakeholders.

2. Which ideas are most feasible? These are timely ideas for which you can envision support and resources.

3. Which ideas are we most enthused about? These are the ideas most of your inventing group *wants* to make happen.

Ideas that make all three lists are great candidates for investment.

Correlate, concentrate, explode, and sort are keys to inventing feasible possibilities. There are also traps that stop this flow of invention. The ear-lier you note the appearance of these waste traps, the quicker you can re-turn to inventing.

 ### Invention Waste Traps

Assuming being right equals being well received. People will not support your idea just because *you* know it is valuable. They will support your idea when they can see how your idea will advance their purposes. Oftentimes, people do not invest in a well-correlated start to inventing and will later battle with "buy-in" problems. Get stakeholders involved early as coinventors and your ideas, if they are great, will gain unforced support. Learn to hear criticism and rejection as interim disconnection rather than a referendum on your creative value.

■ ■ ■

"They damn what they do not understand."

QUINTILIAN DE, *INSTITUTIONE ORATORIA*

Mistrusting yourself. Trusting yourself to fulfill a purpose is an act of courage. Many people stop short of giving everything in order to avoid the potential embarrassment and regret that comes with falling short. Every honest hope brings with it potential pain. Creativity is not always pleasant, for it can be dispiriting to care completely for something, fall short, and continue to care. The drive to invent is easily derailed when the driver is cautious and tepid about trusting himself. To stimulate ideas, we need to be foolish, wrong, embarrassed, and misunderstood without losing heart. It is better to emphatically promise *not* to pursue a purpose than to pursue one with half of a heart.

The absence of every great hope can be disheartening, and yet, no great hope can ever be fulfilled without first being absent. When we commit fully and trust ourselves to invent, we very often turn hope into achievement.

■ ■ ■

"Life shrinks or expands in proportion to one's courage."

ANAÏS NIN

"Worry? I don't worry so much; I just figure it out."

LARRY EDWARD FOLES

Cynicism. Cynicism is not mere doubt. Cynicism is the focused drive to prove impossibility. Wood drenched by water does not catch fire, and purpose drenched by cynicism does not ignite invention. The refuge of cynicism is past-proven disappointment. Wrench attention from the disappointments of the past to the possibility of the future, and cynicism declines. Whatever we concentrate on, we invent support for, so beware of the undermining power of the cynic.

■ ■ ■

"When you realize the value of all of life, you dwell less on what is past and concentrate more on the preservation of the future."

DIAN FOSSEY

"In hell they say heaven is a great lie."

DANIEL BERRIGAN

Confusing a good mood with accomplishment. An explosion of ideas is an emotional high, because possibility is a beguiling pleasure. It is important to tie the ideas back to the real purposes and circumstances of stakeholders. As we sort through the ideas looking for value, we direct our attention back toward reality, which is where invention fulfills its promise. Too many brainstorming sessions end with unedited lists of ideas and a hopeful mood. Do not close invention there—close with clear, high-potential contributions.

Catalyze invention with the invention cascade or kill it with the invention waste traps. When the past is insufficient for the challenges you face, be vigilant about the difference, for high-velocity value is at stake.

The third stage of alignment is investment. The way we spend time and money and assign key people tells the truth about alignment. How we suggest you orchestrate those assets is the subject of Chapter 5.

First, as you have come to expect, we are going to check in on Rev and Walker. Walker promised Rev he was going to come back with a "song," an authentic purpose that he, Sharon, Ray, and Louis could all rally around. Let's check in on how Walker did and hear what Rev has to say about inventing, because he will certainly have his own twist.

CHAPTER SUMMARY

The Heart of the Matter

Invent conversations shift the focus from the discovery of a common purpose to the generation of actionable ideas to achieve that purpose. Invention has more to do with connection, faith, and focus than it does with individual intelligence.

Value Track: The Invention Cascade

1. *Correlate* with a focus on gathering support.

- *Build relationships.* Be vigilant in looking for intersections, practicing high-value perception, and operating in the accuracy and authenticity sections of the conversation meter. Upgrading the conversation upgrades the relationship and the ability to generate valuable ideas.
- *Identify resources.* Ask yourself the question, Who benefits if I succeed at this purpose? The people you identify in answer to this question will be natural resources, building your network of "invent" partners.
- *Forage.* Explore facts, constraints, purposes, and assumptions.

2. *Concentrate* with a focus on a singular future: Fulfillment of our shared purpose. Patterns of possibility will naturally emerge if we proceed with full commitment to ourselves and our common future.

3. *Explode* with a focus on free, energetic inquiry. This is *not* a time of critical interrogation. "Explode" is a chain reaction of ideas. If you attack each idea as it is uttered, you will break the chain.

4. *Sort* with a focus on high-value leverage of contribution. Compare the ideas and rank for the highest contribution to stakeholders. Higher leveraged contributions serve multiple purposes and stakeholders.

Invention Waste Track

- Assuming people will support your idea just because *you* know it is valuable
  Action to take: Connect your idea back to their purposes; get stakeholders involved early on as coinventors of ideas.
- Mistrusting yourself to fulfill the shared purpose
  Action to take: Abandon timidity and contribute boldly to a cascade of ideas.
- Allowing cynicism to be your focused drive to prove impossibility
  Action to take: Shift your focus from the disappointments of the past to the possibilities of the future.
- Confusing a good mood with accomplishment
  Action to take: Make clear, high-value contributions the test for your ideas, not euphoria.

R E V   L E S S O N

■ ■ ■

It's Just Your Imagination

"Tell you, it was just my imagination,
Running away with me."

THE TEMPTATIONS, "IT'S JUST MY IMAGINATION"

"It is surely good to meet y'all. It's like fittin' faces to folks I've only read about in books." Rev was smiling as he shook hands all around.

We were sitting at table number six, the round one in the middle of Rev Baker's Beautiful Central Texas Hill Country Barbecue Café. Table number six is on the other side of the jukebox from the table Rev likes to sit at. I was nervous and eager for them to think well of each other.

"I told Walker if he kept quoting you, I was going to think you were a famous dead person. It's good to meet you myself." Louis Evans looked up at Rev with obvious interest and his customary big smile. I noticed that Louis looked like a smaller, paler version of Rev. Same tight curls and burly, strong body on a shorter frame but from a different lineage.

Ray Garza's deep, black eyes searched out Rev's. "It is good to meet you, Mr. Baker. You have already helped us a lot."

"You must be Mr. Garza. I'm glad to help out. Now, how about I call you Ray and you call me Rev. That alright with you?" Ray, having never broken his gaze, nodded yes.

"I understand I have you to thank for my no longer being referred to as a fire-arm." The former "Shotgun Sharon," now known only as Sharon Scott, stood to shake Rev's hand. It struck me as an intentional act of respect. Rev's checkered pants and white, starched, double-breasted cook's coat did not seem to dull her regard for him.

Rev held the handshake for an extra second and told Sharon, "You've been good for Walker, Ms. Scott. He needed to bump up against someone strong and smart so he could find out some things about himself."

Sharon said, "Rev, I'm glad that Walker's stories left you with that impression. And please, call me Sharon."

Rev nodded and said, "Walker, you promised to come back with a song, as I re-call." He looked at me expectantly.

"Yes, and I think we composed a good one." I looked around the table and added, "Rev's talking about our senior purpose." That evoked nods and smiles.

"Rev," Sharon said, "we took your advice and looked for a common purpose that helps us coordinate everything we're doing. When Walker brought up the subject, I didn't understand right away. I knew we already had a charter, which is our divi-sion job description. After we talked, though, I understood what he meant. We did not have a common purpose that was stimulating a lot of invention."

"That's for sure." Louis nodded with a rueful half-smile. "I was mainly being in-ventive about how to avoid dealing with the rest of you."

"Pure pretense, Lou," Ray chided.

"Except when I got mad, then a dose of sincerity." Louis pointed at me. "Walker, I think you win the pretense crown. I had no idea you were so annoyed."

Sharon stepped in. "I think I take the sincerity crown. I had no problem telling all you guys exactly what I thought was wrong with you. Then, the small number of ideas and proposals you offered frustrated me. Small wonder."

We went on to explain to Rev how we got to our senior purpose. Ray and Louis were working on two major development projects that used to be managed separately. They were bundled together and put under me, along with an advanced research lab that was an incubator for other possible development projects. We all reported to Sharon, who had three other organizations reporting to her. Sharon's organization was called Information Technology Solutions. Many people at MightyTek gossiped about the name. Lots of organizations were putting "solutions" in their name, because it is considered smart to bundle products and services into solutions to customer problems. So far, though, the solutions were only a sales angle and had not changed how we worked. We were promising integrated solutions but not really delivering any.

The first intersection Ray, Louis, and I reached was the meeting we thought Sharon and the rest of her staff would be interested in. We called it "Solution Selling: Cheap Talk or Real Value." They loved it, and we had a meeting with Sharon, her staff, and their direct reports. We put up the conversation meter and explained it to everyone. We put up the intersection graphic and said we were looking for a common purpose that would transform our solution strategy from cheap talk to real value. We also asked for permission to point out when the conversation fell below 50 on the meter and to coach people on accuracy and authenticity. They said "yes" and off we went.

It was a wild meeting. The walls were covered with flip chart lists of purposes, worries, and important facts. We broke into three groups that identified three to five themes from the lists. We posted all of the themes, and then each group suggested a purpose statement that integrated the themes into actionable commitment. Then, two people from each group got together, and those six people suggested a senior purpose we could all rally around. The whole group really liked it and, after minor changes, adopted it on the spot. All of this happened with a few interruptions from Ray or Louis or me as we pointed out conversational waste (pretense and sincerity) and coached people on upgrading to high-value conversation (accuracy and authenticity).

"Well, what's your song? You got to tell me, you know that." Rev was obviously pleased at our progress.

"Walker," Sharon said, "you tell Rev."

"Rev, we looked for the most valuable common thread running through the current products, new ones, and ideas coming out of advanced research. We realized that our own problem of disconnected solutions is also our customers' problem. Some of the best ideas in the advanced lab are ways to connect systems that do not talk to each other now. What we landed on as a senior purpose is, *"We transform current costs into high-return investments by connecting existing Information*

Technology systems to create networks of breakthrough productivity." As I finished, Ray raised his tea glass in a toast and the others followed suit.

"Hear. Hear!"

Rev said, "What has you folks like the purpose so much?"

Sharon responded first. "We all have our best thinking in it. Before, we were
spending considerable time convincing each other of what was the right thing to
do, and now we're in something together with no convincing necessary. Also, it has
enough detail in it to guide our decisions, and it fits our capabilities. Now we don't
just have a veneer of a promise to customers that we all mistrust. We really see
the strategic solution we're eager to provide."

Louis followed, "Rev, that definition of value you gave Walker was a big help.
We kept testing our common themes by asking what the value was to customers,
investors, and ourselves. The purpose we adopted was the best value for all three
groups. We're pretty darn excited about it. A little scared, but excited."

Rev said, "You know, Louis, any great idea will likely scare you a bit. I just want
to know if it is worth being scared about. Sounds like this purpose is worth it to
y'all." Rev finished with a sweeping gesture that took in all of us.

Ray jumped in, "Yeah, and we already have some great new ideas. In fact,
these ideas are so good that we're going to revise our business plan upward and
request more resources. We think we can at least double our contribution to
MightyTek profits over the next three years."

"Ray, that is mighty fine. That's the way you know you have a real intersection—
ideas start poppin' out all over the place. Once you've got an intersection, you can't
help it, you just got to start inventin'."

"Whoa, fellas!" Sharon had her hand thrust out in the middle of the table with
her palm opened wide. "Slow down. We have lots to prove before I get any budget
increases. Let's not let our imaginations run away with us."

Rev said, "That's a fact, Sharon. It's just imagination at the moment. Is it OK
with you if I say a little bit about that?"

"Sure." Sharon laughed slightly. "Who am I to refuse counsel from someone
Sara McGregor listens to." I hoped Rev did not mind my sharing that fact.

It did not seem to bother Rev. "Imagination is us tryin' to have a say about the
future. Changin' how the future's gonna go, well, that's not a little thing. Imagination may not change the future by itself, but you're not changin' much without it.
Imagination is like an excited youngster who needs a bit of guidance."

"Rev, I get the impression that you think our imaginations running away with us
is not a bad thing. Sooner or later, though, we have to deal with reality." Sharon
then asked Rev if he would sit and talk. He said he needed to check in on the
kitchen and the dining room, then he would be happy to "sit and visit."

This was one of those moments when, up to a week ago, I would have just appeased Sharon and let my enthusiasm for our purpose wane. However, I was starting to get good at researching purposes I could respect.

After we ordered lunch, I asked Sharon what was on her mind when she said "Whoa!" She said she did not want us to give up on improving the development processes and have that fund all or part of our new strategic direction.

"As I hear you guys get excited about an increase in resources, I get nervous. Once we demonstrate the contribution to revenue and profit, we'll have the appropriate budget. We've had a good start, but we have not proven anything."

"Sharon, I promise you we will take waste out of the development processes. We're sharing more information with each other now, so Louis, Ray, and I have already seen improvements we can make quickly. We will refocus and reprioritize within our existing budget rather than just coming to you with our hands out. I don't blame you for worrying, because in the past we've blamed too much on 'not enough resources.' I think the real problem is that we were not using each other as resources."

Sharon said, "Walker, I'm glad to hear that you respect my concerns."

I went on. "Ray, I know you said the word *resources,* and I also know that's not what you are excited about. Your enthusiasm is really for our new senior purpose, not for budgets. Your passion is infectious and we all feed off of it, so don't you dare lose it." I noticed Ray sit up straighter.

The conversation immediately became less tense and more animated. In a short while, Rev and the waiter served our lunches and Rev sat down with us. After about 15 minutes of casual comments between bites, Rev reentered the imagination subject.

"When you are inventing a new future, you want a bunch of ideas, more than you will ever make happen. How you overcome the limits folks have on the future is to generate more possibility than they can avoid. Y'all focus on the new purpose and produce so many ideas that folks stop askin' 'Is it possible?' and start askin' 'Which of these great new ideas are we gonna do first?' That's the time you worry about budgets. Don't worry about budgets till your inventin' has broken the grip of the past."

Sharon laughed out loud and pointed at Rev. "Yeah, what he said."

Rev made a lot of sense, as usual. Louis told Rev that we engineers always wanted to know the answer to the question "how." I suspected that a bevnap lesson was on the way.

"Louis, the difference between imagine and invent is just a little bit of guidance. Let's draw a rough map for turning imagination into invention." Rev stood, walked to the bar, and returned with some napkins.

Rev wrote down what he called the "invention cascade." The elements are:

- **Correlate.** Build a network out of potential beneficiaries of the purpose and forage facts, constraints, and assumptions. "While you forage you're hooking up folks and facts and such to make an invention machine," Rev said.
- **Concentrate.** "Give all your attention to the purpose you're inventing for. Write it down, post it, and talk about it till it haunts you in a waking dream. Focus on it like it's all that matters."
- **Explode.** "Free, wild brainstorming is what you want here. It'll be like a chain reaction of ideas, so don't go breaking the chain by worrying about each one. Let it roll till you're surprised, till you've seen things you've never seen before."
- **Sort.** "Make four lists: (1) highest value to customers, investors, and employees; (2) most feasible; (3) most enthusiasm; and (4) best to invest. The 'best to invest' list, that'll be the ideas ranked high on each of the first three lists."

We talked for an hour. Sharon asked more than a few questions and so did the rest of us. We talked about pitfalls and next steps, and asked Rev for examples.

Finally, Rev said, "I believe we've said enough for now. How about some dessert? We've got somethin' special." We did not resist.

Soon, Rev put before us what looked like a dense chocolate pie. I saw the perfect, bronze crust through the glass pie plate and felt my tongue wet my lips.

"I got this from my friends Larry and Guy. I was down on West Sixth Street havin' dinner with them at Z'Tejas yesterday, and Larry served me a piece. Oh my, it's so good I thought I was in God's own kitchen. Chili ancho fudge pie is what it's called. I bought a whole one to bring home."

I must have had an obvious reaction, because Rev said, "Walker, you seem a touch afraid of chili ancho fudge pie."

"Well, Rev, I've never thought of having chili peppers and chocolate for dessert."

"Walker, don't get all trapped in the past. Inventin' great desserts is not all that different than inventin' new Information Technology solutions. It all starts with putting old things together in new ways. What's at the intersection of chili anchos and chocolate is a whole new kind of delicious."

Louis chimed in. "Walker, remember, great ideas will scare you at first."

"Sure, Lou, but everything that scares me might not be a great idea." We all laughed at that point, even me at my own joke. I gave in and we all sampled Chili Ancho Fudge Pie. Oh my, what a heavenly surprise!

As our scraped-clean dessert plates were being cleared away, Sharon thanked Rev for spending time with us. We all added our thanks, too.

"You are surely welcome. And Sharon, you are an unusual leader. I've earned nothin' with you, and yet you come in here interested. Lots of folks in your position would keep their own counsel and just tolerate my chatter. Not you."

"Rev, you've made a valuable difference in how we are working. I've paid consultants thousands of dollars for less value than we received from you just today. I just don't want to abuse your generosity." They shook hands as equals.

Louis spoke up. "Rev, Walker says you always have a song. Have one today?"

Rev turned to the jukebox and pressed buttons. When the song began, we all laughed one more time. We paid our check and Sharon, Louis, and Ray departed while The Temptations sang, "It's just my imagination, runnin' away with meeee."

Rev walked outside with me. "Y'all aren't totally aligned yet, Walker. You will be once you decide how you're gonna change how you spend time and money, and assign your key people. Let me know if you want to talk about that."

I thanked Rev warmly. As I drove away, I knew we would be talking again soon.

CHAPTER FIVE

ALIGN
Invest

■ ■ ■

"For a successful technology, reality must take precedence
over public relations, for Nature cannot be fooled."

RICHARD FEYNMAN

Invest conversations are the bridge between potential and performance.
They turn optimistic agreement into realistic alignment by allocating time,
money, and talent to achieve a purpose. Invest conversations are the third
crucial element of genuine alignment:

1. Intersection of purpose
2. Invention of ideas for achieving the purpose
3. Investment of time, money, and key people

Invest conversations ensure that shared purpose and inspired ideas do not devolve into those good intentions with which the road to hell is paved.

Invent to Invest: A Shift in Emphasis

Last chapter, we were fanning the flames of invention. Valuable invent conversations are optimistic and daring. However, the mood shifts when you are hosting an invest conversation. The interactions move from *generating ideas* to *testing ideas and committing resources*. In the invent conversations criticism is wasteful. In the invest conversations criticism is valuable. In the invest conversations invention gets married to reality.

■ ■ ■

"If you have built castles in the air, your work need not be lost;
that is where they should be. Now put foundations under them."

HENRY DAVID THOREAU

In their own way, invest conversations are just as creative as invent conversations. Invest conversations are creative about discovering and orchestrating resources to achieve valuable ideas. We do not want our great ideas to succumb to reality. Rather, we want to creatively weave our great ideas into reality. Stand confidently in the idea and ask, What purposes and circumstances help the idea? Invest conversations bring the power to invent to the circumstances, sorting them for value. Circumstances, then, are less the limits of creativity than they are the building blocks.

■ ■ ■

"Learning too soon our limitations, we never learn our powers."

MIGNON MCLAUGHLIN

Invest conversations creatively address issues of:

- *Value.* Will this investment produce benefit for which customers and investors will pay? Will our employees (including contractors and allies) be willing and able to provide it?

- *Planning.* Are the right people involved in the planning? Is our plan adequate to assess needed time, money, and talent?
- *Efficiency.* Are the processes the plan assumes in place? Do those processes make smart use of our resources? If not, which people need to meet and in what forum to design valuable processes?
- *Feasibility.* Can we practically expect success? What are the risks? Are the risks worthwhile?

In invent conversations, questions of planning, efficiency, and feasibility break the chain reaction of ideas. In invest conversations, answering those questions roots the idea in reality and grants it credibility.

The Invest Conversations

In any business system constrained by time, money, or talent, investment is an issue of timing. We allocate and reallocate resources inside of the question, What is the most valuable use of time, money, and talent right *now?* If you want to become brilliant at invest conversations, haunt yourself with this question of timing. We have found this general fourfold approach to be valuable in addressing the timing question:

1. *Simulate.* Design and propose realistic scenarios for executing a high-value idea.
2. *Compare.* Filter the scenarios through common criteria and rank for value.
3. *Improve.* Stimulate suggestions for improving chances of success.
4. *Commit.* Dedicate time, money, and talent.

1. Simulate (Focus: Anticipate)

Simulation anticipates and prepares for reality. Even a quick, informal simulation is more valuable than a thoughtless investment. It is remarkable how much people can anticipate if they are only given a chance.

In the mid-1990s, we worked on a construction project that was under enormous time pressure. The financial stakes were huge, and accelerated completion was mandatory. Our client hosted a meeting with a microcosm of the people who would have to get this unprecedented achievement to happen. Attendees included governmental authorities, building contractors, architects, engineers, company management, and other key contributors. We started the meeting by posting and explaining the conversation model (pretense/sincerity/accuracy/authenticity) and asking that we all use it. They agreed. Then, we asked the following questions:

- If we do not get this plant operating in 18 months, what will have happened that explains the failure?
- If we succeed in getting open in 18 months, what will have happened that explains the success?
- What forums or meetings will ensure that we use our time well? Who should participate in each of those forums?
- What suggestions do you have for smart cost management?
- What suggestions do you have for using key people wisely?

These experienced people anticipated the problems and opportunities brilliantly. We were able to add their insights to all the traditional large-project planning that was already in progress. The facility opened on time and on budget. The project manager says two things rise above other factors in explaining the success:

1. Establishing a condition of open, valuable communication
2. Using the experience and commitment of the people who would have to "get it done" to anticipate and simulate failure and success

Another method of simulation was well tested by Edward Lindaman, who wrote *Thinking in Future Tense*. Lindaman's recommendations were based on, among other things, his experience as a successful director of planning in the Apollo space program. He discovered a remarkable dynamic: When people create action plans by working backward from a preferred future, they take less time to plan, increase enthusiasm for the plan, and develop a more realistic simulation of the challenge.

We urge you to test Lindaman's assertions. The next time you are testing an idea, try the following ten steps:

1. Assemble a microcosm of the group who would have to achieve the idea.

2. Post your "who benefits" list from your invent conversation. Explain it to the group and invite them to add to it at any time.

3. Together, create a detailed picture of your preferred future. If you achieve it, what will have happened? What will be the visible, valuable difference?

4. Pick a particularly important milestone associated with achieving the preferred future.

5. Put three charts on the wall labeled "time," "money," and "key people."

6. Draw a timeline on a wall from today out to the time by when you need to achieve the major milestone.

7. Go stand at the future milestone date and turn toward today's date.

8. Walk back to today in very small steps. Each step will be the answer to the question, What happened just before that? Make notes on the three charts:

   - Time: How will time be spent differently than it is right now?
   - Money: What new costs or investments are necessary (equipment, salaries, software, consulting, etc).
   - Key people: Who specifically will need to be involved to achieve this idea? What do you predict as the *real* demand on their time?
   - Note on the timeline when each of these investments in time, money, and talent will be needed.

9. If you get stuck, look at your "who benefits" list and see who can help.

10. Walk all the way back to today. You will have developed a plan that simulates the real challenge of your idea.

Try out this Conversant version of Lindaman's approach. We predict that you will find it engaging and valuable.

■ ■ ■

"I remember sittin' in the dentist's office, I was about

nine years old, doin' the puzzles in the back of *Boys' Life*

magazine. For fun, I tracked one of the mazes from the end

back to the beginnin'. The path was obvious goin' backwards,

so it was fast. I never did a maze the old way after that."

REV BAKER

2. Compare *(Focus:* Illuminate and Accelerate*)*

By comparing alternate uses of resources, you can develop better plans, make quicker decisions, and ensure solid support. However, don't treat comparison like a competition between proposals, with one winning approval and the others losing. The point of comparison is *not* to see who wins. Instead, use comparison to illuminate and accelerate value.

Illuminate. Prepare and present the scenarios accurately. Carefully separate mutually observable facts from explanations of what the facts mean. What do you *accurately* have to say about necessary time, money, and key people? Then, compare your scenario to other uses of the same resources:

- How does this scenario contribute to our senior purpose?
- What else could the same resources be used for?
- What other approaches to this same idea are worth considering?
- Who benefits from each scenario? Would those beneficiaries be willing to subsidize costs and mitigate risks?
- Whom does each scenario damage? What are the implications?
- Can strengths of the different scenarios be combined into a new scenario?

When different groups are preparing scenarios, tell them ahead of time that the comparison is not a competition. Ask them to come as a brain trust with a senior purpose: highest possible value for customers, investors, and employees. The spirit is present, learn, and adjust rather than present and defend. Beware of the presenter who is not there for the greater good. You can recognize him because he uses facts for self-defense rather than illumination.

■ ■ ■

"He uses statistics as a drunken man uses lampposts: for
support rather than illumination."

ANDREW LANG

Valuable scenarios generate discussion. Many presenters mistakenly think that their purpose is to "wow" the crowd and receive wild acclaim and no adjustment to their plan. If your scenario is valuable, then people want in on it. They will naturally compare your use of resources with others they know about. They will question, suggest, and test. Such input is evidence of interest, not disdain. If you want to get nervous, get nervous when you stimulate no discussion at all.

Accelerate. Comparison quickens decision. Highest value is apparent more quickly when it arises from comparison. Think back to a time you were stuck making a decision. Were you laboring over whether or not you should do a particular thing? For example:

- Should we buy that house?
- Should I hire that person?
- Should we make that investment?

Often, stuck decisions can be unstuck by comparison. Explore what else you might do with the time, money, and talent involved. What senior purpose are you out to serve? What is your preferred future? How do the alternatives compare regarding your senior purpose and preferred future? Most of our choices, consciously or unconsciously, are made relative to other uses of time, money, and talent. To accelerate the choice, clarify the other uses and compare. Comparison is significantly faster than laboring over alternatives one at a time.

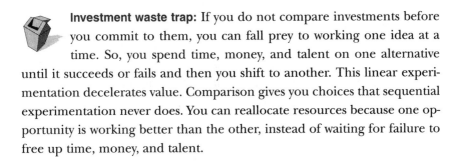 **Investment waste trap:** If you do not compare investments before you commit to them, you can fall prey to working one idea at a time. So, you spend time, money, and talent on one alternative until it succeeds or fails and then you shift to another. This linear experimentation decelerates value. Comparison gives you choices that sequential experimentation never does. You can reallocate resources because one opportunity is working better than the other, instead of waiting for failure to free up time, money, and talent.

3. Improve (Focus: Increase Benefit and Reduce Risk)

Every comparison provides answers to the question, How can we improve our use of time, money, and key people? To ignore this question is to waste the power of comparison. Harness the power of comparison by reviewing:

- *Value.* How can we improve the benefit to customers, investors, and employees?

- *Planning.* How can we improve our plan of achievement? Are there different people to involve? In what forums will they interact?
- *Efficiency.* How can we improve our fundamental processes to better use our resources?
- *Feasibility.* What can we now do to improve our chances of success?

Update your scenario after reviewing value, planning, efficiency, and feasibility. Even if there are no more comparisons, your idea will be better designed.

4. Commit (Focus: Full Support)

Invest conversations are complete when we commit:
- Time, money, and talent sufficient to the task
- Political support sufficient to the task

Commitment to an idea needs to be decisive, not tentative. If support is tentative, then the invest conversation is incomplete. Do not expect inspired, successful execution of the idea. When people in authority shrink from their responsibility to fully commit resources and political support, the foundation for action is weak. Tentative fence-sitting is an investment in failure. In our consulting practice, we frequently hear employees complain about the failure of leadership to commit decisively.

■ ■ ■

"Perhaps your fear in passing judgment is greater
than mine in receiving it."

GIORDANO BRUNO

"There is grief in indecision."

CICERO

A well-designed decision protocol is central to full commitment. Design and commit to your decision protocol well prior to the potentially heated moment of decision making. In *The Communication Catalyst,* our bias is for high-velocity value, and that bias is evident in our recommendation.

Four Decision Protocols

Business decisions tend to be made in one of four ways:

1. *Authoritative* decision making puts prioritizing, deliberating and deciding in the hands of someone in authority. Occasionally, any community needs to depend on leadership for a fast, intuitive decision. If authority is the *everyday* decision protocol, however, these effects ensue:
   - People stop thinking for themselves and await instructions.
   - Decisions depend on the disconnected judgment of a few. If the authority misses something that is obvious to employees, her credibility crumbles.
   - Bioreactions proliferate when people feel dominated. Fear drives behavior more than purpose, and there is less brainpower on the job.

2. *Voting* puts decision making in the hands of the majority. Voting is quick and relieves any individual of the responsibility for the decision. Voting has these drawbacks:
   - Those who lose are often alienated; their compliance is not commitment, it is resistance gone underground.
   - The input of experts is equal to nonexperts.
   - The input of those who have to implement the decision is equal to those who have no such accountability.
   - The input of those who are liable for consequences is equal to that of relative bystanders.

3. *Consensus* decision making requires that everyone deliberates and everyone agrees. The underlying intent is sound: get the entire work community involved and ensure support. It does not work that way, though. The limitations of consensus include the input inequities cited above about voting. Also, there is an effect hardly anyone desires: painfully slow decisions.

   When consensus is the dominant protocol, people only have to think through the decision until they develop a personal preference. You give a virtual veto to people who are not considering what is best for the system as a whole. With no natural call to study system benefit, you accidentally train people to think in narrow terms. Consensus becomes an inadvertent investment in turf protection. Participants protect their own view and avoid truly understanding competing views.

To get everyone to agree in that covertly contentious situation, you must sacrifice creativity for conformity.

The longer consensus is the dominant protocol, the slower decision making will get. Organizations will fragment and protect themselves from each other, hiding and hoarding information and resources. The original purpose of having community support for decisions is lost, and a different reason maintains the consensus habit: mistrust. When you do not trust others to represent your view, you treasure veto power as a way to protect your interests.

■ ■ ■

"Not everyone who can contribute to an important decision has the perspective, information, and courage needed to make the decision."

SARA MCGREGOR

4. *Contributive* decision making harnesses the intelligence of a group to make quick, valuable decisions. A contributive protocol has two requirements: (1) high-value communication and (2) clear roles that connect expertise to business risk.

The roles that we describe below are valuable only in a condition of high-value communication. As you will see, their effectiveness lives in the ability to recognize, raise, and resolve issues. If you are vigilant about managing the quality of conversation, the roles are valuable. The easiest way we have found for ensuring valuable interactions is to use the conversation meter from Chapter 3. Catch pretense and sincerity and correct to accuracy and authenticity.

Contributive roles are designed to connect expertise with risk. Some years ago, we learned a valuable lesson from Chuck Saxe, a scientist and senior manager at Tektronix. Chuck pointed out that in businesses we usually know who is expert in what, and when our biggest problems occur, we quickly fit appropriate expertise with the risk involved.

Think back to the last major problem that struck your organization. Notice how quickly you pulled people off of what they were working on to solve the new, high-risk problem. We naturally try to fit expertise with risk when we face grave difficulty. The purpose of contributive decision making is to fit expertise with risk *before* we face such problems.

Roles in Contributive Decision Making

Decider. The decider has the ultimate authority to decide. He is:

- In the best position to assess the value that is at stake for customers, investors, and employees
- Accountable for learning from every issue raised by the executors and advisors
- Answerable for the consequences of the decision

There should be only one decider per decision. If it seems that there must be more than one, break the decision down into a succession of decisions.

Executor. The executor is the person or persons responsible for executing the decision.

- Executors have the right to give input about feasibility, consequences, and value of the decision.
- Executors must be skilled in raising *accurate* (fact-based) issues with the decider in a way that clearly serves the business purpose at stake.

Advisor. Advisors are subject matter experts who have important perspectives granted by their specific skills and experience.

- Advisors have the right to raise issues related to their areas of expertise.
- They, too, must raise accurate issues that clearly serve the business purpose.
- Frequently, an advisor can help design the decision team to ensure the right participation relative to business risk.

Recipient. The recipient is someone who needs only to be informed of the decision so he can act accordingly.

Uninvolved. The uninvolved person is anyone who does not fill one of the previous four roles.

Commitment of time, money, and talent happens quickly and with conviction when the contributive roles are at work. Remember, though, contributive decision making demands a condition of valuable communication.

We also mentioned political support. When we have committed time, money, and key people to a new effort, it is important to reset the expectations of the population at large. If you have reached the decision by using the principles of alignment (intersect, invent, and invest), you will then be well prepared to clarify what people must:

- *Preserve.* What will you keep doing? To what purposes are you still committed?
- *Eliminate.* What will we stop doing? What do we say "no" to now?
- *Create.* What must we generate that we have not been doing? What new purposes are important? What are the new uses of resources?

Simulate. Compare. Improve. Commit. These are the invest conversations and complete the foundation of alignment. The cycle of value, align⇒ act⇒adjust, operates like any wheel: it takes more effort to get it started than it does to keep it going.

Your well-laid foundation is now ready for rapid action and agile adjustment.

Rev Lesson number five comes up next. When we left Walker and Rev, Walker was feeling good. Ideas were flowing from his newly forged work community. Now, it's time for Rev to coach Walker on how to turn inspiration into investment.

CHAPTER SUMMARY

The Heart of the Matter

Invest conversations turn optimistic agreement into realistic alignment by allocating time, money, and talent to achieve a purpose. They are the bridge between potential and performance.

Invest Value Track

Invest conversations creatively address issues of value, planning, efficiency, and feasibility. By answering questions in these areas, we root the ideas in reality and grant them credibility.

Invest conversations are about timing. What is the most valuable use of time, money, and talent right *now?* Answer the timing question by doing the following:

Simulate

- Design and propose realistic scenarios for executing a high-value idea.
- Simulate by anticipating reality. Walk back from a desired future. Look to the "who benefits" list for resources and plot out the use of time, money, and key people.

Compare

- Begin to illuminate and compare accurately the necessary time, money, and key people for each scenario. You are looking for the scenario that contributes to the senior purpose and creates the highest possible value for customers, investors, and employees.
- Use comparison to stimulate ideas for improvement.
- If you do not compare investments before you commit to them, you can fall prey to working one idea at a time. Comparison gives you choices that sequential experimentation never does.

Improve

- How do you improve the use of time, money, and key people? Look at value (to customers, investors, and employees), planning, efficiency, and feasibility.
- Update your scenarios based on what you learn.

Commit

- Invest conversations are complete when we commit time, money, talent, and political support sufficient to the task.
- A well-designed decision protocol is central to full commitment. There are four decision-making protocols:
  1. *Authoritative* decision making puts prioritizing, deliberating, and deciding in the hands of someone in authority.

2. *Voting* puts the decision making in the hands of the majority.

3. *Consensus* decision making requires that everyone deliberates and everyone agrees.

4. *Contributive* decision making harnesses the intelligence of a group to make quick, valuable decisions. The contributive protocol has two requirements: (1) High value communication (the ability to effectively recognize, raise, and resolve issues) and (2) clear roles that connect expertise to business risk.

Those roles include:

- *Decider.* The person who has the ultimate authority to decide
- *Executor.* The person or people responsible for executing the decision
- *Advisor.* Subject matter experts whose specific skills and experience give them important perspectives
- *Recipient.* Someone who needs to be informed of the decision so they can act accordingly
- *Uninvolved.* Anyone who doesn't fill the previous roles

Investment of time, money, and talent happens quickly and with conviction when the contributive roles are at work in a condition of valuable communication.

R E V   L E S S O N

. . .

Budget Is Policy

"If you've got the money, honey

I've got the time."

LEFTY FRIZZELL, "IF YOU'VE GOT THE MONEY, HONEY"

ff **I**f everybody likes it right away, it's mostly 'cause it reminds them of something they already like. If you water down your great new ideas so everyone approves right off, what's great and new gets lost." Rev's words made their customary sense. However, he seemed unusually subdued.

I responded, "It's still disappointing that everyone did not react as positively as we thought they would."

"Walker, you best give up the notion that a great idea guarantees you a great response. The folks you're talkin' to haven't gone through all you did to think it up. Also, they don't have the same purposes and circumstances as you. If you want a great response, you'll need to weave the idea into their lives." Rev's voice was quiet and certain.

"Rev, you told me last week that I was likely to run into a lack of alignment. I have. Can I come out for lunch today or tomorrow? I'd enjoy the barbecue and the counsel." For a moment, all I heard over the phone was Rev's quiet, even breathing.

"Walker, I won't be available the next few days. There's somethin' that I need to attend to. Come out anyway, though. I'll have to see which day works best."

"Rev, I'll come out for lunch alright, but if you're gone why does it matter when I do?"

"It's time you get a little input from someone else. Hold on a minute." While Rev was off the line, I sat at my desk and wondered. I wondered why he did not say more about not being available. I wondered who he wanted me to meet. I wondered if I was having Rev's Mighty Fine, Mighty Tasty Barbecue today or not. In the midst of my wondering, Rev returned.

"How about the day after tomorrow, Walker, about one o'clock?"

"Okay. Who is going to meet with me?"

Rev chuckled softly. "I believe we'll just let that be a surprise, Walker. You just come out on Wednesday. It'll be worth your while."

I thought, "What exactly is he up to?" All I said, though, was, "Thanks, Rev. I'll be there for whomever." Rev told me he would talk to me pretty soon and we got off the phone. I kept right on wondering.

Two days later, I rolled into the gravel parking lot of Rev's barbecue café at ten minutes before one o'clock in the afternoon. Since I was early, I strolled down past the magnolias to the lakefront and walked through the grass to Rev's hammock, which hung parallel to the shoreline between two trees. I sat in the middle of the hammock facing the water, my feet on the ground, and rocked slightly in the breeze. I reflected on the events of the past week.

The Research and Development Council for MightyTek was having its semiannual meeting with the Marketing Council. The agenda was to share customer feedback on our products and services and preview new possible offerings coming out of the labs. I thought it would be a good place to test our new senior purpose. I told the assembled R&D and marketing managers: *"We transform current costs into high-return investments by connecting existing Information Technology systems to create networks of breakthrough productivity."* Then I paused briefly to allow for applause. None came.

First, there was silence and then, a storm of comments, like: "Do you have approval for that charter change?" "What projects are you going to kill?" "What customer data supports the strategy?" "Where will you get the money to do this?" "What extra resources are you going to need? Where will they come from?"

I started responding to the questions and that spurred more questions. The person chairing the meeting asked that we not take up more time for this "off-agenda discussion." I told everyone I would respond to the comments and questions by e-mail and voice mail. The next day I found out Sharon got e-mails objecting to our "freelance strategy development." It was sure not the response I'd hoped for. I never even got to all the great ideas we had for making our new purpose a success!

As I watched the waters of Lake Austin lap up against the grassy shore, I reflected on what I'd learned from Rev so far. I was already seeing some things to do when I heard footsteps on the path behind me. I turned and my back stiffened slightly at the sight. I suddenly felt like I needed to be on my best behavior.

"Hello, Walker O'Reilly."

"Hello, Ms. McGregor." She always seemed cool and poised. I wondered if anything ever disturbed her composure. The beige, collarless suit she wore looked less wrinkled than suits get on the rest of us.

"Let's dispense with last names and get to work." Sara Mac jerked her head up toward the café, a suggestion that we move in that direction.

"Are you my lunch appointment?" I was startled.

"Yes, and I would prefer you did not relate to it as an unwelcome shock." Sara smiled as she noted my discomfort.

"It's welcome, believe me. I'm just surprised you would take the time to help me. And a little nervous, I guess, about being worth your while."

"I'm here because Rev asked me. If he says you're worth it, you're worth it." She was turning up the path while she spoke. I scrambled to catch up. As we walked, she told me what she knew about my situation. By the time we finished our sandwiches, I'd filled her in on the latest events.

"I'm impressed." Sara Mac said. "That was an accurate report, something rare and useful. Thank you for not peppering your account with explanations masquerading as facts."

"You're welcome."

"Rev wanted me to talk with you, because he said the invest conversations were next for you. Investing is what I do, so I'll tell you some things I've learned, if you're interested."

"Interested? Anything you're willing to share I'm eager to hear. Please, go on."
I was very, very interested.

"We'll go on, then. First, a fundamental point: *the evidence of investment is time, money, and talent.* What does that mean to you, Walker?"

"I guess that no one is really invested in something if they don't risk those things." My voice went up an octave at the end of my sentence, turning a statement into an appeal for approval.

"Perfect." Sara Mac nodded, and as her short brown hair moved, light caught the flecks of gray. She seemed young and old at the same time: too vital to be old and too wise to be young.

"Walker, go for investment, not just approval. Among the veterans in Washington, D.C., there is a saying: Budget is policy. There is practical truth to that. People approve of a whole lot of things that they don't spend time, money, and talent on."

"Do you think I got too caught up in looking for approval at the council?"

"It seems that way. Approval is a dangerous focus for someone seeking investment."

"What makes it dangerous?"

"People going for approval tend to design their ideas to avoid controversy and conflict. Invest conversations should confront reality head on. Otherwise, people agree to things without confronting the real demand on time, money, and talent. Invest conversations are not about convincing people. Rather, they are about weaving your idea into current purposes and conditions to make it achievable. A great, achievable idea easily gathers support."

"We really haven't done that yet, not even for ourselves. It sounds like I unveiled our new purpose too soon." I was starting to see why we got objections and not much else at the council.

"It was too soon only if you were expecting them to promise you time, money, and key people. If you wanted their help in troubleshooting your purpose, you timed it perfectly. Invest conversations turn the possible into the plausible. They asked those tough questions, because plausibility was missing in their eyes. You need plausibility to assess timing."

"Timing?" I wanted to hear more.

"That's right. Invest conversations are all about timing. They answer the question, What is valuable *now?*" Sara Mac's right forefinger came down on the table to punctuate her point.

"That seems shortsighted. Am I missing something? What about long-term investments?"

Sara smiled slightly. I suspected she was about to patiently correct my flawed reasoning. "Any investment, short term or long, starts with action now. Tomorrows are built out of what we do today, Walker. Invest conversations build enough of a bridge between tomorrow and today to merit spending time, money, and talent *now*."

"OK, now I think I understand. What's valuable now? is one of those smart questions Rev talks about. I think I've confused What do I wish was happening now? with What's valuable now?"

Sara smiled again, this time a bigger smile. "Don't feel lonely, Walker. Understanding the difference between those two questions is all too rare. You are a quick study. It took me years to grasp the difference between my preferences and good timing. It's an intersection issue, not an issue of isolated desire."

"Is that because What's valuable now? is at the intersection of my view, other people's views, and the circumstances?"

"Absolutely, Walker!" Sara leaned over and slapped my shoulder as she spoke. "The intersection governs investment. In invest conversations, enrich the original intersection with the question, Who benefits if our idea succeeds? The people who benefit can help convert your possible idea into a plausible idea."

Sara Mac went on to say that the critical questions I received were the natural way people interact with ideas to test their plausibility. Sara also said you could harness that critical tendency to develop an idea into an investment.

"There is a flow to an invest conversation, Walker. The stages are simulate, compare, improve, and commit. *Simulate* several ways to achieve your idea. For each simulation, pick a milestone achievement in the future and anticipate the time, money, and talent needed to accomplish the milestone. *Compare* the simulations by asking two questions. First, What produces the highest value for customers, investors, and employees? And second, What is there to learn from this comparison? *Improve* your use of time, money, and talent by applying the comparison lessons. *Commit* the time, money, and key people necessary for a plausible chance of success."

I was madly taking notes. "Wow, Sara, I can see I was not ready to ask for support. We could have done a good job of making our new ideas plausible in less than a day and then asked for input."

"Yes, and you can include a lot of the known purposes and concerns the council members have in your simulations. When you present your ideas, they will already be represented in your thinking. That does not guarantee immediate support, though."

I nodded. "Now I can see that if I'm going for approval, I'll keep watering down the ideas until no one disagrees. With your approach, we'll build the value of the idea so that it naturally attracts support."

"Great point, Walker. Everyone wants to be valuable, to improve things. When people are faced with a new idea, their method of improvement can be criticism.

Listen to their criticism as pure contribution, and you'll build a successful approach together. I get more worried if my ideas are greeted with yawns than if they provoke criticism."

"You and Rev think alike. Your explanation of their questions is a heck of a lot more valuable than mine. I just wrote them off as nonsupportive, and you turn them into design partners." I was awed at both Rev's and Sara's ability to explain facts in a valuable way. "I still pay too much attention to my first explanation." I shook my head at my own incompetence.

"Walker, explaining takes practice. Any explanation is a simulation of what certain facts might mean. The simulations that launch invest conversations are really explanations with a timeline. If you don't simulate several explanations before you commit to one, you lose the chance to compare and improve. There is major value in comparing and improving explanations before you commit to one."

I laughed. "It sounds like you think of explanations as investments!"

"You're darn right, I do. Every explanation I entertain is a potential investment. If you want to get straight about that, I'll give you a hot tip."

"Tell me, please."

"Okay." Sara leaned toward me. "You explained the R&D and Marketing Council members' questions and comments as nonsupport, right?"

I nodded in agreement.

"Promise me that those people are and will continue to be nonsupportive." Her eyes sparked as she spoke.

"Why would I do that?"

"To confront what you are investing in with that explanation. Go ahead, do it."

I thought this was a strange assignment. "I promise that the council members are and will be nonsupportive of our new purpose and the ideas we have for achieving the purpose." I couldn't say it without laughing.

"You ought to laugh. That would be an irrational promise, right?"

"Sure. I suspect I explain things all the time without confronting what I'm investing in. I like this explanation ROI. I'm really interested in increasing my explanation return on investment."

"Good for you, Walker. The 'I promise' exercise is also a good practice when you are assessing where you might commit time, money, and key people. After you simulate, compare, and improve, you still have to decide what to invest in. For the remaining simulated ideas, say them as a promise. You will notice which ones you have confidence in."

"I have a meeting tomorrow with Sharon, Ray, and Louis. They are going to love your suggestions. If we have good invest conversations, our own confidence will go way up. That will make it easier to solicit support when we need it."

"It will. And never lose sight of time, money, and key people as the evidence of investment. Dedicated resources are the test for thorough alignment, not a bunch of nodding heads." Sara slid her chair back from the table.

"Are you leaving? Is that all about the invest conversations?" I was disappointed to see Sara Mac stand to go.

"Yes, I'm leaving, and no, that's not all there is to the invest conversations. You have enough for a good start, though. Maybe another time we'll talk about effective processes and well-designed forums."

"Processes. That makes sense since the best ones make good use of time, money, and people. What are forums?"

"Forums," Sara said, "are groups of the right people to answer important questions. Many times organizations lack forums for the right people to deal with important business issues. For instance, several product organizations may need to cooperate to deliver an integrated solution to a customer. The vertical product hierarchies don't cover the conversations that take place between organizations. Valuable forums emerge naturally. The problem is that we inadvertently kill them off or trivialize their importance, which wastes massive time, money, and talent. That is for another time, however."

Sara Mac waved in parting. I freed one hand from paying the check to wave back. My wave lacked enthusiasm. I did not want to see her go.

Sara stopped, turned, and said, "Enjoy converting your ideas from possible to plausible, Walker. You are building something valuable. Don't stop." She disappeared into the kitchen. Moments later I heard the back screen door squeak open and slam shut.

I said my good-byes to a couple of Rev's associates and left. As I walked toward my car, I saw Sara Mac walking toward a storage building about 75 yards behind the restaurant. As she disappeared around a corner, I realized I never thanked her for my lunch lesson. After a twinge of embarrassment, I headed up the hill. "Thank you" would only take a moment.

The 20-by-20-foot storage shed is made of dark, weathered wood. I'd seen it from a distance and noticed the windows were covered with shutters, unusual for Austin, Texas. As I drew close, I noticed one of the shutters was open and glanced in as I walked by. The sight stopped me in my tracks.

Rev was focused on the conversation he was in, his face relaxed yet alert. His eyes were clear, steady, and confident. He was standing with his arms at his side, his head draped with a telephone headset. One hand held a pad of paper, the other a pen. When Rev spoke, even though I could not hear, the words seemed measured and important. Rev's red-and-black plaid Pendleton shirt and faded blue jeans seemed incongruent with the surroundings.

The room was not outfitted like a storage shed. There were three large flat-panel computer screens and what looked like a high-speed fax machine. There was also a large television screen split into four images. On one wall was an eight-foot whiteboard covered with writing and Post-it notes. At one end of the board was an eight-by-ten picture of a man. Rev walked over to the board and removed a yellow note, dropping it into a waste can as he continued to speak. I could not decipher what was going on, although I was sure of one thing: this wasn't about barbecue.

A man in shirtsleeves and tie sat at a small desk between the whiteboard and a bulletin board covered with what looked like a floor plan. His suit coat hung on the back of his chair. He, too, wore a headset and wrote rapid notes on yellow Post-its. Transfixed, I watched him stick several notes to the whiteboard under Rev's watchful eye. I squinted my eyes, straining to read the writing.

"I don't think you should be here."

I flinched and turned my embarrassed face to see Sara McGregor. She took my arm and firmly steered me away from the window and back toward the café.

ACT
Engage, Clarify, and Close

■ ■ ■

"Even the best cooking pot will not produce food."

AFRICAN PROVERB

". . . and never hope more than you work."

RITA MAE BROWN, *STARTING FROM SCRATCH*

Once resources are committed, action remains. The actions of real people in real time convert plausible plans into visible achievement. Many a fine plan has fallen in the gap between committed resources and effective action.

After more than a few missteps, we have learned a few things about bridging the resource/action gap.

Align to Act: From Prognosis to Promise

Conversation changes dramatically from alignment to action. Some words stay the same, like *intersect, purpose,* and *value,* while others are very different. Alignment conversations are peppered with these kinds of words: *possible, plausible, probable, might be, we could, we hope, maybe, I like it,* and *what if.* As you get to the end of the invest conversations, the language begins to change. Allocating resources begins the shift toward the language of action, to new words like *commit, yes, I promise, accountable, responsible, we'll do it,* and *make it happen.* The relationship to time changes, too. In the align conversations, time is a prognosis ("We could probably get that done by late fall with the right people"). In the act conversations, time is a promise ("We will have our first shipment on store shelves by October 1st").

■ ■ ■

> "Promises are the uniquely human way of ordering
> the future, making it predictable and reliable to the extent
> that this is humanly possible."
> **HANNAH ARENDT**

Consider romantic courtship as an example. Courtship, while not a business, illuminates the shift from align to act. Dating is all about alignment. If we truly intersect with someone else's purposes, preferences, and personality, we want to keep dating. We begin to invent things to do together, both immediately and far into the future. We get so enamored with being together that we start seriously considering a big emotional, spiritual, intellectual, and physical investment: marriage. When we set the wedding date, we commit time, money, and talent to getting married. The language of dating is filled with words like *what if, maybe, I like,* and *I hope.*

Marriage adds high-stakes action to dating's alignment. Like all valuable conversations, the action is an expression of aligned purposes. It is not that we leave alignment behind, for it is earned repeatedly over time. We do shift the conversation, though, from "I really like being with you" to "Until death do us part." The language represents a firm move from prognosis to promise.

Moving from alignment to action can occur in a mood of confidence, fear, or both. It is exhilarating to take confident responsibility for producing a visible, valuable result. It can also be frightening to confront: "Do I control enough of the variables to promise and deliver success?" To assess how fear and confidence affect action, we return to the Conversation Meter from Chapter 3:

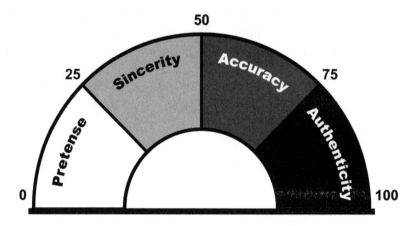

The Conversation Meter

The farther to the left of the meter, the more fear governs. The farther to the right, the more confidence governs. Imagine that I have promised you, "We will have our first shipment on store shelves by October 1st." Note your level of confidence in the outcome in these four different types of promises:

1. *The pretentious promise.* A dishonest pledge to deliver a result. I do not intend to deliver, or I do not believe it is possible to deliver, or both. However, the pretentious promise helps evade an imminent perceived threat.
2. *The sincere promise.* An honest promise to perform. My promise, while well intended, does not accurately confront what will really be demanded of me, and I am disconnected from conditions and key partners. Those who promise sincerely tend to talk big and deliver little.
3. *The accurate promise.* A confident promise informed by conditions, clear expectations, measurable outcomes, key relationships, and available resources. The source of confidence is the plausibility of the promise.
4. *The authentic promise.* A full investment of myself in a valuable, important opportunity to contribute. This full investment of self drives me to connect accurately with conditions and partners and ensures resilience and resourcefulness. I am the author of this promise, even if

it came to me by way of another's request. The source of confidence is my unyielding devotion to delivering the value at stake.

The next time you are asked to make a promise, use the conversation meter to assess the likelihood of success. Promises, implicit or explicit, are the conversations that spur action. It is wise, then, to attend to the quality of promises.

You can increase the likelihood of accurate and authentic promises by practicing the *act* conversations: *engage, clarify,* and *close.* If you want people to accept responsibility for performance, engage with them to connect their interests to the need for action, clarify precisely what you are asking them to provide, and close the conversation with a request for accountability.

Engage: Connecting the Doer with the Deed

"Why don't they just do what I say? This is the right thing to do, why don't they just do it? I'm the boss; I shouldn't have to justify my instructions." Wouldn't it be grand to have everyone hanging on your every word, waiting for even a hint of your desires so they can leap into inspired action? Too bad, it doesn't work that way. For people to fully engage, you need clear senior purpose to coordinate action, and people need to perceive the needed action is in their own best interest.

The source of teamwork is a common future. If we have no future in common, we will not coordinate action today. A clear senior purpose ensures that our common future is the basis for resolving differences and accelerating action. Senior purpose is born in the intersect conversation, transformed into actionable ideas in the invent conversation, and made feasible in the invest conversation. The word *senior* matters for three reasons. First, the important purpose for action must govern the methods we use and the measurable results we promise. Second, the purpose must be senior to the separate agenda of the people who need to collaborate. Third, tough choices must be made in favor of the purpose.

■ ■ ■

"A thought that does not result in an action is nothing much,

and an action which does not proceed

from thought is nothing at all."

GEORGE BERNANOS

Here is a case in point. Some years ago, we worked with a division of a large consulting company regarding a new corporate directive: decrease operating costs by 10 percent over the next quarter. Meetings convened and the cutting began. The following pattern emerged: Arguments broke out and attendees could not agree on resolution, the question escalated to a higher authority, and the higher authority requested more information. This time-consuming pattern of behavior ate up two of the three months, and no significant costs had been cut. We were asked to help. Initial conversations told us that the managers were working on an outcome (cut 10 percent) disconnected from purpose.

We interviewed the three executives who had signed the cost-cutting directive. We asked, "For you, what is important about this cost-cutting initiative?" We looked for common themes and composed a senior purpose using vocabulary present in all three interactions. Then, we sent the purpose statement back to the three senior executives and asked, "Is this an accurate statement of your senior purpose for this cost-cutting initiative?" After two minor word changes, they endorsed the senior purpose. The three executives publicized the statement via e-mail, voice mail, and a large conference call. They made it clear that all decisions about what to cut and what to keep had to serve the senior purpose: *Increase profit by taking costs out of our system that are not valued by a majority of our top 500 customers.* The senior managers could use any cost-cutting methods that were true to the purpose. The measurable outcome requested was still 10 percent by the beginning of the next quarter.

The groups involved immediately made more cost-cutting decisions and sent fewer escalations to upper management. One smart manager suggested that the parties make a list of potential cuts that they all agreed fit the purpose and see how close to 10 percent they came. That got them to 6 percent. When there were disagreements, everyone referred to the senior purpose for direction. When the tough choices still were not clear, they escalated. Within two weeks, they identified reductions totaling over 11 percent of expenses. Differences melt in the presence of a senior purpose that is valuable to customers, investors, and employees.

■   ■   ■

"There can be no acting or doing of any kind, till it be
recognized that there is a thing to be done; the thing once
recognized, doing in a thousand shapes becomes possible."

THOMAS CARLYLE, *CHARTISM* (1839)

To ensure genuine accountability, connect the senior purpose to the *best interests* of the people you are counting on. If you do not perceive an action to be in your best interests, you will not carry it out. You only accept domination when you think it is more in your best interest than resistance. Proactively engaging with best interests stimulates creative and resourceful action by connecting organizational commitment to personal commitment.

There are common best interests and unique best interests. The more unique you can make the connection between requested action and the best interests of the actor, the better. However, connecting to the seven common best interests is a reliable catalyst for action. It will be much more valuable for you if you review the best interests with a real request for action in mind. Do you have any important request for action to make soon? If so, keep it in mind and use the "engage" comments to plan the conversation. We refer to the person you need action from as the actor.

1. Agency. Each of us relates to free choice as evidence of worth and the opportunity to freely contribute.

Engage: Has the actor already accepted this request by virtue of his job description? If not, there should be a real option to refuse. If refusal is a possibility and the actor's support is crucial, intersect with the other best interests to gain support.

A crucial element of agency is access to the truth. If anyone feels duped into accepting an assignment, agency is betrayed. The wisest choices are made in the presence of the truth. If you "protect" people from challenging facts, they will be unable to rise to the challenge.

 Waste trap: Give people no choice and assume that they then have none except the one you offer. The "no choice" ploy fails to engage wholehearted effort. Authentic support can be given, but it cannot be coerced.

▪ ▪ ▪

"Assets that cannot be controlled by rule are the most critical to success. People's ideas, their commitment to high standards of competence, and their connections of trust with partners are what set apart great organizations. All these requirements can be enhanced by leaders, but none can be mandated."

ROSABETH MOSS KANTER

2. Being heard. Being heard is our constant test for inclusion and trust. *Engage:* Once you explain the need for action, ask if the actor has questions or concerns. Make sure she knows you understand her view. The time spent on mutual understanding is an investment, not a cost.

 Waste trap: Act like people should not have the purposes and concerns they do. Treat their concerns as inappropriate and not worth resolving. Later, wonder at the broad lack of support.

3. Contribution. We long to make a meaningful, valuable difference; especially potent when our unique contributions are fully utilized. *Engage:* Let the actor know what specifically makes him important to the task. What expertise, purposes, or personal qualities does he have that you need? Ask if he sees any other contribution he can make that you may not know to ask him for. The chance to contribute value is far more engaging than obligation.

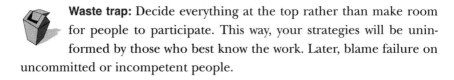 **Waste trap:** Decide everything at the top rather than make room for people to participate. This way, your strategies will be uninformed by those who best know the work. Later, blame failure on uncommitted or incompetent people.

4. Relationship. The experience of connection, of belonging, of being an important element in a larger whole. *Engage:* Tell the actor the valuable purpose that is at stake and how it will contribute to customers, employees, and investors. Ask the actor, "For you, what is important about this effort?" Her answer tells you her current relationship to the effort.

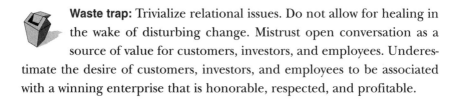 **Waste trap:** Trivialize relational issues. Do not allow for healing in the wake of disturbing change. Mistrust open conversation as a source of value for customers, investors, and employees. Underestimate the desire of customers, investors, and employees to be associated with a winning enterprise that is honorable, respected, and profitable.

5. Time, money, and safety. The ability to care for our most basic needs and meet important commitments. *Engage:* Ask the actor, "Is it plausible for you to get this done, given your other commitments?" If he says "no," then ask, "Do we need to redesign your workload in any way?" or "What would you need to stop doing so that you could do this?" If you do not resist time and money concerns, the actor will usually join you in solving them.

 Waste trap: Treat people as expendable in times of difficulty. Keep asking for more without considering how stressed and stretched people are already. Blame a perceived lack of loyalty on ingratitude and irresponsibility.

6. Learning. The experience of insight and possibility that tells us our best days are still to come.

Engage: Ask yourself, "What is the actor's learning opportunity if she takes this assignment?" Let her know what you think the learning opportunity is and ask if she sees any opportunities that you did not. How can you support the learning opportunity?

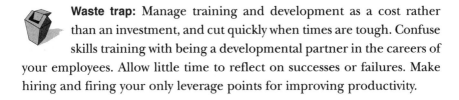 **Waste trap:** Manage training and development as a cost rather than an investment, and cut quickly when times are tough. Confuse skills training with being a developmental partner in the careers of your employees. Allow little time to reflect on successes or failures. Make hiring and firing your only leverage points for improving productivity.

7. Appreciation. Being known for the value we create.

Engage: Ask yourself, "What do I appreciate about this person? How has he been uniquely valuable? Does he know what I appreciate about him? What is the best way to express my appreciation?"

 Waste trap: Only appreciate people when you need something from them. That way you can earn a reputation as a shallow manipulator.

Any request for action connected to these seven best interests has a very high probability of acceptance. Appealing to all these best interests can seem complex and difficult. Remember, you have been setting yourself up to appeal to them before you ever get to the act conversations. If you arrive at the request for action via the three dimensions of alignment (intersect, invent, and invest), you have much of the information you need to connect to the best interests of the work community.

Clarify: Preempt Mischief with Precision

Unclear expectations are "cancer" to collaborative action. This element of action is simple: How exactly will you assess success? We bet that anyone reading *The Communication Catalyst* could tell a tale or two about messes caused by conflicting expectations. Imagine that you just accepted a new assignment as the leader of an important project. You are smart enough to ask for support from a very experienced project manager, Josie Jones. "Josie, since you have so much experience with this technology, I've come to ask you for your support in this new project," you say. Josie replies, "Certainly, you have my support." You walk away pleased, expecting Josie to attend all of your project meetings and provide counsel. Josie walks away thinking that she completed all obligations by endorsing your leadership. The only action she contemplates is an occasional supportive comment should she see you in the hallways. Some weeks later, the relationship is damaged because of your disappointment in Josie's integrity. She has not attended even one meeting! Do you have similar stories? As singer Tom Jones once warbled, "It's not unusual."

To cure the cancer of unclear expectations, we pay strict attention to *precision*. There are three precision factors:

1. What precisely is at stake for customers, investors, or employees? What senior purpose is being served, and what makes it important now?
2. Why choose this person to do this task? Precisely what is it about his skills, position, and leadership (or anything else) that explains your interest in his contribution?
3. How precisely will you assess success? Precisely what needs to be delivered and when? What measures will you track?

When people first start managing precise requests, it can feel strange. Just remember that collaborative action demands clarity about what we need from one another. There is bonus value, too. The more precise you make your request, the more you evoke a no response from the people who were never going to get it done. This leaves you free to keep going until you connect with someone who really will perform. We have often been asked, "Aren't there times when you shouldn't have to give that much detail?" Our answer is "Sure, if the parties are familiar with the situation and each other, then the precision factors *might* be already known."

Without precision, we have assumption, presumption, and invalid expectations. Collaborative action is a gamble at best, and we find ourselves constantly disappointed.

■ ■ ■

"Expectations are resentments under construction."

ANNE LAMOTT

In his uniquely valuable book on leadership, *Stewardship: Choosing Service Over Self-Interest,* Peter Block takes a rigorous look at the practical challenges facing the participatory leader. When Block and his associates delved into the mischief of expectations, their discoveries were illuminating and entertaining. By asking people to exaggerate their unsaid expectations, they uncovered a medley of desires that are familiar to many of us. These invalid expectations belong to that class of desires no one has ever agreed to fulfill. Still, we resent the nonperformance. The expectation lists from *Stewardship* are reproduced in Figure 6.1.

Clear, precise outcomes bounded by time are the antidote to invalid expectations. If you are sponsoring high-performance action, then clarity is especially important in times of sudden or radical change. For example,

---

FIGURE 6.1 / *Unspoken Expectations*

When people are asked to state their normally unstated wants from those around them, and to exaggerate, here is what they long for:

EXPECTATIONS OF A RELATIONSHIP

Place my needs above all others.
Provide me with safety at all times.
Include me in all decisions.
Never argue with me.
Want to be with me always.
Take care of me so I don't have to be responsible for myself.
Trust and agree with all my decisions.
Give me my freedom . . . all the space I need.
Never need anything I don't want to give.

(Continued)

FIGURE 6.1 / Unspoken Expectations, continued

WHICH GET EXPRESSED IN EXPECTATIONS OF A BOSS

I want to be your favorite.
Ask my advice before you do anything impacting me or my work.
Make me your confidant.
Make my advancement your personal responsibility.
See my weaknesses as charming.
Leave me alone . . . except when I am in trouble, then rescue me.
Protect me from powerful foes, run interference for me.

On the flip side, as bosses, we have our own emotional demands of our subordinates. The ones that meet these expectations affirm to us that we are good at what we do, and we tend to call them high performers.

A BOSS'S RECIPROCAL EXPECTATIONS OF A SUBORDINATE

Value me more than any boss you have ever had.
Know what I need and want without my having to ask.
Accept my controlling behavior as timely and helpful.
Don't bother me with problems.
Come to me only with solutions and successes.
Even though I occasionally embarrass you in front of peers, consider
    me your friend.
Be loyal to me, regardless of how I operate.
Be grateful for the opportunity to work for me and learn from me.

Finally, those in service or staff roles have their own desires of their "clients."

SERVICE/STAFF PERSON'S EXPECTATIONS OF A CLIENT

Don't act without asking my advice. Tell me you have learned more from
    me than anyone else.
Tell others how good I am, especially up the line.
Keep needing me, don't get too independent.
Teach me what I need to know, and be grateful for the opportunity.
Accept my desire to control you as an act of service.

Reprinted with permission of the publisher. From *Stewardship: Choosing Service Over Self-Interest.* © 1993 by Peter Block. Berrett-Koehler Publishers, Inc., San Francisco, CA. All rights reserved. www.bkconnection.com

commercial airlines sponsor rigorous training of flight attendants. One element of the training is how to communicate during an emergency. In those moments of sudden, radical change, a flight attendant's communication is very precise: "Reach down between your knees and find the red canvas handle under the front of your seat cushion. Do that now. Next, pull firmly on the handle to release your life vest from beneath the seat. Do that now. Next, unfold the yellow vest and pull the vest down over your head. Do that now." In more stable times, or after a work community has developed reliable patterns of collaboration, this level of precision is in the interaction without you having to recite it.

Making precise needs known completes the issue of clarity. Next, we close the matter: Is someone going to actually do this or not?

Close: Authentic Acceptance of Accountability

Once you engage and clarify, closing the issue of personal commitment firmly establishes accountability for action. Notice the natural flow:

- *Engage.* What senior purpose is at stake? How does that senior purpose intersect with your best interests?
- *Clarify.* Precisely why am I the person to do this? What is at stake for the company? Precisely what must I achieve and by when?
- *Close.* Do I promise to do this or not? Who needs to know? Tell them and go to work.

If you only engage and clarify, authentic accountability is absent. Among the definitions of *close* are: to bring the parts together; to join; to conclude; to come to an agreement. Up to the moment of closure, we are only discussing, not acting. Post-closure we are acting, not discussing. The key to closure is in the words *I promise.*

A promise is an assurance from one person to another that he or she will or will not do something. With an authentic promise, a specific human being assumes responsibility for producing a valuable result. The etymology of promise extends back to the Latin *promittere,* "to send forward." When we authentically promise a result, we send a purpose forward from good intention to action. Without promising, there is tentative intent, which is easily derailed by difficulty. With a promise, there is a focused drive to achieve that is fueled by telling a community, "You can count on me."

To close an act conversation, use the precise information from the clarify step and ask for a promise: "Do you promise to have this new product on store shelves by October 1st?" You can sort any response into one of three categories:

1. Category one: "I promise to do that."
   "Yes." "I accept." "Count on me." "I commit." "I will." These are all category one responses.
2. Category two: "I promise not to do that."
   "No." "I refuse." "I won't." "I can't." "Maybe." These are category two responses. Hot tip: Treat "maybe" as a promise not to perform.
3. Category three: "I promise something else."
   "I won't, but how about this?" "I counteroffer." "As an alternative I will ___." "I cannot tell you now; how about if I tell you by six o'clock tomorrow?" These are all category three. If you accept a category three response, make sure the new promise is precise regarding visible result and time. If you cannot get precision, file it in category two.

Many a manager has said, "But what if I can't accept 'no' for an answer?" Asking for a promise can occur on a spectrum ranging from fearfully expecting no (begging, pleading) to demanding yes ("I order" or "I command"). However, it's best never to forget that the fuel for authentic accountability is intersected purpose. When you demand acceptance, you are requiring others to act out of your purpose rather than a shared purpose. Managing the commanded is far less effective than managing the committed. The commanded take more time, more supervision, and produce less value than the committed.

If you frequently cannot take no for an answer, then you need to revisit job descriptions. You should be able to anticipate the kinds of promises that are necessary and not up for negotiation. Those promises belong in the job description. When someone says yes to that job, they say yes to the promises that come with it. Additionally, in times of emergency it can be valid and valuable to issue an order. If you customarily manage the intersection between you and those you lead, they will respond beautifully. If you do not normally manage the intersection, each order you issue will weaken the foundation for high-velocity value. When "no" is not allowed, "yes" is inauthentic. The person who utters an inauthentic yes will be impotent in the face of difficulty.

Now, what do you do when you are on the receiving end of a request? Everything we have said applies, and we add one important point: Focus on what you *can* say yes to. In a work community, an unexplained no is very unsettling. When someone is soliciting a promise from you, ask yourself, "How can I contribute?" Can you say yes to their need? Can you direct them to another prospect? Can you offer any aid at all? We do *not* suggest that you agree to anything asked of you. That is a recipe for an undoable, overwhelming workload. What can you say yes to that does fit with your workload? No matter how apparently small your offer of help, your relationship with the people involved will be enriched, and the people around you will think of you as an affirmative personality rather than a negative personality. Responding in an affirmative spirit builds the foundation of trust and collaboration. Without taking on work you should not, your affirmative spirit will deepen the foundation of trust and collaboration. Your workload will be lighter, not heavier.

■ ■ ■

"After the final no there comes a yes. It is on that yes that
the future of the world depends."

WALLACE STEVENS

The act conversations move us from shared, plausible ideas to collaborative action. Now, people are doing the work their promises reveal. Of course, that work will not go as imagined. There will be surprising opportunities, unsettling disappointments, and changes in the circumstances. The proof of aligned action is adjustment to change. The adjust conversations are coming up right after a visit with Rev. He and Walker have much to discuss, given what Walker stumbled onto at the end of his visit with Sara Mac. What exactly is going on?

CHAPTER SUMMARY

The Heart of
the Matter

Once resources are committed, action remains. Act conversations convert plausible plans into authentic individual commitments.

The "Promise Meter"

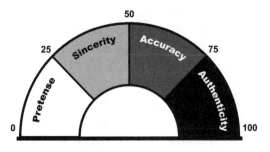

Promises, implicit or explicit, are the conversations that spur action. A promise is an assurance from one person to another that he or she will or will not do something. We can use the conversation meter to formulate promises that will result in valuable actions that move us toward fulfillment of our shared purpose.

Act Waste Track

- *The pretentious promise.* A dishonest pledge to deliver a result. There is no intention and/or belief that it is possible to deliver as promised.
- *The sincere promise.* An honest promise to perform. Although well intended, it does not accurately confront what is called for and has little chance of being delivered on.

Act Value Track

- *The accurate promise.* A confident promise informed by conditions, clear expectations, measurable outcomes, key relationships, and available resources.
- *The authentic promise.* A full investment of self to deliver the value at stake in a resilient, resourceful manner.

Action to take: The next time you make a promise, use the promise meter to assess the likelihood of your success. Low likelihood of success means there is weakness in one of the three aspects of action: *engage, clarify,* or *close.*

Act Conversations: Engage, Clarify, and Close

If you want people to accept responsibility for performance, engage with them to connect their interests to the need for action, clarify precisely what you are asking them to provide, and close the conversation with a request for accountability.

Engage. Connect the doer with the deed. A clear senior purpose ensures that our common future is the basis for resolving differences and accelerating action.

Connect the senior purpose to the best interests of the people you are counting on. Following are seven best interests that we all have in common:

1. *Agency.* Each of us relates to freedom of choice as evidence of worth and the opportunity to freely contribute. Access to the truth is crucial to agency.
2. *Understanding.* Being heard is our constant test for inclusion and trust.
3. *Contribution.* We long to make a meaningful, valuable difference.
4. *Relationship.* Each of us desires the experience of connection, of belonging, of being an important element in a larger whole.
5. *Time, money, and safety.* We want to be able to care for our most basic needs and to meet important commitments.
6. *Learning.* All people desire the experience of insight and new possibility.
7. *Appreciation.* It is profoundly satisfying to be known for the value we create.

Clarify. Preempt mischief with precision. Without precision, we have assumption, presumption, and invalid expectations. As you clarify, answer the following questions:

- What precisely is at stake for customers, investors, and employees? What senior purpose is being served? What makes it important now?
- Is this the person to do this task? What skills, position, and leadership does he or she have that serves your purposes?
- How will you assess success? What needs to be delivered by when? What measures will you track?

Close. Ask for authentic acceptance of accountability. To close an act conversation, use the precise information from the clarify step and ask for a promise. Refer back to the promise meter to ensure that requests and promises launch you on the road to high-value achievement.

R E V   L E S S O N

■ ■ ■

It's Not the Skillet, It's the Cook

"Wishin' and hopin' and thinkin' and prayin'

Plannin' and dreamin' each night of his charms

That won't get you into his arms."

DUSTY SPRINGFIELD, "WISHIN' AND HOPIN'"

(WRITTEN BY BURT BACHARACH AND HAL DAVID)

"So, you got yourself an eyeful. That so, Walker?" Rev was cooking flour and butter together in a skillet to make a roux, a crucial step in the preparation of his crawfish etoufee. This occasional departure from barbecue was highly prized by the small, passionate group of long-time customers who somehow knew when it was available.

"Yes, by accident. I was looking for Sara to say thank you." I was uncomfortable. Clearly, Rev had not intended to include me in whatever he was up to.

"About how long did it take for you to find out Mac wasn't in there?"

"Uh, just a second, I guess."

"About how long did you keep watchin'?" Rev kept stirring and looked up at me.

"Longer than I needed to. Sorry." Trying to get an irresponsible excuse past Rev, as Satchel Paige once said about getting a fastball by Josh Gibson, is like trying to get sunrise past a rooster.

"Thanks for being straight with me, Walker."

I heard the shuffle of steps behind me, and then a voice. "Hey now, Rev, it's my turn to make the etoufee." Willie Caldwell, Rev's kitchen manager and old friend, was grinning and putting on an apron as he headed for the eight-burner gas stove. "My daughters are coming to lunch for my etoufee, not yours."

"Willie," Rev said, "I make a fine crawfish etoufee, and those beautiful twins of yours know it. I learned directly from Jim Pertuit, the Pepper King of St. Tammany Parish, Louisiana." He stepped back from the stove, letting go of the wooden spoon just as Willie's hand was there to catch it. A couple more stirs and Willie pulled the skillet off the fire.

"Rev, great cooks like Jim and me, we keep some secrets private, you know." Willie grinned at Rev. "Look at this. I can tell I'll have to do extra work 'cause you started off a little sloppy. Gimme a dollar."

This was an old routine. Rev told me that Willie found a reason to demand a dollar every day. It was a long-time dance, one they both enjoyed.

"Here's a dollar. I did leave a bit of a mess. However, Willie, you *are* gettin' to cook with my fine personal skillet." Rev paid up, pulled his apron over his head, and hung it on a hook by the back screen door.

"C'mon, Walker, we'll leave Willie alone so he can do secret stuff." Rev waved at Willie, Willie laughed at Rev, and I followed Rev out the back door.

Rev walked across the parking area and crossed into the grassy area in the middle of the magnolia trees. A round redwood table is there on a small rock patio, with six surprisingly comfortable redwood chairs. We sat in two of them.

"Walker, I'm going to let you in on a little history."

"Rev, you don't have to explain anything to me."

"No, I don't. I didn't tell you before 'cause you have no stake in what's goin' on. I generally don't invite people into serious situations unless they've got a role to play. Now, though, I have my reasons for talkin' just a bit."

Rev leaned back in his chair, rocking the front legs off the ground as he looked through the leaves at the blue summer sky. "It's mighty pretty today, Walker, mighty pretty." I merely sat and waited, wondering what was coming. It was a few minutes before Rev spoke again.

"Walker, I've only owned the café for about eight years. My dad used to haul around a barbecue pit on wheels behind his truck and cook for folks. I've learned from him and other fine cooks, like Willie, Jim Pertuit, Larry Foles up at Eddie V's, and I guess I've tried nearly every recipe Marcella Hazan has put to paper. Yes, I truly enjoy bringin' people together over a good meal." Rev stood, stretched, and walked a few steps before he turned back to me. "Bein' a café owner is not what I've done most of my life, though."

"I've noticed you have talents that don't seem to come from owning a café, Rev." He nodded, and then he told me a few things.

Rev said he was an indifferent student in high school, finishing low in his senior class. However, he took the Air Force Qualifying Test, because one of his buddies did not want to do it alone. When the results came back, the officer told Rev, "You have some of the highest scores I've ever seen." Rev said it was the first time he ever thought that he might be smart. Even though he did not enter the service then, the officer's comments stuck with him.

Some months later, in the thick of the Vietnam War, Rev's buddy wanted to check out being a paratrooper and Rev thought that sounded "fun." They both ended up in the 101st Airborne Screaming Eagles, and that began Rev's government career. His personal path after that was interesting. After some successful drops behind enemy lines, Rev was invited into activities that were more clandestine. He spent time undercover and, after wriggling out of a couple of dangerous situations, was told he had natural skills as a negotiator. That led to training in high-stakes negotiations. Rev said over the next 20 years, he was in "some" treaty negotiations and hostage negotiations. I found out later from Sara Mac that the number was over 300, and included Strategic Arms Limitation Talks (SALT). She also told me Rev's employers over the years had been the CIA, the National Security Agency, the State Department, the NYPD, and the Bramshill Police College just outside of London, England.

"I got real interested in what has folks act the way they do, Walker. Along the way, I got myself to college and earned a doctorate in social psychology. The biggest insights for me were all about how conversation and language affect everybody and everything all the time. That's what I've been researching and applying the last 20 years." Rev stepped back to the table and sat down. It seemed like an invitation to ask questions, and I did.

"Rev, how did all that lead to you advising people like Sara McGregor?"

"Well, after spendin' time in the military and the State Department and workin' with defense contractors, I started to see that all organizations have similar challenges. It's all people working together to try to do things bigger than they can do by themselves. They just measure success in different ways. I met Mac on Capitol Hill while she was with the Federal Reserve Bank. We've done a lot together since then."

"Rev, what makes you tell me all this now?"

"I've got plans for you."

That jerked me to attention. "What do you mean?"

"Walker, you have a chance to make a big impact. You are smart, honorable, and hardworkin'. And, you're a natural learner. You're worth investin' in."

"Thank you, Rev." Sometimes thank you is only a reflex. Not this time.

"The things you and I've been workin' on have broad application. The kind of conversation someone is in affects the kind of action he takes, and that's true in hostage negotiations, product development, cookin', and just about anything else you can name. I'm tellin' you all this 'cause I want you to know the advice is well tested. In fact, that has a lot to do with what I was doing in the shed last week."

"How so?"

That's when Rev first told me about the Catalyst. He called it a "natural network," which he said is a group of people who stay connected simply because of the value they give and get. No obligation, no manipulation, just value.

"Natural networks are all over the place, Walker. They cover everything from nuclear safety to quilting. These networks of conversation grow naturally 'cause there's a valuable intersection. The Catalyst is one of those."

"What's the intersection that grew the Catalyst? Not quilting, I bet."

"Conversation grows the Catalyst, Walker."

"I don't understand, Rev, everybody talks, nuclear scientists, quilters, everybody."

"A conversation isn't people talkin'; that's just noise. Conversation comes from Latin for 'turning with.' A conversation is people turning to each other and listenin', discovering what they can only see in light of the other's view. In a conversation, there is always more value at the end than either party started with. It's a discovery every time out. In the Catalyst, we do one thing: develop our ability to converse. We help each other, we learn from each other, we meet big challenges, and we solve big problems. Also, we enjoy provin' that we can produce faster, more valuable results with conversation than anyone else can any other way."

"What are other ways?"

"Position power, manipulation, violence, and trickery of all kinds. Generally, all the dressed-up fight, flee, freeze, and appease reactions."

"Where did the name Catalyst come from?"

Rev had a look of pleasant recollection. "From a chemist named Patricia Fairchild. She was one of the early members of our group. Pat was workin' on one of the nuclear safety projects that came after the Chernobyl disaster. Mac worked with her to turn a bunch of turf-protecting bureaucrats into a high-performance team. After the project was back on track, she said Mac was a human catalyst, because she accelerated performance without gettin' in the way. Mac said conversation was the catalyst, and that belonged to all of us, not just her. Pat gave us the name Catalyst then and there."

"How do you know these Catalyst people? And how many are they?"

"We know each other from working together. On negotiations, projects, emergencies, all kinds of things. We're people who know that how we converse is important to how we perform. I don't know how many for sure. We grow every time someone new gets interested in how a Catalyst member helped a remarkable thing happen. For me, it started when I saw Clark Williams handle a hostage situation in a way I'd never seen before."

"What was different?"

"Clark didn't treat the hostage taker like a target. He was interested, truly interested, in what drove the man to take 36 kids hostage in a grade school. The other negotiators I'd seen had mostly fallen into two camps: the 'get 'em in view for a clear shot' camp and the 'follow the standard escalation path' camp. The 'shot' group put everyone at risk way too quickly, and the 'standard escalation' group followed the manual like robots. Both groups were proud of being able to predict exactly how the situation would unfold. 'This one is irrational, we're going to have to take him down,' for instance. There was not much discovery and few surprises.

"Clark did and said things that day that changed how I think. I heard him talking to the hostage taker and ask, 'For you, what's important about what you're doing?' Then, the guy hung up on Clark. I said, 'What's next?' When Clark said, 'We'll talk again in a few minutes.' I asked him how he knew that. He told me that the man was thinking about what was important to him. 'I asked him a question he wants to answer and that I'm interested in hearing about. With those two ingredients, he'll answer soon.' In five minutes, they were back on the phone. An hour later, it was over. Clark walked the man out of the school himself and no one was hurt.

"In the debrief Clark said, 'For great negotiators, the hardest work is researching what legitimizes the hostage taker. If you aren't tough enough to ask that question, you're not going to produce miracles. It's easy to make him inhuman. It's hard to make him legitimate. That is the only way you'll uncover a surprising solution, though. I'm not saying approve of his action. I am saying find out what's important to him that legitimizes the action in his eyes. Then, work with him to figure out better ways to handle what's important.'"

Rev kept recounting Clark's comments. "He told me, 'A criminal has to dehumanize his victim to be able to kill. If you won't humanize the potential killer, he won't humanize the victim, and that gets people killed. To defeat evil, you first have to meet the evildoers, really meet them. Bad negotiators don't connect with their adversary out of fear, ignorance, or a lack of discipline.'"

Rev said, "He also told me, 'If you see *anyone* take actions that damage his own best interests, whether it is a hostage taker, a government official, or a family member, place a bet. Bet that buried somewhere behind the bad act, no matter how objectionable, is a purpose you can understand and maybe even respect. You can also bet that, whether awake to it or not, he is asking your help to find better options. Your first job is safe rescue. Your best job, though, is having the hostage taker see better ways to achieve his purposes. Then, there's no blood on anyone's hands.'"

"Wow." I was stunned. "Were you doing something like that last week?"

"Yes. I was bein' a shadow advisor, consultin' the people on the scene who are accountable for the result. If a Catalyst friend calls, I do what I can to help. They do the same for me. It turned out fine. I won't be tellin' you more than that, Walker."

"Rev, will you wait here for a minute?"

"Surely."

I ran into the café and grabbed a handful of bevnaps. I still liked to capture Rev's comments that way. When I returned, Rev was at the lakefront skimming stones across Lake Austin. I counted eight skips after the final stone left his hand.

"Walker, you and Mac talked about the invest conversations last week. What'd you get out of that?"

I put the bevnaps on the little green metal table that was, for this day, on the grass a few feet from the water. It has a spike in the bottom so you can stick it in the ground wherever you like. After I weighted the bevnaps with a rock, I answered.

"I learned that you have to fit an idea with the conditions—with purposes, circumstances, and resources—to get people to invest in it. We talked about ways to compare and improve ideas, so I can have enough confidence to commit time, money, and talent. I saw that I could invite criticism instead of avoid it and have stronger investments. Sara gave me some of your notes on fast, smart decisions, too."

"Sounds just right, Walker. What do you think comes next?"

"Making it happen! We redesigned three of our ideas so they are plausible investments. Yesterday, we got the time, money, and people we need for one of them. Now, we need to do it."

"You sound ready to go. Mind if I share a few thoughts?"

"I definitely want your thoughts. I have to admit, though, I'm still caught up in what you said about the Catalyst and Clark Williams."

"I'll hook it all together, Walker. Clark needed that man to take an action: let the kids go. It may seem strange, but how he got a valuable action applies to how you put *your* plans in action." Rev turned to walk back to the redwood table. I grabbed the bevnaps and followed. It was prime time for note taking. We resumed our seats, and Rev shared a few thoughts, good ones.

Rev said that it was "highly unlikely" that I would ever run into the dysfunctional hostility that Clark had handled. He noted that I had the good fortune to be working with good people who, for the most part, wanted to do good work. I also had done lots of pre-work in the align conversations to set the stage well. Still, I could move any idea into action by observing the same principles Rev and his associates do: engage, clarify, and close.

Rev pointed out that Clark first had to *engage* with the man and thoroughly understand his purposes and concerns, searching for a way to connect with the hostage taker's best interests. Then, Clark needed to *clarify* the situation, using facts both people respected, to show a disconnection between the man's purposes and the current situation. Clark also brainstormed alternatives with the hostage taker and clarified possible actions and consequences. Finally, to *close*, Clark gave the man a precise proposal and asked him to accept, reject, or counterpropose.

"Now, the reason things worked out at that school is because the man found a better way to get what he wanted. He and Clark found a way out together since Clark earned a relationship in a very short time."

Rev leaned toward me. "Clarify means nothing without engage and close. Lots of folks make clear statements and don't achieve much at all. When you engage, you earn the right to collaborate. Only then does anybody care about clear roles and measures and such.

"And, if you don't close, it's like harvestin' acres of wheat and then lettin' it all rot in a silo. We call it close because it's finishin' the question of whether or not something will be done. It's about closin' the door on 'may be' so you can give everything you got to 'will be.' With all the tools we have, it's easy to forget how much a human matters. 'I promise' stops fence sittin' and starts focused, devoted action. Authentic closure is powerful, Walker."

"What do you mean by authentic closure, Rev?"

"Well, you recall the conversation meter, right?"

"Of course. It's up in my office, on a Post-it note on my coffee maker at home, and on a business card I have in my wallet. I'm getting better at catching pretense and sincerity and switching to accuracy and authenticity. When I make the switch, something valuable happens fast." That little meter was a big asset.

Rev continued, "What's the project you just committed time, money, and talent to?"

"Enterprise Software is the information sharing system that lets different parts of a business communicate. Financial reporting, production tracking, customer data, forecasting, and many other forms of information are accessible to everyone on the same system. There's a problem, though. The four most popular Enterprise Software systems don't talk to each other. Information sharing across organizational boundaries is very inefficient. It's a problem for alliances, mergers, working with vendors, customers, and even other divisions in the same company. Our new project, code name Converge, is a software interface that lets those four systems talk to each other." I was getting used to explaining Converge. I'd done it a lot in the past week.

"That sounds valuable, Walker, and I imagine the sooner it's on the market, the better."

"You bet. We have an aggressive development schedule. I think we can go faster than we used to because we are communicating so much more effectively."

"I'm glad to hear that. Now, Walker, think of someone whose promises are important to meeting your schedule." I told Rev that Theresa, the R&D project manager, was very important.

"If Theresa promises you a prototype of Converge by October 1st, what does it mean if that promise is authentic?"

I thought for a few seconds. "That she is connected enough to the situation and the other players to know what she is promising, why it matters to all of us, and how she is honestly assuring Ray and the rest of us that she'll make it happen."

Rev smiled. "What if her promise was a pretense?"

I winced. "She wouldn't mean it and it wouldn't get done."

"Sincere?"

That one I had to consider for a moment. "It would be honest, but it would be disconnected from important facts and the other people involved. It would be impulsive, and she wouldn't really know what she was promising."

Rev nodded. "Accurate?"

"Theresa would have a factual understanding of the situation. She would have a good sense of what it would take to keep the promise. And, she'd have the time, money, and talent available to get it done."

"Mighty fine, Walker. Anything else about authentic promises?"

"Theresa's authentic promise would have everything an accurate promise does, plus she would be aware of the stakes for customers, employees, and investors. It would be personal for her, something she thought was important. Almost a vow, I guess." I was basking in the idea of authentic promises all over the place.

"That's right," Rev said quietly. "The Greek root for authentic is *authentikos*. It means 'the doer of a deed.' When any of us truly says 'I am the doer of that deed,' we have taken responsibility for a piece of the future. Authentic promises can be scary, excitin', or both. Once you make one, things look different, Walker. You set up powerful radar that hunts for chances to make it happen. You listen differently, you think differently, and you set different conversations loose in the world."

"Rev, my promise for this new project is authentic. You just described what it is like for me."

"Yes, Walker, and that's why I have plans for you. You make authentic promises. You let them bother you and provoke you. I admire how unsettled you get when you tell me you're gonna do somethin'. You're a doer of deeds in a world where there's a lot more talkin' than doin'. I don't see you wishin' and hopin', son, I see you workin'."

"Thank you, Rev. Your opinion matters more than I can say." I was slightly awed.

"You don't need everybody to make authentic promises. If you have mostly accurate promises around you, many great things will happen. You do need a critical few people who put the deed in their own hands. The authentic actors set the stage for everyone else."

Rev said that setting the stage is what *engage, clarify,* and *close* allow me to do.

He asked me a barrage of questions to make sure I could apply the principles in my work at MightyTek. With a collection of full bevnaps, I felt well prepared to make proposals and solicit promises from the people who could make it happen.

"I'm satisfied, Walker. Thank the Lord you're not in hostage situations. Still, you have to proactively make the link between alignment and action. That puts you in good shape to deal with surprises, and I imagine you'll have some." Rev's statement about surprises was prophetic. In retrospect, I'm glad I didn't know what was coming. You will hear all about it, just not now.

Rev stood and pushed his chair under the redwood table. "I'm hungry. You want some lunch?"

"Yep, but what about those plans for me?"

"My plan is to hook you up with other Catalyst folks. That's why I asked Mac to spend time with you. I don't know where all this will lead. I do know that the Catalyst is a natural network for you, too. If you're interested, I'll show you our archives and let you look at what we've learned over the years. You can access all of it through the Internet. You need to know, though, that the Catalyst is not for the faint of heart. What holds us together is a promise we all make. It's a near impossible promise, Walker, and you best not make it lightly."

"What is it, Rev?"

"We promise that we can meet any challenge, no matter how difficult, by havin' the right people in the right conversation."

"Rev, that's a huge promise. It scares me to say that seriously."

"Good, Walker, I respect your integrity. Any big promise is likely to scare you. The question isn't, 'Do I already know how to do this?' The question is, 'Does this promise wake up something important inside of me?' Only you can say. I recommend you not say today. Sleep on it. If you decide you want to make the Catalyst promise, Mac and I will tell you a bit more about the whole idea."

I stood up. "Thanks, Rev, I need to think about this. I know you're a serious man. Your bold promise raises some questions for me. Let's close on it by the end of our next meal together, okay?"

Rev agreed, slapped me on the back, and we walked back up to the kitchen. When we entered, Willie's crawfish etoufee was warming on the stove. Rev spooned some onto a plate and sampled the dish.

"Mmmmmmmm! Walker, you best have some of this. Mighty fine, mighty tasty." Rev spoke loudly enough for Willie to hear him at the other end of the kitchen. Willie looked over at Rev with a smiling nod.

"You are a cook, Willie Caldwell, you are a cook."

Willie laughed out loud. "You're right, Rev. It's the cook, not your fine skillet. I promised great etoufee and that's what you're tastin', yessir."

Rev bowed deeply toward Willie. Willie said, "'Bout time someone around here bows to me!" He was obviously pleased with Rev's acknowledgment.

I served myself a full plate, and Rev and I walked into the dining room. Rev said a few hellos and then joined me at our table next to the jukebox. As he sat, I was scanning song titles.

"Lookin' for a tune, Walker?"

I smiled at Rev. "Yeah, it's become a habit. I like having a song to remind me of what you and I talk about."

"Now, we happen to have a song on the box that's a good one for the act conversations. Mind if I play it?" Rev's eyes lit up, like they do every time he thinks of the right song to make a point.

"Play away, Maestro." I waved my right arm at the jukebox buttons. Moments later, we were listening to Dusty Springfield sing her signature hit from long ago. Must have been some baby boomers in for lunch that day, because a few people started singing along. One more time, a Rev tune had me laughing as I heard Dusty admonish us all that "wishin' and hopin' and thinkin' and prayin'" aren't quite enough. I guess even romance has to make the jump from hope to action.

CHAPTER SEVEN

ADJUST
Review and Renew

■ ■ ■

"The only person who is educated is the one who has
learned how to learn and change."

CARL ROGERS, *FREEDOM TO LEARN*

Agile. Resourceful. Resilient. Tenacious. These are the adjectives of adjustment. It is inspiring to see agile adjustment in the face of change. Many of
our most enduring myths celebrate such resilience, from Robinson Crusoe
to Star Wars. Whether it is "The mail must go through!" or "The show must

go on!" we admire those who are agile in the face of challenge. Leaders who learn and adjust are of that same character and tradition.

At the Grammy Awards in 1998, opera star Luciano Pavarotti cancelled due to illness halfway through the show. He was to sing *Nessun dorma,* a demanding aria from Puccini's *Turandot.* Aretha Franklin was on hand, having already wowed the audience with the high-energy soul of *Respect.* Aretha offered to step in. She had eight minutes to rehearse with the 72-piece orchestra. Ms. Franklin sang the aria in Pavarotti's key, three steps lower than her own, and astonished the spectators with her glorious performance. It is now one of the legendary moments in Grammy history.

In 1974, Barbara Jordan was a freshman member of the U.S. House Of Representatives from Texas. Jordan sat on the Judiciary Committee and was soon in the middle of the Watergate uproar. As the committee considered impeachment, the day came for all members to make a statement. Ms. Jordan was the junior member, and her turn did not come until well after midnight. She composed her remarks only after listening to and learning from many hours of comment. Jordan electrified the numbed, tired audience with one of the most affecting speeches in the history of the U.S. Congress. Her comments crossed all party lines and, according to the *New York Times,* gave the assembled legislators "a much needed lecture on constitutional law." Many Washington insiders say her 15-minute intervention accelerated Richard Nixon's decision to resign and the resolution of the Watergate scandal overall.

In the early 1990s, IBM was reeling from business losses. The company's long-time success was receding into memory as deficits mounted. In 1993, Lou Gerstner, Jr., assumed the role of CEO. After early, intense investigation, he is rumored to have told key employees "we are six months from bankruptcy." Difficult decisions led to massive layoffs, accompanied by a complete overhaul of the business strategy. Ten years later, IBM has recovered its position as one of the most profitable companies in the world. Sources of revenue are radically different, and the company has transformed itself from hardware giant to services juggernaut. Gerstner left the CEO role in 2002 with the company in far better shape than he found it.

Each of these examples is worthy of our admiration. How accessible are those deeds, however? How can the rest of us be so agile and valuable? Taking a conversational approach to adjustment can help.

In the cycle of value, the align conversations get shared purpose rolling, the act conversations produce actual value, and the adjust conversations translate experience into improvement. Leading high-velocity value requires it all: rapid alignment, early action, and frequent, valuable adjustment.

Adjustment is the proof of purpose. When you fully give yourself to a purpose, you naturally find your way through dynamic and even disappointing conditions. A purpose for which we are unwilling to adjust is mere preference. People with authentic purpose can fail temporarily, learn and adjust, and succeed finally. However, preferences are too weak to endure inconvenience, much less difficulty. The short story about adjustment is this: Stay true to purpose and adjust as necessary. All else in this chapter serves this inescapable point: adjustment relies on fidelity to purpose.

■ ■ ■

"All success is due to constancy of purpose."

BENJAMIN DISRAELI

Waste trap: *Relating to adjustment as an embarrassing indicator of incompetence.*

When a new purpose emerges, how likely is easy achievement? Unlikely, in our experience. A new strategy often emerges in unsupportive conditions, for example. Habit, history, current processes, and familiar concepts are consistent with old strategies, not with the new one. Understanding the merit of a new strategy is only the beginning; from that starting point, the ultimate strategy comes to light in a flow of adjustment. Adjustment is not evidence of strategic flaw; it is the emerging integrity of strategy. Few, if any, major strategies happen as originally imagined. The successful ones are a combination of the original intent and what materializes on the path of action. For new purpose to take root and succeed, adjusting must be a state of mind.

■ ■ ■

"He who rejects change is the architect of decay."

HAROLD WILSON

The Natural Attraction of Improvement

Conversations for adjustment are of natural interest to most human beings. To test our assertion, please read the following and note your response to it.

Some years ago, Charles Schulz's great comic strip *Peanuts* featured Lucy, the resident expert on everything, at a booth selling wisdom for five cents. Lucy loved to get Charlie Brown, the well-intended, beleaguered "every boy" of the strip, to pay for her advice. The strip went something like this:

Responding to Charlie Brown's reluctance to pay, Lucy says, "Charlie Brown, today I have been thinking about life itself."

Charlie Brown considered the risks of missing out on some important point about life itself and decided to pay his five cents.

Lucy: "Well, what I've been thinking is, in life, there are good days and bad days."

Charlie Brown nodded. "Yeah, I have good days and bad days, that's true."

Lucy: "Well, that means one day would be really bad, the worst day you ever had in your whole life."

Charlie Brown looked downcast as he considered a day that was the worst day of his entire life. "Yeah, one day would be the worst day ever . . ."

Lucy: "But wait, Charlie Brown. That also means one day would be the best day, the very best day you ever had in your whole life!"

Charlie Brown liked that thought a lot. He cheered considerably as he thought of the best day in his whole life.

Lucy, still on the subject of the best day: "Charlie Brown, what if you've already had yours?"

Here is where you check yourself out. If you recoil at the thought of already having had your best day, you have a natural affection for adjustment. The adjust conversations are for people who cause great days and still know the best is yet to come. For those people, valuable adjustment is magnetically attractive. Well then, why do people resist change?

"People resist change" has been said so often and with such conviction that it sounds like a fact. It is not. It is an explanation. As a fact, the statement will not stand up to scrutiny. How do you account for our interest in a new movie, a new restaurant, or the exciting fascination of a new relationship? What about the sense of anticipation that accompanies a new product, a new service, or any new opportunity? Absent change, nothing new can happen. We offer an alternate explanation: people resist threat.

The bioreactive responses to threat are often triggered by change. Fight, flee, freeze, and appease reactions abound when a change is perceived as a threat to our best interests. We resist change that threatens our purposes, our safety, and our opportunity to contribute. We greet change that seems valuable to our purposes and concerns with enthusiasm and offers of support. One wrinkle: If the amygdala cannot "match" a change with a quick, safe response, it assumes the change is a threat until proven otherwise.

The Attraction Keys

These are the keys to unleashing the natural attraction of improvement: purpose, facts, appreciation, and contribution.

In Chapter 2, we spoke of flipping the brain switch. A connection to a worthy *purpose* is the best antidote to thoughtless bioreaction. When significant adjustment looms, clarify the purpose at stake. Show its value to customers, employees, and investors. Demonstrate your commitment to the purpose in word and deed. Clear, shared purpose is the steering wheel of adjustment.

A common set of *facts* is a reliable antidote to fearful explanation. Danger provokes explanations that are often wildly inconsistent with facts. Make sure there is a common ground of facts, if you expect a common response to change. Purpose takes root in facts and is then not easily dislodged by the winds of change. Any community connected to a worthy purpose can deal valuably with known facts. The unknown sends us reeling into the wasteful world of fearful explanations.

■ ■ ■

"It is only when proofs are lacking that people
try to impose their opinions."

ANDRE GIDE

Appreciation gives a work community a connected past, present, and future. Appreciating past contributions develops a tradition on which to stand. Appreciating current efforts makes today's work meaningful. Appreciating what we might build together gives us a future worth the challenge of adjustment. The leader who proactively searches for chances to appreciate value is investing in effective adjustment and the pleasure of high achievement. The leader who takes effort for granted is investing in resentment, disloyalty, and mediocrity.

As a leadership competence, appreciation is adding value, not just witnessing it. An appreciative leader adds value to purpose, facts, and contribution. In Chapter 2, we introduced the notion of valuable questions. The question, What value can I appreciate? sets a filter in place that sifts input for opportunity.

Waste trap: *Deflecting appreciation.*

When someone offers appreciation, it is often greeted with depreciation. "Oh, it was nothing. I didn't do that much. Really, I made a lot of mistakes." Appreciation is a gift. It is not an accurate and exhaustive description of all of your merits and demerits. If you refuse a gift, you train people not to give again. Receiving appreciation gracefully is as important as giving it: "Thank you. I'm glad you found it valuable."

Waste trap: *Appreciation as manipulation.*

Fraudulent compliments and false kindness make skin crawl and toes curl. If dishonest concern is not perceived immediately, it will be ultimately. In the Dilbert cartoon in Figure 7.1, Scott Adams artfully communicates employee disgust with inauthentic appreciation.

The final attraction key is *contribution*. At the intersection of shared purpose and changing conditions, there is always the opportunity to contribute

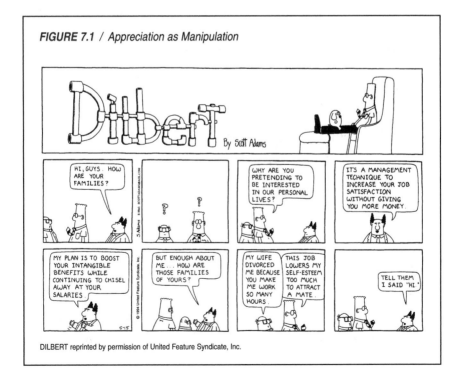

FIGURE 7.1 / Appreciation as Manipulation

DILBERT reprinted by permission of United Feature Syndicate, Inc.

value. We recommend that you develop a bias for constructing a response to change rather than instructing a response to change. *Construct,* from the Latin, means "to build with" or "to build together." If we merely *instruct* change, the wisdom of a few is substituting for the commitment and intelligence of many. Clarify purpose and facts, appreciate value, and create opportunities for contribution. Ask for help. Solicit suggestions. Show where important questions remain unanswered. One of the antidotes to the amygdala is the chance to be valuable. When we are creating value for customers and investors, we tend to feel safe and satisfied. When we are a pair of hands to carry out someone else's instructions, we tend to feel unsafe, disrespected, and dispensable.

The conviction that contribution is possible is central to leading valuable adjustment. In our consulting practice, we are often in adjustment conversations. Clients call when an important purpose is challenged by a change in conditions or poor execution of plans. One of our promises to ourselves is that we will accept no assignment without the wholehearted conviction, *"It is achievable from here."* We have found that conviction to be a reliable source of creativity and resilience. As a leader, authentically communicating your faith in achievement is a profound influence on contribution.

For Aretha Franklin, Barbara Jordan, and Lou Gerstner, the tumultuous conditions were the field of play for making a valuable contribution. They brought personal purpose to the facts at hand, appreciated the opportunity, and contributed. Vital contribution is natural when there is a clear opportunity to be valuable. Consider, then, a thought counter to popular conversation: Valuable change is magnetically attractive.

■ ■ ■

"Growth itself contains the germ of happiness."

PEARL S. BUCK

When to Adjust

In the Chapter 1 overview of the cycle of value, we gave examples of valuable occasions for adjustment. Here they are again, plus some additions. The timely occasions for adjustment are:

- In standard forums for debriefing performance (e.g., quarterly reviews) and at other obvious milestones (e.g., new leadership, major deadline)

- When results are far better than expected and you do not know why
- When results are worse than expected and not improving
- When key players are having major disagreements or losing interest
- Performance evaluations, project debriefs, and process improvements
- Times of shocking change: major (sometimes sudden) changes in conditions, personnel, strategy, and/or tactics
- When you are overwhelmed by work and lack the time or other resources to get it all done

In general, adjust whenever you wish to accelerate the creation of value. Once you are in action for any purpose, lessons begin to mount. When you debrief early and often, you can take advantage of the information that arises from action.

Waste trap: *"We are too busy to stop work and debrief."*
The "no time" impotent explanation is popular. Often, people relate to the act conversations as work and the adjust conversations as what we do when we have extra time. Waste, waste, waste! The most important time to debrief is when we are overwhelmed with work and cannot see how to get it all done. When we are overburdened, it is especially important to revisit priorities and practices. After all, our current practices got us into the overwhelming mess. Stopping to adjust accelerates the production of value. It is just counterintuitive to think of *stop* and *accelerate* in the same sentence.

■ ■ ■

"We cannot solve our problems with the same thinking we
used when we created them."

ALBERT EINSTEIN

What to Adjust

When goals are threatened by challenging conditions, what is the most popular thing to change? In our experience, it is the goals themselves. There are certainly times when it is valuable to just change a promise. However, we have found that adjusting commitment instead of adjusting performance is a frequent cause of waste. We recommend that you attempt to improve performance *before* you settle for revoking commitments.

In his elegant book *The Path of Least Resistance,* Robert Fritz describes the reliable desire of humans to release tension. When there is tension between our purposes and the situation, we naturally mobilize to resolve it. Fritz uses the term "creative tension" to show the value of crystallizing the difference between a desired future and the current state. In *The Communication Catalyst,* we purposely create tension between ideal align, act, and adjust conversations and the current state. By contrasting current conditions with the ideal cycle of value, we make improved conversations the path of least resistance.

Adjusting conversation is effective for at least two reasons:

1. People can alter the conversations they are having without falling into the cycle of waste. Almost any other method of adjustment is ripe with opportunities for personal blame. Personal blame obscures the system solution by catalyzing disagree⇒defend⇒destroy instead of align⇒act⇒adjust. Blame triggers bioreaction, people separate from one another, and improvement (if it happens at all) is isolated rather than integrated.

2. Conversation is the context in which we relate to each other, our work, and ourselves. If we adjust the right conversation, the right conduct will follow. Try to alter conduct without altering the conversations that generate it, and you produce temporary improvement at best.

The seven-step debriefing protocol in *The Communication Catalyst* views adjustment through the lens of conversation. The conversation categories are: align (intersect, invent, invest), act (engage, clarify, close), and adjust (review, renew).

The Standard Conversational Debrief

In the *act* conversations, we set the stage for accountability. Adjustment is the true test of accountability. To build a culture of accountability, host frequent debriefs of performance. Have the debriefing sessions be open, public conversations including all significant stakeholders. Initially, many people balk at public debriefing because of the threat of embarrassment. High-velocity value requires the system of interests to debrief and adjust together. Personal discomfort must be junior to the acceleration of value.

Stage One: Review

1. *State the original purpose and any specific results that were promised.* If the first step is difficult, you have your first lesson: You were never aligned regarding purpose.
2. *State the accurate outcome to date.* Separate facts and explanations. Only accept mutually agreed facts. Treat facts under dispute like explanations.
3. *What worked well in achieving the purpose and promised results?* What were valuable insights, methods, and mindsets? Sort the input into the cycle of value conversations: align (intersect, invent, invest), act (engage, clarify, close), and adjust (review, renew).
4. *What worked poorly since the last review?* Acknowledge goals unmet, disappointments, and mistakes of commission and omission. Sort the input into the conversations: align (intersect, invent, invest), act (engage, clarify, close), and adjust (review, renew).
5. *Who is there to appreciate?* Who specifically? What specifically did they provide? How and when will you recognize them?

Stage Two: Renew

6. *What actionable lessons will produce value going forward?* How will what you learned change how you act? What new action(s) will you take immediately? Share the lessons with whoever would benefit.
7. *What area of improvement is our highest priority focus?* What cycle of value conversation is it in? Is it an issue of insight (information, analysis, concepts), method (skills, processes), and/or self (mindsets, personal patterns)? What structures and measures are needed to support adjustment?

We have found it very important to close debriefing with a single, important focus. To find the focus, look through the responses to the previous six questions for themes. Then ask yourself, Which theme will make the most essential contribution? At this point, you have a valuable focus known to the entire community. When all members of a team focus on a single area of adjustment, improvement accelerates dramatically.

In step seven above, we introduced three new terms: *insight, method,* and *self.* You can adjust any of the cycle of value conversations in one or more of these three ways. When to use each is the subject of the next section.

The Integrity of Adjustment

In Chapter 1, we spoke of the architecture of conversation to show that you can design and build value through conversations. Architectural integrity normally refers to the relationship of the various elements of a design. For instance, if the foundation of a building lacks integrity, it is insufficient for the structure and might crack or crumble. The same can be said of adjustment. Relative to the purpose at stake, do the adjustments have architectural integrity? Are the changes we are about to make sufficient to achieve our purpose? Are they more than is needed, or less? People gravitate to the leader who adjusts with integrity.

Any of the cycle of value conversations can be adjusted in one or more of three ways: (1) *insight* (information, analysis, concepts), (2) *method* (skills, processes), and (3) *self* (mindsets, personal patterns). For instance, you decide the area of adjustment is the act conversations. Do you just need to explain the value of clear promises (insight)? Do you need to train people in the steps to a clear promise (method)? Do you need to confront a cultural habit of avoiding responsibility via vague promises (self)? For adjustment to produce high-velocity value, the adjustment must fit the need for change. All too often, it does not.

For example, vision statements have become much the rage. The actual fulfillment of vision statements is rare. We have seen two major reasons. First, the statement does not intersect with the authentic purposes and concerns of customers, employees, and investors. Second, the statement is an inactive desire rather than an instrument of adjustment. Reason one means the vision was never taken seriously at all. Reason two means the vision evoked support and then betrayed it. A vision statement, like any purpose, starts out as a theory. As an instrument of adjustment, the statement is a permit to point out and resolve inconsistencies with the purpose. Resolving these inconsistencies grants integrity to vision, escorting it from theory to reality. The romantic notions in these glib statements have too often beguiled the proponents of new vision. They become too satisfied with the emotional uplift and too weak at confronting the disparity between tomorrow and today. The integrity of a vision lives in learning to fulfill it. The lessons come in three forms: insight, method, and self.

Insight: Thinking a new thought. Insights are the least intrusive adjustment. If insight is the issue, then someone needs to understand something that they do not already. You may hold a conference call, a meeting, send a memo, or recommend a book. The hope is that by understanding something new, the people involved will take new, valuable actions. You explain it, they understand it, and a valuable change follows. However, new insight only produces valuable change in a very specific situation.

New insights are valuable to people who already have purposes allied with the insight. Insights unsupported by adjustments in method and self catalyze *existing* purposes; they do not conquer fear, transform attitudes, or break long-lived habits. Think of an area that is currently of interest to you. Perhaps you have been looking into successful employee evaluations, for instance. If someone sends you a reprint of a *Harvard Business Review* article on employee evaluation best practices, you are probably going to find it valuable. If someone sends you an article to try and change your interests, you probably will not even read it.

 Waste trap: *Sending out memos and reprints of magazine articles expecting an alteration of entrenched habits and attitudes.*

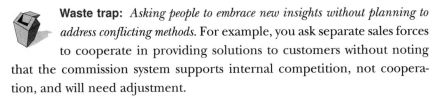 **Waste trap:** *Asking people to embrace new insights without planning to address conflicting methods.* For example, you ask separate sales forces to cooperate in providing solutions to customers without noting that the commission system supports internal competition, not cooperation, and will need adjustment.

Method: Taking new actions. Method interventions are adjustments in technique, process, and/or personnel. They are the answer to the question, How can we do it better? Best practices, process improvement workshops, and how-to trainings are examples. New actions are a bigger intervention than new thoughts, because they take more time and money. Designing and implementing new methods can also be highly valuable. Method interventions can conquer fear by demonstrating feasible practices. Experiencing a new method can shatter ignorance and reveal new occasions for action. New methods that are discovered and implemented by a group can be an inspiring asset to new effectiveness. Improving processes can produce dramatic increases in profit and customer satisfaction. For all this remarkable value, new methods do not solve everything. A method contribution only tends to be adopted if one of two things is true: It contributes to a purpose the person already cares about, or it is the only alternative available.

Many leaders have used the "only alternative available" path to ensure adoption of a method. There are times "no alternative" works well, as when the method is in the person's best interests and he discovers that by using it. However, if someone perceives that a new method is not aligned with his purposes and concerns, he will be astoundingly creative in undermining the new system.

Waste trap: *Confusing a how-to recipe with self-development.*

There is a disease run rampant in for-profit education: the how-to solution to everything. A tool that substitutes for developing our own competence is the daydream of our time. If you listen closely, you can hear a great, collective whine: "Tell me howwwww." Brochures in the mail, television commercials, and "breakthrough" training programs promise the risk-free remedy to whatever ails you. Hundreds of thousands of images in radio, television, billboards, and print inflame the fantasy. The false promise of the sure-fire solution has created a disabling expectation: The quality of the method should be responsible for my success. "What? I failed? Well, someone did not give me sufficient information. The process was unclear. I'm confused, and that is not my responsibility. I don't see what to do, and that certainly is someone else's fault." Developing our power to be resourceful and creative has been usurped by the fantasy of the fail-safe method. Methods can serve purpose; they cannot substitute for purpose.

■ ■ ■

"All means prove to be blunt instruments

if they lack a living spirit."

ALBERT EINSTEIN

How many success recipes for management, leadership, employee coaching, weight loss, golf, or parenting fall short of desire? Try this experiment: Go through your office and home collecting all the books, videos, and audio programs that promise a how-to solution. Stack them on a table so you can see the titles on the bindings. Now, what percentage of those purchases has lived up to its promise? However many failed, consider that the source of their failure is disconnection between self and method. A method inconsistent with your self can produce no value.

■ ■ ■

"You can't teach an old dogma new tricks."

DOROTHY PARKER

Self: Closing the gap between authentic purpose and habitual conduct. In every acorn is the complete design for an oak tree. Of course, not every acorn an oak tree becomes. Similarly, in every human being is the complete design for something he or she may or may not become. Developing oneself is realizing some aspect of that design. There are times in the pursuit of purpose when adding an insight or a method is not enough. In those moments, only self-development will do.

■ ■ ■

"If education is always to be conceived along the same

antiquated lines of a mere transmission of knowledge,

there is little to be hoped from it in the betterment

of man's future. For what is the use transmitting knowledge

if the individual's total development lags behind?"

MARIA MONTESSORI

Self-development is a topic for the ages. Great minds have given it lifetimes of attention. William James, Erik Erikson, Anna Freud, and Carl Rogers have delved deeply into the psychology of self. Thomas Merton, Martin Buber, and Abraham Joshua Heschel have passionately explored the theology of self. Add to that list philosophers from Plato to Heidegger to Bateson and modern thinkers like James Hillman. We cannot possibly honor their work or the size of the subject in the few pages to come. However, ignoring the place of self-development in creating value for customers, investors, and employees would be irrational. What follows is a simple, practical look at self-development in business.

If sponsoring self-development is too daunting, you can just change personnel. However, if you change personnel too frequently, you disintegrate the social system. Institutional memory weakens. New people may not know where to go and what to do. Informal connections are unclear and problem solving can suffer. A change in personnel is often worth those disruptions. Sometimes, it is more valuable to improve the performance of the people you have.

The Law of Large Numbers, a mathematical theorem, strongly suggests that no large business system can maintain a long-term advantage in the quality of people. The larger the system, the less likely the distribution of talent is much different than the population at large. In that case, improving the performance of the people you have can be a major competitive advantage. Such improvement can occur via insights and methods. It can also occur through people adjusting their own mindsets and patterns of behavior.

"If I only knew then what I know now." Is this something you have reflected on? If you compare your mindset at 20, 30, or 40, do you see substantial change? All of that is your personal development. Who in your career has been important to those changes? Who has been remarkably influential? Those people contributed to the realization of your self. Now, in whatever supervisory position you occupy or hope to, you have the opportunity to contribute in the same life-changing ways. Sponsoring self-development is not simply sharing insights and methods; it is penetrating into the important purposes of a human being to appreciate and catalyze contribution.

The similarities between acorn development and self-development end sooner than later. Acorns only develop if circumstances conspire to allow it. While our self certainly can develop circumstantially, we can also develop on purpose. We can, because we, unlike acorns, are capable of awareness, reflection, and choice. If you want the best from yourself and those around you, make sure you (and they):

- Are *aware* of your important purposes and the results you produce relative to those purposes.
- *Reflect* on how you specifically contributed to those results, learning more about your competence in the cycle of value in the process.
- *Choose* to either *cultivate* the explanations and habits that fulfill your purpose and discard the ones that do not, or revoke the purpose.

■ ■ ■

"I wanted to change the world. But I have found that the only thing one can be sure of changing is oneself."

ALDOUS HUXLEY

In our experience, the crucible of self-development is authentic accountability: an unflinching relationship to the results we produce relative to purpose. In order to reflect on those results, you often need help to hold up the mirror. You can arrange help in the form of standard forums for reviewing results. It can come in the form of a developmental partnership with people you respect. In a developmental partnership, each party is obliged to hold up the mirror for the others, acknowledging when conduct fulfills or departs from purpose. You can arrange help in the form of a personal

discipline that is supported by scheduled occasions for awareness, reflection, and choice. Regardless of how you do it, if you want self to develop
naturally, make sure there are honest mirrors around.

If you are ever dissatisfied with the development of someone in your employ, first look at the quality of the connection she has to the results she
produces. Make sure you are providing conditions that compel awareness,
reflection, and choice. You never develop anyone else; however, you can
create the conditions in which self-development is possible.

There is far more to be said on this subject of self-development and business value. Space and time do not allow us to say as much as we would like
in *The Communication Catalyst*. Still, here are a few things we have learned:

- *Appreciate heroism.* All around us, every day, people are doing what must
  be done. They endure inconvenience, misunderstanding, and insufficient resources. Somehow, they find it within themselves to be valuable.
  A culture of self-development can be built, in part, by appreciating the
  self-propelled heroes who produce value beyond the norm.
- *Do not just point out error; more important, put people in possession of the
  truth.* Citing error is a cheap imitation of leadership without accurate
  facts and actionable lessons. Help people stay connected to the real
  effects of their conduct and the real progress of their purposes.
- *The only things that can be adjusted are inauthentic patterns.* These are patterns of behavior that are inconsistent with genuine purpose. People
  adjust themselves for their own purposes, not yours. If you can support their purposes, you can support their development.
- *You can sponsor self-development only if you demonstrate self-development.*
  Hypocrisy does not play well in the honorable challenge of self-
  development.
- *You can only be an agent of development for someone that you believe in.* If you
  already characterize people as insufficient, you will have little influence. Entrust their development to someone who has not despaired
  of their contribution.
- *Crystallize the conflict between a wasteful explanation and reality; this is not
  always comfortable.* For example, a manager we know was hosting an
  evaluation for an employee frustrated by being passed over for promotion. The employee was convinced that "everyone" knew he was the
  most qualified candidate, and he was not chosen because his boss's boss
  did not like him and thus ignored the input of people in the department. The manager said: "This level position has opened three times

in the last year. We have solicited recommendations for the opening from all employees in the department. None of your peers has ever mentioned you as a qualified candidate." The stunned employee could not maintain his wasteful explanation in the face of those facts.

- *Crystallize the conflict between purpose and mindset.* We worked some years ago with a restaurant organization whose owner was worried about losing a very talented young chef. The woman in question wanted dearly to be the operating partner in the next restaurant to open. The next restaurant was to focus on "high pleasure, low calorie" meals. The idea was to feature healthy foods that required no sacrifice of eating enjoyment. The owner was reluctant to name the young chef as the operator. According to the owner, "Katherine was trained at a classic French restaurant in Paris and worships at the shrine of butter. She has told me numerous times that the new concept is a pure marketing ploy, because she knows that if you cut calories, you cut enjoyment. I need someone with faith in the concept." We recommended that he meet with Katherine and express his faith in her talents and his concern about her ability to lead the new restaurant concept. He told her that if she firmly believed that the concept was only a "ploy," that belief would prevent her from being a candidate for the position. Although the information was upsetting, Katherine could not help reflecting on her situation.

- *Invite the person to generate and compare explanations.* The restaurant owner told Katherine she was welcome to work with one of us if she wanted to explore her options. When Katherine called, we explained the difference between wasteful and valuable explanations. She agreed to come up with three explanations for her current dilemma that did not help her achieve her purpose. She also came up with three explanations that could help her achieve her purpose. We asked her to select the explanation that most supported her purpose. Katherine chose, "There is something for me to learn, which, if I learn it, could get me a partnership position."

- *Show a way out of the dilemma by revealing a developmental focus.* Ask the person if he is committed enough to his purpose to explore a new mindset. If yes, give him a single, fundamental adjustment to explore. Make the person's most basic wasteful explanation observable, plus a question to explore when he observes it. With Chef Katherine, we asked her what was important to her about being a chef. She responded with, "creativity, exciting new dishes, people being awed by wonderful smells and tastes," among other comments. We asked, "Is the new concept a violation of those purposes?" She said, "No." We then asked, "Are you willing to conduct a two-week learning experiment?" She said she was. We agreed to an experiment. For two weeks, every time Katherine caught herself reaching for butter, she agreed to ask and answer the following question: "What fresh ingredient will give me the taste I want?" At the end of the two weeks, Katherine reported several exciting discoveries and apologized to the owner for doubting the honesty of the concept. She said, "The things that had always worked for me were limiting my imagination." Katherine's learning and adjustment made a valuable impression on the owner, and he gave Katherine the position.

Waste trap: *Trying to improve everyone else first and yourself last.*
If you lead any system, big or small, you are the most effective leverage point for valuable change. To lead adjustment, look to your self first. Yours is the most influential mindset of all.

■ ■ ■

"Although the connections are not always obvious, personal change is inseparable from social and political change."

HARRIET LERNER

Full value of any conversation in the cycle of value requires insight, method, and self. We need it all, each in its own time. Some corrections require only one, others all three. In each of the align, act, and adjust conversations, look at insight, method, and self as if they are three floorboards to stand on. Is each strong enough for your purposes? You get to say. Just having the question puts you ahead of the crowd.

Thanks for exploring the adjust conversations with us. Adjusting can be magnetically attractive, personally challenging, and enormously valuable. The leader with the courage to adjust strengthens alignment and launches new cycles of value. Those strengthened relationships generate valuable new challenges, and "the beat goes on." Walker is about to discover how important such relationships are, because shocking change is on his doorstep. Let's move on to a Rev Lesson. It will be entertaining to see how well Walker adjusts.

CHAPTER SUMMARY

The Heart of the Matter

Adjust conversations translate experience into improvement. Authentic accountability lives in *reviewing* performance and *renewing* efforts via the actionable lessons learned. The opportunity to accelerate value is senior to the threat of personal embarrassment.

The Natural Attraction of Improvement

People are magnetically attracted to improving the value of their contribution. Why then do people seem to resist change? People resist threat, not change. A change that threatens our purposes triggers the amygdala to produce a fight, flee, freeze, or appease response. A change that supports rather than threatens our purposes is magnetically attractive.

Keys to Unlocking the Natural Attraction of Improvement

Purpose. Clear, shared purpose is the steering wheel of adjustment. Connection to a worthy purpose is a powerful antidote to thoughtless bioreaction.

Facts. A common set of facts is a reliable antidote to fearful explanations. Make sure there is a common ground of facts, if you expect a common response to changes.

Appreciation. Appreciating past contributions develops tradition on which to stand; appreciating current efforts makes today's work meaningful; appreciating what we might build together gives us a future worth the challenge of adjustment.

Contribution. Create opportunities for contribution. A vital contribution is natural when there is a clear opportunity to be valuable.

When to Adjust

Value track: Adjust whenever you wish to accelerate the creation of value. Timely occasions for adjustment:

- In standard forums for debriefing performance (e.g., quarterly reviews) and at other obvious milestones (e.g., new leadership, major deadline).
- When results are far better than expected and you don't know why.
- When results are worse than expected and not improving.
- When key players are having major disagreements or losing interest.
- Performance evaluations, project debriefs, and process improvements.
- Times of shocking change: major changes in conditions, personnel, strategy, and/or tactics.
- When you are overwhelmed by work and lack the time or other resources to get it all done.

 Waste track: *"We are too busy to stop work and debrief."* The most important time to debrief is when we are overwhelmed with work and cannot see how to get it all done.

What to Adjust

Adjusting conversation is effective for two reasons:

1. People can alter conversations without launching the cycle of waste.
2. If we adjust the right conversation, the right conduct will follow.

How to Adjust: The Conversational Debrief

Stage One: Review

1. State the original purpose and any specific results that were promised.
2. State the accurate outcome to date. Separate facts and explanations.
3. What worked well in achieving the purpose and promised results? What were valuable insights, methods, and mindsets? Sort the input into the cycle of value conversations: align, act, and adjust.
4. What worked poorly since the last review? Acknowledge goals unmet, disappointments, and mistakes of commission and omission. Sort the input into the cycle of value conversations: align, act, and adjust.
5. Who specifically is there to appreciate? What specifically did they provide? How and when will you recognize them?

Stage Two: Renew

6. What actionable lessons will produce value going forward? Share the lessons with whoever would benefit. How will what we learned change the way we act? What new action will we take immediately?
7. What area of improvement is our highest priority? Identify a single, important focus. What cycle of value conversation is it in? Is it an issue of insight, method, and/or self? What structures and measures are needed to support adjustment?

The Integrity of Adjustment

For adjustment to produce high-velocity value, the adjustment must fit the need for the change. The cycle of value conversations can be adjusted in one or more of three ways: insight, method, and/or self.

Insight: Thinking a new thought. Insights are the least obtrusive adjustment and come into play when people need to understand something they currently do not. In order for an insight to result in valuable action, however, the person must have a purpose that is aligned with the insight.

Examples of insight adjustments are sending memos, recommending a book, and calling a meeting.

Method: Taking new actions. Method interventions are adjustments in technique, process, and/or personnel.

High-value methods adjustments align with the purposes and concerns of the individuals involved.

Methods can serve purpose; they cannot substitute for purpose.

Examples of method adjustments are best practices, process improvement workshops, and how-to trainings.

Self: Closing the gap between authentic purpose and habitual conduct. Authentic adjustments are accomplished by being aware of your important purposes and the results you produce relative to those purposes; reflecting on how you specifically contributed to the results; and choosing to cultivate mindsets and habits that fulfill your purpose. Otherwise, revoke the purpose.

As you complete your conversational debriefs, assess the integrity of your adjustments:

- Are you truthfully adjusting to serve your purposes?
- Are the changes you are about to make sufficient to achieve your purposes?
- Are they more than is needed? Less than is needed?

R E V   L E S S O N

■ ■ ■

Stompin' on Dreams

"Each time I find myself

Layin' flat on my face

I just pick myself up and

Get back in the race."

FRANK SINATRA, "THAT'S LIFE" (WRITTEN BY KELLY GORDON)

"Walker, I guess I'd be about as upset as you, if it happened to me. It's about like drivin' down the road and havin' a tree fall on your car." He let the axe fall, rise, and fall in an easy rhythm. For Rev, chopping that dead tree into manageable chunks was a pleasant recreation for this Saturday afternoon.

"Rev, we've worked too hard to deserve this. It's wrong, and it makes me mad as hell!" I felt like I was in a nightmare. Disbelief and anger competed for my attention.

"Walker, I'd like to hear exactly what happened." Rev straightened and leaned the axe against the remaining stump. "How about you tell me while we load this wood in the back of the pickup?"

I picked up one of the tree chunks and heaved it into the truck bed with a bit more force than necessary. Then, as I continued to heave, I gave Rev the enraged version of the story. For you readers, I'll give a more accurate report, which seems easier now than it did then.

Things were going great. We moved the Converge project into action quickly, and Sharon was very pleased with our progress. Feedback from potential customers was enthusiastic. She had presented two other project ideas for funding, and we were optimistic about getting resources. Our new strategic purpose seemed to be rapidly gaining momentum. Then, the figurative roof caved in.

Sharon asked Ray, Louis, and me to come to her office. We were hoping to hear good news about our two other projects. Instead, we found out all further funding was stopped, because MightyTek had decided to put our division up for sale.

It had been a tough year for MightyTek. Sharon said that the board of directors had decided to divest some assets to improve MightyTek's cash position. Our division was selected for sale, because our business strategy was marketable, our major projects were outside MightyTek's core strategy, and there were interested buyers. The possible buyers were big companies who had lots of people with credentials as good or better than Louis's, Ray's, and mine. MightyTek's CEO told Sharon her boss was going to retire, and the job was hers as soon as the sale was closed. Good for her.

When we left Sharon's office, Louis exploded in anger. Ray joined in and I just walked along in shock. Their rage sounded muffled, like it was coming from another room. I was too stunned to be mad. That came later. One thing we did have in common was the dreadful realization that the result of our great work was joblessness. We all believed that it was our new strategy and projects that made the division marketable enough to sell. That morning, our accelerated development plan for Converge was an exciting challenge. Now, who cared?

"How did Sharon Scott react to all this, Walker? What does she think about it?" Rev was sliding the rough leather gloves off his large hands. I was breathing heavily from the dual exertion of lifting wood and angry storytelling.

"She seemed to take it in stride. Sharon just laid out the facts. Come to think of it, she didn't express an opinion at all." I realized I never even asked Sharon what she thought. My self-absorbed shock displaced my interest, I think. In retrospect, I was embarrassed. I should have at least asked.

"Let's go for a ride." Rev shoved the gloves into the waistband of his Levi's, picked up the axe, and stowed it in the back of the truck cab. He slid behind the wheel, and I sat in the passenger seat, still in the grip of a quieter version of my anger.

We rode in silence. When Rev is quiet, it seems exactly right, like nothing is exactly what there is to say. In the quiet, I felt my anger morph into sadness, the kind of sadness grown men tend to keep to themselves. I came out of my reverie as the truck passed the Dry Creek Saloon. Soon, we slid into an angled parking space at the foot of Mount Bonnell.

"What are we doing here?"

"Walker, when I'm facin' problems I like to think from a high spot. Seems to help me reflect; thought you might like it, too."

I didn't know that it would help, but we certainly were at a high spot. As far as I know, Mount Bonnell is the highest spot in Austin. Rev and I climbed up from the car park to the top, stepped over the low retaining wall, and sat beneath a tree overlooking Lake Austin's winding path through the hills.

"Rev, I don't think I even have a problem to solve, other than finding a new job. I don't have the energy or the ability to fight the sale of the division."

"Walker, what was that purpose you, Sharon, Ray, and Louis came up with?" Rev's voice was calm and interested.

I snorted, sounding somewhat like an annoyed pig. "It *was*, 'We transform current costs into high-return investments by connecting existing IT systems to create networks of breakthrough productivity.'"

"Last time we were together, I think I remember you sayin' that was an authentic promise for you? That so?"

"At the moment it feels like a mistake. I guess it's easy to claim authenticity when things are working well. I still care about it; it just seems out of my hands." My comments ended with a pronounced exhale and a rueful head shake.

"Walker, if you care about it, it's your problem. That's what a problem is, carin' about a purpose when it's not goin' well. If it's an authentic problem, it's one you promise to solve in a way that helps the original purpose."

"What? You mean I should help the new buyers with the purpose until they dump me and the others?" Injured indignation was rearing its head.

"No," Rev said. "An authentic purpose is at an intersection that includes you. There's no authentic solution if it doesn't take care of your purposes and concerns, too."

"I don't see how *that* can happen, Rev."

"It can't, Walker, unless it's your problem. At the moment, it's not yours enough to work on it."

"You just lost me, Rev."

"Walker, some years back, we had big rains up here in the hill country. All the lakes were fillin' up, LBJ, Travis, Austin, and Town Lake. As you know, dams connect the lakes. Rumor is, someone at the controls up at the Tom Miller Dam fell asleep and didn't let the water out of Lake Austin in time to stop a whole lot of floodin'. Then, the water got let out all at once and Town Lake flooded. A bunch of downtown was underwater. Damaged a lot of people and property."

"Rev, I'm sorry that happened, but what's it got to do with the sale of the division?"

"Now, Walker, you know I'm about to make a point, don't you?" Rev's slight smile nearly evoked one from me. He continued.

"My dad was livin' on Lake Austin back then. When I arrived to help out, Dad and his neighbors were rippin' out carpets, puttin' furniture out on driveways to dry, and shovelin' mud out of their houses. Dad was on the muddy driveway with a shovel singin' 'Baby, the Rain Must Fall,' and one of his neighbors was laughin' out loud. That neighbor told me, 'We got to work pretty quick, about the time we figured out it was *our* flood. We didn't do much good at first, 'cause it was someone else's flood, some fellow up at Tom Miller Dam. Now, it's our flood, and a lot's gettin' done.'" Rev stopped talking and let the silence provoke my response.

"Rev, I don't think I'm up to a lesson yet. I'm still in a bioreactive funk."

"Good to notice that, Walker. You best finish up bein' mad and such. You do just as much of that as you need to. Let's go get some lunch." Rev stood up and stretched, looking up and down Lake Austin.

"It's beautiful, isn't it, Walker?" I agreed.

"Some folks say that the lawns and gardens have never been better, ever since the flood." Rev turned, stepped over the retaining wall, and headed across the stone terrace. I trailed behind him as we headed down the hill.

We drove into town and stopped by Hut's for a hamburger. Rev said, "My friend Jim Pertuit is the curator of the Hamburger Museum. He thinks so much of a Hut's burger that he has a framed T-shirt on the wall that says God Bless Hut's." Jim and Rev are right. Even in my sorry state, this was a fine burger.

Rev stopped to get his wood ground into wood chips at a lumberyard. "I use 'em in the garden," he said. It was about three o'clock when we drove back down the quarter mile driveway and parked next to Rev Baker's Beautiful Central Texas Hill Country Barbecue Café.

Standing next to the truck, Rev said, "I'll be around tomorrow, Walker. You want my help, you ask for it. It's true that folks need to grieve a bit when things go badly.

Grieve just long enough to honor what really matters to you, and not so long that you lose it."

It seemed Rev was inviting my departure. "Thanks for talking with me, Rev. Coming out here and complaining was the closest I could come to not giving up on everything you and Sara Mac have taught us. I'm in a deep rut, for sure."

Rev nodded and picked up a sack of wood chips and rested it on his right shoulder. "You know, Walker, the only difference between a rut and a grave is how long you stay in it."

Rev turned and headed for the garden. I turned and headed for my car and a restless night.

■ ■ ■

"Rev Baker's Barbecue Café, this is Willie, can I help you?"

"Good morning, Willie. This is Walker O'Reilly. Is Rev around?"

"Not just now, Walker. He'll be back soon, though, 'cause he told me he'd be around for lunch. He said if you called, I could transfer you to his cell phone, though. Hold on." I held.

"Rev here." I could hear Rev's confident baritone through the cell phone crackle.

"Rev, this is Walker. I called to close an act conversation."

"Mornin', Walker. What act conversation is open that you need to close?"

"Last week, you invited me into the Catalyst, but you said the ticket in was a big promise. I said I'd close on it with you at our next meal. Yesterday at Hut's, with my cortex on vacation, I forgot about it."

"Walker, it sounds almost like a sense of humor, a bioreaction joke and all." I could hear Rev smile.

"A little black, but humor nonetheless. Rev, I kept being haunted by that promise last night. 'We promise to meet any challenge, no matter how difficult, by having the right people in the right conversation.' I figured something out about that."

"What's that, Walker?"

"I figured out that I can make a promise because it is authentic, not because I already know how to do it. I need to make that promise or I may never know how to do it. This is a good time for the Catalyst promise to become my promise. Feels a little bit like when your Dad made that flood his flood. So, I promise."

"That's fine, Walker, that's mighty fine. Let's meet at the café at one o'clock this afternoon. I've got something to show you."

"Rev, is it okay if I bring Sharon? I'm having coffee with her in a few minutes and she may want to come."

"You bet, Walker. Sharon is welcome. See you soon."

I met Sharon Scott for coffee at the Upper Crust Bakery at 45th and Burnett. It was a perfect place to nurse our coffee and our wounds, and I thought our conversation was the best we'd ever had. To my surprise, Sharon was not all that interested in the promotion she'd been offered.

Sharon told me that she was in shock herself when she delivered the news to us. She even called it a "freeze" reaction. Sharon believed the stock market would reward the sale in the short term, but that it was a long-term strategic loss to MightyTek. The more she thought about it, the more she did not want to abandon our new strategic purpose. She said she had spent most of Saturday analyzing the division as an asset, exploring the possibility of trying to sell the new buyer on the benefit of keeping our whole team. Sharon had arrived at the same sober conclusion Ray, Louis, and I had. On paper, at least, our skills were replicated in the company most interested in the acquisition. Sharon accepted my invitation, and we left the Upper Crust to go meet Rev.

When we arrived at Rev's he heartily recommended the beef brisket. The beef had spent 18 hours over oak and mesquite. It was smoky, tender, and succulent and required no sauce at all. We agreed to have lunch first and solve problems second. Rev wasn't eating. He had eaten already, enjoying brunch with his father at Guero's on South Congress. As Sharon and I ate Rev punched in a medley of tunes he thought fit the occasion. By mid-meal, our serious demeanors had given way to laughter.

"Rev," Sharon chuckled, "you are something. I can tell you don't feel sorry for us, not with that string of songs. Let's see, 'Baby, the Rain Must Fall,' 'Mama Said There'd Be Days Like This,' 'That's Life,' and really, Rev, Ray Charles singing 'I'm Busted'? That last one is bordering on cruel."

Rev grinned at Sharon, and spoke. "If Keats wrote 'Ode to Melancholy,' I think it's fair for me to do a medley to melancholy. Besides, music can help us go ahead and get as sad as we are gonna get. Then, we can move on."

I joined in. "Alright you two, let's do it. Let's move on. Rev, you said you had something to show us. Can we see it?"

A few minutes later, we were up in the shed. It was my first trip inside. There were two rooms, and I'd only seen one through the window that day. There was the one I'd seen, with all the whiteboards, bulletin boards, computers, and telecommunications equipment. There were no pictures and no lists, so I guessed nothing big was going on. The other room was Rev's office. Maybe it's better described as a library with a desk.

The wall behind Rev's desk is a floor-to-ceiling built-in bookcase. The wall with the windows has a built-in bookcase running the length of the wall from the windowsills to the floor. The other wall is dominated by a large Picasso print, in a museum-quality frame, of a dove hovering over swords, knives, and other tools of war. It was another visit when I noticed Picasso's original signature at the bottom right of the picture. Below the print is yet another bookcase. On top of that bookcase sits a framed quotation from someone named Kabir: "I laugh when I hear the fish in the water is thirsty." Every bookshelf is full. There is a dazzling array of titles, from philosophy to military tactics to fiction.

A small round table fits nicely between Rev's desk and the wall the doorway is on. There are three dark red leather chairs, swivel chairs with cherry frames and brass studs to hold the leather to the wood. The fourth chair sits behind the worn, scratched wooden desk.

As I took one of the seats, I noticed a book open on Rev's workspace, Robert Hellenga's *The Fall of a Sparrow*. Sharon spoke first.

"Rev, you are a fascinating human being." Sharon's eyes were taking in the details of Rev's environment as she spoke. "Plumbing the depths of you would be no small task. For whatever you have gone through to be you, and for sharing your discoveries with us, I thank you." I nodded in agreement.

"You're welcome, Sharon. You too, Walker. And, as Walker said, let's move on." We did.

Rev reminded us that the cycle of value is a conversational architecture for achievement. He told us that adjust conversations are as normal a part of achievement as doors are in a house. Rev said, "Adjust proactively to keep improving things or reactively to unexpected change."

Rev's example of proactive adjustment was Clifford Roberts, the legendary head of Augusta National Golf Club, where the Masters Golf Tournament is played. In the 1970s, after the Masters had already become the preeminent golf tournament in the world, Roberts founded an Improvements Committee. The task of the Improvements Committee was, and still is, to make the course and tournament better every year for golfers and spectators. Rev's example of reactive adjustment was our predicament at MightyTek.

"Reactive or proactive, adjustment is served by debriefing well. Any adjust conversation should be an inflection point, a start of a new trajectory of value. The debriefing protocol helps relaunch value when you are in the middle of a mission. It's not complicated. Most folks just don't take the time to do it, though."

Rev pressed the wood paneling on the wall above the table and a hidden door opened. Behind it were a whiteboard and a large pad of paper. Across the top of the whiteboard was written, "A Conversational Debrief." Under that were seven steps organized into two stages: "Review" and "Renew."

Rev said that you can't renew your efforts without first reviewing your efforts. He, Sharon, and I did what Rev called a "quick and dirty debrief," since we were missing important contributors like Ray, Louis, and Theresa. Still, we saw some very good things by looking for the conversation that was, in Rev's words, "screamin' for attention."

"Sharon, I think you're right on the mark," Rev said. "From laying out your new strategic purpose as a series of conversations, the invest conversation is what needs attention."

"It looks obvious now, Rev. Do you think so, Walker?" Sharon looked my way.

"Absolutely. Our intersection of purpose is still strong, and the ways we invented to achieve it are still valid. The third part of alignment is up in the air, though. The commitments to invest resources have been cancelled. The act conversations are still strong on our team, and we are doing a good job at adjust today. 'Align: Invest' is definitely the issue." I was enjoying the analysis. I could understand the design of our situation without having fits of blame and despair.

Sharon stood, walked a few steps away, and turned back to Rev and me. Her eyes were very bright. "We've been looking at this in the wrong way. The value is not *in* the resources. Value is what *attracts* resources. We've been acting beaten because we've lost resources. The value in this business is in our relationship, our ideas, our abilities, and our courage, and it's up to us to make that case. We just need to replace resources, Walker. We shouldn't resist this deal; we should lead the charge to find the right buyer!"

Sharon was electric. I was awed by how much I learned from her in about one minute's time. Then Rev spoke.

"That's the way Mac thinks."

Sharon looked at Rev, and then her head spun toward me. Our eyes locked. I said, "Are you thinking what I'm thinking?"

It was in that moment that the wild ride really began.

PART / THREE

. . .

Moments of Truth

"I wanted a perfect ending. Now I've learned, the hard way, that some poems don't rhyme, and some stories don't have a clear beginning, middle, and end. Life is about not knowing, having to change, taking the moment and making the best of it . . . "

GILDA RADNER

We have covered much in Parts One and Two. We do not recommend that you try to remember it all. Instead, focus on the critical moments that send you either into the cycle of value or the cycle of waste. Tend well to these everyday occasions, and you will live your way to high-velocity value, leaving a legacy of value rather than a residue of waste.

RAISING AND RESOLVING VALUABLE ISSUES

■ ■ ■

"If the truth were self evident,

eloquence would be unnecessary."

MARCUS TULLIUS CICERO

"It makes little difference how many university degrees or

courses a person may own. If he cannot use words to move an

idea from one point to another, his education is incomplete."

NORMAN COUSINS

We achieve important purposes by resolving the issues that separate the future we envision from the way things are now. As a term of law, an *issue* is "a point in question between parties to an action." As a term of conversation, an issue is *an uncommunicated opportunity to improve achievement of a purpose.* An issue can be a deviation from purpose that needs correction. An issue can also be an unrecognized opportunity you wish to bring to light.

A leader who raises and resolves issues promptly preempts waste and accelerates the creation of value. A leader who does not, sponsors the accumulation of waste. Business cultures weak at raising and resolving issues have a distinguishing characteristic: intermittent, or chronic, change initiatives. In our experience, the majority of "radical change" projects are born of sustained failure to raise and/or resolve issues. Those unresolved issues mount over time into a major need for change. Then, you need a change management initiative, management of change consultants, change management meetings, reports on the progress of change, and so on.

In Chapter 1, we said that "rate of adjustment" is the way to build wealth in dynamic times. The collective proficiency of an organization to raise and resolve issues dictates rate of adjustment. This proficiency is to rate of adjustment what bricks are to a brick building. No senior manager, no matter how brilliant, sees all the dangers and opportunities that call for valuable adjustment. However, each person in the system sees early warning signals that only he or she can see. When a culture is accustomed to freely raising and resolving issues, we tap into the intelligence and commitment of every person in the system.

A brief aside: the ability to raise and resolve issues is good for your career. Managers get eased out or thrown out when they build a mountain of unresolved questions regarding strategy, structure, resource allocation, and poor performance. These discarded leaders often are talked about as conflict averse, delegating poorly, or not building support for their ideas. That is all smoke. The fire is not handling the day-to-day issues of the business.

■ ■ ■

"If we are to be a really great people . . . we cannot avoid meeting great issues. All that we can determine for ourselves is whether we shall meet them well or ill."

THEODORE ROOSEVELT

The Minimum Ingredients for Raising and Resolving Issues

For raising and resolving issues to be a source of business value, *accountability, competence,* and *occasions* are minimum ingredients.

Accountability

Accountability is a hot topic. In education circles, the word is freighted with controversy as our teachers are "called to account" for the education of our children. We want accountability from politicians, accountability from corporate leaders, and accountability from anyone who has ever promised us anything. After all, we need to know who to blame when things go poorly, right? The conventional approach to accountability is a perfectly reliable way for provoking fear and finger pointing. It is not a reliable way for a social system to produce high-velocity value. The flaw: We have made accountability disintegrated rather than integrated.

Manage *disintegrated accountability* by having very clear individual promises. Make sure the individual consequences for failure and success remain crystal clear. Assume that people will not do a good job unless you motivate. Consider the source of good performance to be punishment and reward. Have one-on-one performance discussions.

Manage *integrated accountability* by having very clear senior purposes and transactions. The senior purpose is the system benefit to which all parties are committed. The transactions are what we need to give to and receive from one another to achieve the senior purpose. Make the interdependencies graphically clear to all involved. Assume that people want to be valuable. Consider the source of great performance to be the desire to be valuable in the network of relationships committed to the senior purpose. Have public conversations regarding performance and require individual responsibility and adjustment.

Integrated accountability inspires responsibility and creativity. Based in our interdependent devotion to a senior purpose, we make promises, track results, and debrief performance in a public conversation. We each have individual promises, but those promises are in a clear web of contributions, each requiring the other to succeed. Because we require each other to succeed, we require each other to debrief. No secret one-on-ones. The relationship of the team is the source of accountability, not the relationship of boss and subordinate.

In an environment of integrated accountability, the stage is set for raising and resolving issues. Raising issues becomes a matter of honor, because the success of the community is at stake. Make raising issues a matter of honoring your promises to customers, investors, and each other. You will need a clear, valuable senior purpose, clear interdependent promises, accurate performance data, and the competence and opportunity to interact.

■ ■ ■

"For the strength of the Pack is the Wolf,

and the strength of the Wolf is the Pack."

RUDYARD KIPLING, *THE SECOND JUNGLE BOOK*

Competence

Raise the issue at the intersection. You have been hearing about this intersection business for many chapters. Raising and resolving issues is a great practice field for everything we have said about it.

You can raise issues to respond to a problem or an opportunity. If it is a problem, you are usually noticing something inconsistent with senior purpose that you want to remedy. If it is an opportunity, you are usually in a forward-thinking conversation that is not a response to imminent threat. In either case, you will want to practice the ten steps to raising and resolving an issue. When we design a well-raised issue with clients, we use the chart in Figure 8.1 for steps three through ten. We suggest you reproduce the chart on a large space, like a flip chart or a whiteboard.

A *warning:* it is not true that because your cause is just your issue will be well received. The time it takes to follow the ten-step path is an investment in being heard and stimulating valuable action. Simply saying what *you* think is not enough. As Cicero's comment above implies, the truth is not self-evident. The path below is an investment in eloquence.

The Path to a Well-Raised Issue

1. Stay connected. For any valuable senior purpose, collect real-time data on progress. Have the network of relationships that are committed to the purpose develop not more than three measures of performance and review them early and often. When people track more than three measures for any single purpose, they tend to get bogged down in information and respond sluggishly. Wander around. Check in with people who are close to customers or are otherwise on the front lines of action.

 Waste trap: *Forming opinions about performance with no accurate connection to what is happening in the field of play.*

2. If you start with a concern, shift to a purpose. Many issues come to mind first as concerns or disappointments. The bioreactive response to threat awakens! Without our own permission, focus shifts from what we are *for* (purpose) to what we are *against* (concern). Note the well-justified fight, flee, freeze, or appease response. Since disappointments are simply imperiled purposes, you can regain your poise by asking yourself:

- What valuable senior purpose gives me this concern?
- What exactly happened that I am responding to?
- What opportunity does this issue give me to contribute to the senior purpose?

FIGURE 8.1 / *Raising Issues at the Intersection*

My initial issue:

Name	Purposes	Concerns	Relevant Facts	Relationship Status 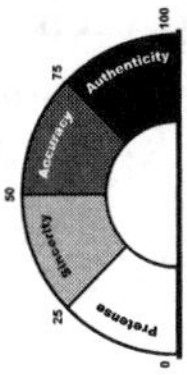

Themes

Issue to raise

If the issue came to mind as an opportunity, then you may be connected to senior purpose without having to navigate a disappointment.

 Waste trap: *Heeding the sirens' call of a bioreactive explanation.* Like the sailors in *The Odyssey*, listening to bioreactive noise can cause you to crash into rocks. Bioreactive explanations of unwelcome issues can seduce you into abandoning purpose. Never quit a purpose while in a bioreactive fit. Reconnect to purpose (and the cortex) first. Only consider quitting with your poise recovered.

3. Name the issue in your own words. Write the issue at the top of the chart. Allow how you express the issue to change as you include other points of view.

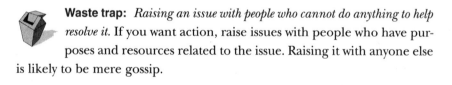 **Waste trap:** *Assuming that the first description of the issue is the most valuable.*

4. Identify the critical few stakeholders in the issue. Who must be in the conversation to fully resolve this issue? It is very common for a concerned group of people to belabor an issue unsuccessfully without having the right people in the conversation. It is smart to ask a few questions: Who are the minimum participants to fully resolve this issue? Who promised something related to this issue? Who has purposes that would make this issue of crucial interest? Who has the resources and authority to resolve this? Who can keep it from being resolved?

Waste trap: *Raising an issue with people who cannot do anything to help resolve it.* If you want action, raise issues with people who have purposes and resources related to the issue. Raising it with anyone else is likely to be mere gossip.

5. For each critical stakeholder, what are his or her most essential purposes and concerns? This is not your opinion of the others; it is your best effort to recreate their point of view. First, write down the purposes you know. If there are people whose purposes you do not know, then who does know? Ask them. If you cannot connect with someone who knows, then ask yourself, If I held his or her accountability, what would my essential purposes be?

Regarding concerns: What are they worried about? What do they complain about? What problem(s) would they love to have resolved?

 Waste trap: *Using purpose statements that demean someone.* If your statement of another's purpose is insulting, it is not their purpose.

6. For each stakeholder, note relevant facts. Pay particular attention to recent events.

7. Identify valuable themes. Stand back from the chart and look for themes. As you identify themes, you are creating a larger, more valuable context in which to resolve the separate issues. Identifying valuable themes sets the stage for system value. What are the common threads? Which have mutual value for a critical mass of the stakeholders (including you)?

■ ■ ■

"Always design a thing by considering it in its next larger

context—a chair in a room, a room in a house,

a house in an environment . . ."

ELIEL SAARINEN, *TIME* (JULY 2, 1956)

8. Name the issue you are going to raise. Look through the themes for a magnetic issue that will attract interest and resources from the stakeholders. We recommend the "Name that issue!" exercise to hone your ability to raise a magnetic issue. As an example, we will use a breakdown in customer service.

Name the issue in all four quadrants of the conversation meter:

1. *Pretense* (avoiding any direct confrontation).
   "Customer service really is important to our business." (Then, wait hopefully for someone to take the pretentious bait.)
2. *Sincerity* (righteous indignation).
   "Customer service around here is disgusting. You people in charge of customer contact need to get your act together, and fast."
3. *Accuracy* (factual inquiry).
   "The customer data log says that we have had a 12 percent increase in customer complaints this month over the same month last year. The only theory I have is that it may be a process problem, and I

don't want to make up my mind about that without hearing from you. What do you think caused the increase? Any ideas for remedies?"

4. *Authenticity* (contributing to a shared purpose).

"The mission we all signed on for this year is to gain five points in market share. Our bonuses are tied to that goal, and so is our professional pride. As we all know, we rely largely on word-of-mouth advertising. The first month of the year we had a 12 percent increase in customer complaints, which threatens our word-of-mouth strategy. What can we do together to dramatically decrease customer complaints and increase positive word-of-mouth?"

Do the "Name that issue!" exercise with the next five important issues you need to raise. We predict that you will develop very sensitive radar for a well-raised issue.

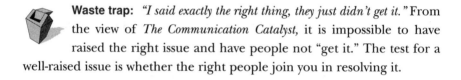 **Waste trap:** *"I said exactly the right thing, they just didn't get it."* From the view of *The Communication Catalyst,* it is impossible to have raised the right issue and have people not "get it." The test for a well-raised issue is whether the right people join you in resolving it.

9. Converse, don't convince. Raise the issue, listen, and learn from differences before composing a response. If your view is the most valuable, it will contribute to a critical mass of purposes and concerns. Make sure they know that you are sensitive to their view. Either your ideas will take natural root or the valuable differences will illuminate something even better.

■ ■ ■

"It is difference that makes interdependence possible,

but we have difficulty valuing it because of the speed

at which we turn it into inequality."

MARY CATHERINE BATESON

10. Propose, don't oppose. Propose ideas you can support rather than oppose the ideas you cannot. Resolution arrives much more quickly when you propose, receive feedback, and repropose until there is an agreement to act. If you oppose something, you launch the cycle of waste (disagree, defend, destroy). If you propose something of mutual value, closing an act conversation is just a matter of real-time learning and adjustment.

Suggestion: When considering two or more viable proposals, consider developing plans for the multiple proposals to learn from points of comparison. You may even put both proposals in action and debrief frequently. When the value is clear, you can stop one and put all resources behind the other, or you may see a hybrid of the two as the best investment of all.

 Waste trap: *Habitually disagreeing with someone else's view prior to stating yours.* This is a pervasive habit in organizational life. "I don't agree." "I'll have to push back on that." "Your reasoning is flawed." Many people gleefully defend this habit, saying they believe in telling the truth and open argument. That view is definitely more useful than pretense. However, it polarizes people, cements positions, and lengthens time to resolution. Accuracy and authenticity allow for complete honesty and productive conflict without all the waste that attends the "I disagree" tactic. It is simply not true that you have to destroy their point in order to make room for yours.

Of course, you cannot just read about competence, you have to earn it. Use the ten steps on real issues until raising issues at the intersection is a natural, graceful act. Become skillful at raising and resolving issues by raising and resolving issues.

Occasions

If you are to build a culture adept at raising and resolving issues, you need occasions for doing just that. Those occasions do not happen automatically.

The typical occasions for conversation in any enterprise tend to be a function of organizational structure. If you are organized by product lines, there will be typical meetings and forums to support that structure. If you are organized by geography, by function (e.g., engineering, marketing, or finance), or by process, there will be typical, unforced occasions for conversation. Each of those occasions is an appropriate venue for raising certain kinds of issues. In almost every company, though, some important issues are not supported by the organizational structure.

Any major purpose that is not supported by organizational structure needs an occasion for raising and resolving issues. In many companies, crucial strategic purposes go unachieved simply because there is no occasion for conversation. For example, we commit to bundling our products and services into customer solutions. Before long the complaints begin:

- "We don't have processes to support solution sales."
- "We don't have the right compensation system to support this strategy."
- "We must not really be committed to this solution selling strategy."

The complaints do not clear up, and there ensues a downward spiral of frustration and failed purpose.

Here, we think, is the dilemma. Innovative purposes usually break the bounds of existing structures. The day-to-day gravitational pull is toward familiar meetings and processes. The innovative purpose is left up to good intention. The new purpose is not understood well in the beginning, so it is nearly impossible to support it with reliable processes. Between the old structure and the needed processes, there is a deadly gap: an occasion for raising and resolving issues.

A simple case in point is how we got *The Communication Catalyst* from book contract to submitted manuscript. Our practice is organized around the services we provide clients. *The Communication Catalyst* is an anomaly. We have not written a book before, and we have no natural occasions for doing so. Still, it is an important purpose. In fact, there is a signed contract with a promised delivery date. This important new purpose brings with it many issues we are not structured to resolve. Guess what happened? We got behind on the delivery schedule. Then came the explanations:

- "We don't have processes to support writing books."
- "Maybe we are not really committed to writing a book."
- "We had no idea what we were getting into."

Of course, none of those explanations was getting the book written. Then, being well-intended people, we made a rigorous time line with lots of deadlines. Guess what happened? We got further behind. Finally, we created some valuable occasions for raising and resolving issues.

The first occasion was a series of meetings between Sue Rhodes, a member of the Conversant fold, and Mickey Connolly to edit the first-draft manuscript. These were the first regular occasions devoted solely to the book. Out of those meetings, the real time demand on completion became clear. All of us working on the project, including Mary Good, our Dearborn Trade editor, met to debrief and restart. The second occasion was born of that debrief.

Julie Naster, who chairs the process transformation practice for Conversant, became the chairperson of a new group: the book team. Julie got all stakeholders together and used their input to redesign the project. She arranged regular check-ins, facilitated problem solving, and in general guaranteed an occasion for discussing issues related to timely submission. With our new occasion for raising and resolving book issues, we discovered how to support writing and the rest of the work of our practice, too. The processes became clear because we had appropriate occasions for conversation. Our stuck purpose was suddenly back on track.

Does our simple dilemma remind you of anything? Do you have purposes that lack occasions for conversation? Do you have issues with no occasion to resolve them? Any purpose that lacks an occasion for conversation cannot evolve. Examine any purpose that is not naturally supported by your structure and ensure:

- *Regular occasions.* A standard forum including all necessary constituents to raise and resolve predictable issues. Clarify the senior purpose served by this occasion. Members commit to the senior purpose as the best way to create value for their individual purposes and concerns. Establish what decisions will be made by this group and instate a decision-making protocol (see Chapter 5).
- *Ad hoc occasions.* Occasions for specific issues that regular occasions do not resolve.
- *Impromptu occasions.* All stakeholders live up to their accountability for the success of the purpose by raising and resolving issues with people as necessary. The development of regular or ad hoc occasions arises from impromptu occasions.

Issues—we all have them. An unraised issue gets no attention, and none of us has the right to expect resolution of an issue we will not raise. A poorly raised issue is either dismissed or causes unproductive conflict. A well-raised issue serves an intersection of purpose, refocusing people and resources on valuable improvement. All you need are accountability, competence, and an occasion for conversation. The accountability comes first, because without it competence is accidental and occasions are wasted.

■ ■ ■

"One can present people with opportunities.

One cannot make them equal to them."

ROSAMOND LEHMANN, *THE BALLAD AND THE SOURCE*

Walker O'Reilly has lots of issues, if you recall. His job is in jeopardy, and his most important business purpose is at risk. In this next Rev Lesson, you will meet new characters and old characters in an issue-resolving jamboree. Walker's life, among others, will never be the same. Check it out.

CHAPTER SUMMARY

The Heart of the Matter

A leader who raises and resolves issues promptly preempts waste and accelerates the creation of value. A well-raised issue serves an intersection of purpose, refocusing people and resources on valuable improvement.

The Minimum Ingredients

An *issue* is an uncommunicated opportunity to improve achievement of a purpose. Ingredients necessary in raising and resolving issues as a source of business value are:

Accountability. *Integrated* accountability is based in the interdependent devotion to a clear, valuable senior purpose; explicit, interdependent promises; accurate performance data; and the opportunity to interact and adjust.

Competence. Raise issues at the intersection; simply saying what *you* think is not enough.

Occasions. Create opportunities for people to raise and resolve issues. A purpose without an occasion for conversation cannot evolve.

The Path to a Well-Raised Issue

1. *Stay connected.* Collect accurate data on progress. Develop not more than three measures of performance and review them early and often.
2. *If you start with a concern, shift to a purpose.* Ask yourself: What valuable senior purpose gives me this concern? What exactly happened that

I am responding to? What does this issue give me to contribute to the senior purpose?

3. *Name the issue in your own words.* Write the issue at the top of the chart.
4. *Identify the critical few stakeholders in the issue.*
5. *For each stakeholder, what are his or her most essential purposes and concerns?*
6. *For each stakeholder, what events and facts are currently important?*
7. *Identify valuable themes.*
8. *Name the valuable issue you are going to raise.*
9. *Converse, don't convince.*
10. *Propose, don't oppose.*

 Waste trap: *"I raised the issue well, they just didn't get it!"* The test for a well-raised issue is whether people join you in resolving it. If they did not join, you did not raise it well enough.

R E V   L E S S O N S

∎ ∎ ∎

Change Partners and Dance

"Won't you change partners

And dance with me?"

FRED ASTAIRE, "CHANGE PARTNERS" (WRITTEN BY IRVING BERLIN)

"**R**ev!"

"Good mornin', Walker."

"I've never seen you look like *this*!"

Rev laughed. "'There are more things in Heaven and Earth, Horatio,/

Than are dreamt of in your philosophy.'" We both laughed.

Rev looked distinguished. He was wearing a three-button, single-breasted, wool suit. It was dark gray with a light gray pinstripe. The spread collar of Rev's crisp, white cotton shirt framed a precisely knotted burgundy-and-gray silk tie. The fit of the suit was perfect, the kind of drape fine tailors achieve. The cuffs of his pants broke slightly where they touched the soft shine of laced black leather shoes. In that moment, Rev reminded me of a larger-framed version of Sidney Poitier. He had that kind of dignity and presence.

"Walker, I dress to fit the occasion. In meetings where the outcome is in question, I like the issues to be front and center, not clothes." Rev was still completely himself. The substance of him clearly steers whether the dress of the day is blue jeans or a Brioni suit.

"Did we pick this spot because of your friends, Rev?" I pointed to the entry of Eddie V's Edgewater Grille.

"Larry and Guy? Partly. Also, It's close to MightyTek's headquarters and The McGregor Fund."

"Gentlemen." I heard Sara's voice and turned to see her and Sharon approach from the tree-studded parking lot.

Rev bowed slightly and, in greeting, sang two lines from a Guy Clark song: "'Now there's a pair to draw to, I would not steer you wrong.'" Amid the smiles, Sara bowed back and Sharon mouthed, "Thank you."

In my experience, time froze. Everything stood still, giving me a chance to be awed by them individually and collectively. A pair? These were three aces. Whether we won or not, playing the game with these three over the last month was reward enough.

It was just over four weeks earlier that Sharon Scott and I met with Rev at his office in "the shed." In our adjust conversation, the fog of disappointment cleared, and we saw where to go to work. My fear that "all was lost" proved to be only a bio-reactive explanation. What was lost was an investment of resources sufficient to our strategic purpose. It was then that we thought of Sara McGregor, the founder and CEO of The McGregor Fund, Texas's most successful venture capital firm.

I called Sara Mac and requested a meeting. I told her about MightyTek's decision to sell our division (she already knew, of course) and asked if she had any interest in supporting the purchase. She did, and Sharon, Sara, and I became immersed in analyses of strategy, revenue, expenses, and profits. After only two days, my growing optimism took a hit.

We were at the offices of The McGregor Fund on Highway 360 in northwest Austin, right next to the arboretum. Sara Mac said, "This is not a good risk as a stand-alone business. I think it will take around $100 million to close the purchase, and another $40 million for working capital. If you are late with any of these first three products, that working capital number will rise. You have good ideas about distribution channels, but no solid agreements. Your strategy is now being thoroughly examined by two Fortune 500 companies. If they decide to pursue the market, they will be formidable competitors. Even though I respect your talent and business vision, I cannot yet justify a $140 million risk."

"What's missing that would justify the risk, Sara?" Sharon asked the question with conviction, as though she knew Sara had more to say.

"Anything that mitigates these risk factors: competitive threat, time-to-market, distribution channels, customer acquisition, and a clear path to positive cash flow. That leads me to a question: Who benefits if you purchase the division? Besides you, I mean?" As Sara spoke, she stood and wrote "Who benefits?" in large letters at the top of a whiteboard.

It was a valuable inquiry. We saw an array of people and institutions that could benefit. Then Sara asked, "Which of the beneficiaries can help deal with our risk factors, and how?" We began to formulate a few scenarios involving different beneficiaries. Then, Sharon stood, stretched, and paced. She did that when she was working through a new insight.

"Let's get our senior purpose straight. It's to preserve our opportunity to achieve the strategic purpose in which we have so much confidence, right?" Sharon was looking at me as she asked the question.

"That's it as far as I'm concerned."

"Okay, then we can give up a lot of ownership to mitigate the risks, because ownership is not our essential purpose. Sara, we need your help in designing a few scenarios involving trading percentages of ownership for addressing our risk factors. I just ask that all scenarios include at least a three-year management contract for our senior team."

"Fine, Sharon, let's do it." Sara's assent launched days of scenario planning. Each of the scenarios included a different array of financial transactions. I felt dizzy at times, grateful that Sara McGregor and Sharon Scott were so financially savvy. They were patient, answering all my questions without irritation or disdain. We called, met, and e-mailed various people as we explored possibilities. Eventually, we developed options that Sara Mac declared worthy of the risk.

It was fascinating to watch Sara lead weeks of conversations from the cycle of value. Rev's teaching unfolded right in front of me. Sara Mac was in a recurring rhythm: Align (turn separate agenda into *intersec*tions of interest that evoked *in-ven*tive ideas, and test and compare the ideas to see where she would be willing to *invest* resources); Act (*engage* Sharon and me in a specific course of action, *clarify* who would need to do what and when, *close* open proposals and promises); and Adjust (*review* actions often and *renew* our efforts with lessons learned). I was relieved to see all the theory in useful action.

I found one thing strangely inspiring: how easily she caught, noted, and corrected threat reactions. For instance, one morning Sara Mac discovered a mistake in one of our financial models. The light freckling across the bridge of her nose darkened as her neck and jaw muscles tensed. I thought a Scotch/Irish explosion was coming. Instead, she took a deep breath and said, "A fight reaction will just waste time, right? Throwing a brick at the computer won't fix the numbers, right? I guess we should find out what happened and move on." We did.

Rev came and met with us several times, always asking smart questions that strengthened our scenarios. As we approached our big meeting with the MightyTek CEO, Sara asked Rev for help.

"Rev, this meeting is do or die. Our value proposition has to be obviously better than the others, or this becomes a bidding war. We need the best. Will you help prepare and conduct the negotiation?"

"I'm happy to, Mac. Let's start now."

We had developed two scenarios to which Sharon, Sara, and I were willing to commit. Rev asked us, "What essential purpose explains why those two scenarios are acceptable to you?"

We had discussed that thoroughly. Sharon said, "Fund our business plan by leveraging the resources of natural beneficiaries while leaving us with at least three years of management control."

Rev nodded. "That's clear, and a good start. That's not the purpose for the upcoming meetin', though. The purpose has got to attract the decision makers like a magnet. We'll get to that in a bit. Now, who are the crucial players?"

That was the birth of our preparation chart for the big meeting. One whole whiteboard was taken up with a list of the players, and the purposes, concerns, and recent events associated with each. There was MightyTek's CEO, Grey Davis; MightyTek's CFO, Madeline Archer; MightyTek's Business Development Officer, Troy Dennis; Sharon Scott; me; Sara Mac; and Glen Gardner, the CEO of Enterwise, the enterprise software firm that seemed most interested in purchasing our division. Rev also asked us to use the conversation meter to assess the current quality of relationship Sharon and I had with each player. The chart had several iterations. The one we ended up with the day before the meeting is reproduced on the page following this one.

As you see on the bottom of the chart, our meeting purpose became: Get MightyTek's response to a proposal to acquire InfoBridge Division that:

1. Immediately increases MightyTek's revenue.
2. Strengthens MightyTek's cash position.
3. Fits the profile of transactions being highly valued in the stock market.
4. Creates new revenue streams for MightyTek.

The meeting purpose came out of examining the whole chart for themes. Rev said, "Intersections just about leap out at you when you look for themes." He was

Valuable Meeting Preparation Chart

SS & WO Purpose: Fund business plan by leveraging resources of beneficiaries while retaining management control (3Y)

Players	Purpose	Concerns	Recent Events	Relationship Status
MT Chairman and CEO, Grey Davis	• Focus on core business • Grow revenue & profit • Customer friendly process • Strengthen cash position • Preserve long-term growth • Increase stock price	• Selling out LT growth for ST problem solving • Stock market perception of MT stock value • Cash reserves • Support of key MT Board members	• Stock price decline • Earnings decline • Board requests action • Austin business press speculates about MT layoffs	Sincerity
MT CFO, Madeline Archer	• Support CEO • Smart investments • Decrease expenses • Increase cash • Ethical dealings	• Weak performance & cash position could hurt credit ratings • IT systems give slow updates on business performance	• Stock price decline • Earnings decline • Incorrect earnings forecast last quarter	Accuracy
MT BDO & Staff Attorney, Troy Dennis	• Grow revenue through select acquisitions • Bring valuable deals to table • Succeed in new position	• Need cash to close deals • Credibility with CEO • Career prospects on new career track	• Stock price decline • Revenues decline • CEO declared one of acquisitions a "failure" • Moved from ACQ attorney to BDO 18 months ago	Pretense
Enterwise CEO, Glen Gardner	• Develop business model with fewer "peaks & valleys" • New source of revenue • Strong relationship with MT	• Extended revenue declines • Time-to-profit of new revenue streams • Integrating new acquisition	• Revenue decline • Enterwise SW spending down this year over last worldwide • Submitted letter of intent to buy the MT division (under consideration by Grey Davis)	Pretense
Sara McGregor	• Invest in undervalued growth opportunities • Invest in quality executives & managers	• Clear path to cash flow • Clear path to customers • Time-to-market performance • Spreading risk	• Sold part of portfolio (has cash) • McGregor Fund return to investors is up over last year (in a down market)	Authenticity
Themes	• Reliable profitable growth • Valuable use of cash • New sources of revenue	• Credibility • Cash flow • Potential damage	• General weakening—financial performance • Activity to grow revenue and profit	• Need to improve relationship to make the deal
Meeting Purpose	Get your response to a proposal to acquire information bridge that: 1. Increases MT current revenue 2. Strengthens MT cash position 3. Fits the profile of transactions being highly valued in the stock market 4. Creates a new future revenue stream for MT			

right, of course. We got energized about the meeting purpose, because it was authentic and we knew we could deliver. However, there was a weak point.

We realized that our current relationship with the players was fine for our historical needs but insufficient to pull off this acquisition. We needed to intersect with them in an unprecedented way and improve the relationship at least one level (pretense to sincerity). Rev gave us some coaching.

"Most of these folks think they already know you. You need to update the relationship. Do some things that they do not think you would do that produce value they don't expect. Do that about three times, and they'll update their opinion of you."

We worked on some ways to update the relationship. In our final prep session, we acknowledged that we still were not confident that we had an authentic intersection with Grey Davis. It would have to happen in the meeting itself. That brings us back to the moment in the parking lot when Rev and I hooked up with Sharon and Sara.

Sharon spoke, her brown eyes radiating confidence. "Here we go, gang. Sara will present the basic deal points, Walker and I will cover our parts, and Rev will be in charge of any mid-meeting adjustments, including calling for breaks as he sees fit. Rev, I told Grey you are a McGregor Fund board member here at Sara's request, and you are advising us in all aspects of this proposal."

"Sharon, Mac, Walker, I'm going to listen quite a bit before I say or do anything. Don't be waitin' on me; you trust your judgment. I'll step in when it's valuable and not before."

Sara smiled. "As I have come to expect, Rev. Everyone, this meeting is a conversation, not a presentation. If a presentation were sufficient, we would have sent over a videotape. We are aligned enough to trust any one of us to speak up at any time. Also, we need to learn as we go from Grey, et al., and adjust along the way. Let's come out of here smarter than we go in."

With that, we turned to walk inside Eddie V's. Crossing the parking lot four abreast, I had a fleeting thought that Rev might burst into a song-and-dance number, but he did not. Still, the energy and rhythm were there, because we were in this together, watching out for each other each step of the way.

Eddie V's is usually not open during the day, but we were expected, and a gracious young woman named Josie escorted us to a private dining room overlooking the restaurant and bar. The mahogany paneling reminded me of Rev's office. The black-and-white photographs on the walls were of the Deep South, featuring forebears of solid citizens like Rev Baker. The table was set with a white tablecloth, legal pads, pens, glasses, and two glass pitchers filled with ice water. Josie turned to Rev and spoke.

"Mr. Baker, we followed your instructions precisely. Here are your place cards." Josie pointed to a set of off-white table tents with names beautifully lettered in calligraphy.

On the back of each tent in impeccable, hand-printed block letters was our meeting purpose. Rev wanted that purpose in front of people all the time. "Also," Josie continued, "the books came." Josie pulled a box from under the table and produced a very slender, dark-green hardbound volume. On the cover in simple stark white print was, "InfoBridge: a proud offspring of MightyTek."

It surprised me how quickly and inexpensively we got our proposal printed in an elegant, hardbound book. On the first page were a promise and a list of quotations. The promise was: "We will only propose what achieves your goals." The quotations were comments our invitees had made in the recent past. To find them, we combed the annual report, press conferences, news articles, and notes from meetings we have attended:

"I have never made a mistake betting on the talents and commitment of the people who love this company."—Grey Davis

"Don't expect me to believe it if you can't prove it."—Madeline Archer

"Sometimes the best deals are right under your nose."—Troy Dennis

"We will be aggressively seeking new alliances that allow Enterwise to serve customers in innovative ways."—Greg Gardner

We set the place cards and books at the appropriate places. Josie performed finishing touches on our beverage and snack setup. Then, our MightyTek guests arrived. There was a flurry of introductions, and we sat.

Grey Davis said, "Sharon, I was impressed with your bold stroke of inviting Greg Gardner. I was even looking forward to the drama. However, our legal team frowned on it, since we have an existing letter of intent from Enterwise."

"Thanks, Grey." Sharon was nonplussed. "Greg Gardner called last night and let us know he would not be here." Sharon shifted to our purpose.

"To begin, we ask that you review our purpose for inviting you here. It is on the back of your place card, facing you. Afterwards, I'll ask everyone to add any other intentions you have for our time together." As the purpose reading began, I surveyed the participants.

Grey Davis, MightyTek chairman and CEO and local Austin legend, wore a dark blue suit, white shirt, and red-and-gray tie. His close-cropped black hair was beginning to turn the color of his name. Grey is famous for being smart, tough, and generous, an interesting combination. Grey speaks his mind and expects others to do the same.

For the first time in Grey's 20-year tenure, MightyTek was struggling. Corporate purchasing was in a slump. Competitors had finally developed comparable technologies. The previous week he had told senior managers, "Revenue is no guaranteed annuity. Our competitors have fed off of our complacency. It is time to fight for our customers and *earn* their spending like we never have before."

Madeline Archer, the chief financial officer, seems to always look like she just stepped in from a windstorm. Her wild red hair and slightly disheveled clothes belie her rabid attention to financial detail and her pristine ethics. She is fiercely devoted to MightyTek. Madeline respects people who respect data. She does not speak a lot. When she does, it is usually with passionate conviction.

Troy Dennis had been MightyTek legal counsel for divestitures and acquisitions for most of the last nine years. Eighteen months earlier, he took a job he had coveted: business development officer. His first acquisition as BDO was widely regarded as a failure. He was looking, some say desperately, for a "win." Troy was partial to Italian suits, contrasting solid-color silk ties, and glove leather loafers. Any time I saw him I thought of that old Billy Crystal routine: "You look mahvelous!"

Then, of course, there were the three aces and me.

Troy Dennis commented on the purpose statement first.

"Well, Sharon, are you people going to solve peace in the Middle East, too? This seems a little ambitious for a couple of managers trying to put together their first deal."

Troy's remark struck me as wasteful. With Rev's influence, I was beginning to observe conversations, not just react to them. I glanced at Rev, and he was looking pleasantly impassive. Before Sharon could respond, Grey spoke, waving a dismissive hand in Troy's direction.

"Sharon, I do not share Troy's view. I assume your associates stand behind this purpose?" Sharon answered affirmatively. "Ms. McGregor, I apologize to you in particular for that remark. You have certainly earned the right to make bold statements." Sara gave a single nod in response.

Troy said, "Hey, just a little needling, no need to take it seriously. We're all friends here, right?" I found his comment jarring, since Troy just met Sara and Rev and had few dealings with me in the past.

Sara said, "No harm done. Now, you have seen our purpose, and we need to make sure it fits yours. Can each of you tell us what you want to come out of this meeting?"

We were rolling. Rev had told us to give each of them a chance to communicate very early in the meeting. "Y'all need to intersect with what's present for them in that moment, not just what we put on our prep chart. Listen to them like they have never been listened to before, and acknowledge what you learn." We listened and we learned.

"Madeline, I did not appreciate all of the demands on your time. Your decision to conduct a proactive review of all accounting practices in the post-Enron climate must be adding to your heavy workload. We accept your request to give you whatever you need to form a fast opinion of our offer."

"Thank you, Walker." Madeline's head raised slightly, and her eyes opened wider as she spoke to me. I think she was surprised to hear me speak for us all.

We finished hearing from everyone, and we saw that our purpose was valuable to all. In fact, we had learned a few things that gave us even greater certainty. Then, Sara went to work.

Sara Mac asked everyone to open their InfoBridge book. She gave them a moment to read their own words. Again, we had surprised them. I watched the relationship being updated before our eyes. Then Sara gave them the basic points:

- We were willing and able to meet their asking price, plus leave MightyTek with a significant ownership position in InfoBridge for two reasons:
  1. We knew InfoBridge was worth more with existing management at the helm, so we were willing to value the business accordingly.
     - No learning curve meant faster time-to-market.
     - No one else was as invested in the business strategy.
     - No one else could be as sure about identifying and retaining crucial personnel.
  2. We knew MightyTek could make important contributions to InfoBridge without distracting from MightyTek core strategy.
     - Distribution channels
     - Marketing information
     - Purchasing power
     - Other easily shared services
- We intended to negotiate alliance agreements with the four major software firms stating that they would receive a royalty payment for every incidence in which our software products connected to one of their systems.
  1. This strategy would preserve MightyTek's relationships with all the major enterprise software firms. Selling to one could jeopardize relationships with the others.
- We requested that Grey Davis accept a seat on the InfoBridge board for at least two years, so that we could continue to learn from him.
- The portion of ownership to MightyTek would be a function of three variables:
  1. How much of the purchase would be in cash versus debt
  2. What shared services we agreed to
  3. A favorable lease for InfoBridge's current premises

Watching Sara Mac communicate those points was a lesson. She was so poised and focused that no one interrupted her until she was inviting comment. Later, when we debriefed, Rev said, "'Poised' is what you say about folks whose purposes are the context for their concerns, instead of the opposite. For Sara, concerns are background music she only listens to when valuable. Mostly, people get interrupted because their relationship to what they are saying is weak and riddled with worries."

The comments did come, however. We fielded them with ready facts. Grey complimented us on our preparation. Madeline kept challenging our figures, and we kept substantiating them. I could tell we were earning her respect. Then, Troy stepped in.

"Well, theoretically this sounds good." Troy was tapping the proposal book with the pen in his right hand. "But, I happen to know that Greg Gardner would *never* go for this royalty deal; he really wants to own InfoBridge." Troy emphasized his assertions about Gardner with a broad sweep of his left hand. "Besides, there are antitrust concerns."

"Mr. Dennis, may I ask you something?" Rev's voice was a sudden, relaxed penetration of the conversation. Everyone was immediately riveted on Rev. He has that effect on people.

"Yes?" Troy seemed disturbed by the intrusion, his "yes" more a question than an invitation to converse.

Rev said, "Those are important statements about Mr. Gardner. Can you please tell us exactly what has happened that has you say that?" Rev's tone was friendly. His eyes stayed focused on Troy's eyes. Troy broke the gaze and looked at Grey Davis, then around the table, and, finally, back to Rev.

"Well, I'm not free to say."

"That's fine, Mr. Dennis. If it's confidential, then we respect that. It seems, though, that you expected your last comment to influence the outcome of this meeting. Is that so, sir?"

"I certainly have an obligation for Grey and Madeline to know my view of things, so yes."

"That is honorable on your part, sir." Then, turning to Grey, Rev continued.

"Mr. Davis, may I suggest a brief break? We have promised Madeline a quick resolution of this acquisition proposal. That will be served by you hearing, in private of course, the basis for Mr. Dennis's statement about Mr. Gardner. Then you can decide what effect those facts should have on this meeting."

"Mr. Baker . . . or should I say Reverend?"

"I'm not a reverend, Mr. Davis. 'Rev' is a nickname I picked up in government service. I was able to speed up the resolution of some things that used to drag out.

Some folks took to calling me Rev 'cause of the acceleration, and the name stuck. After 25 years, I'm accustomed to it. Please call me Rev."

"I will, Rev, and you call me Grey, all right?" Rev nodded. The two men looked into each other and I saw a connection form, a good one.

Grey continued. "Rev, you're right, this is a good time for a break and some private discussion with Troy and Madeline. "

"Good, Grey, and I'll use the time well myself. The antitrust concern is a smart one, too. I'll do a little research on the break. I know a member of Congress in Washington, D.C., who is spearheadin' a review of the Sherman Antitrust Act and its application to technology mergers. She's about as knowledgeable as they come; I'll see what she has to say on the matter."

I glanced around the room. Sara Mac had a slight smile on her face, like she was seeing more than the rest of us. Madeline looked intensely interested, and Troy seemed uncertain and off-balance. Grey was picking up his legal pad and pen. Sharon spoke.

"A break it is. Let's come back in 30 minutes. Grey, the room is yours. If you need more time or less, just call my cell phone. We're going to take a walk outside." With that, our break began.

Rev went off to call his congressional friend, and then joined Sara, Sharon, and me next door on the Z'Tejas patio. We all took in the view of the hill country, with Highway 360 winding through it like a frame that sets off a beautiful picture. Sara talked first.

"Rev, you are unfailing entertainment; a good piece of work, partner. Sharon, you are doing well at running this as a conversation, and Walker, your comments have been well timed. We have definitely met our goal of updating the relationship."

"Before we debrief everything, can someone tell me what happened there at the end? Sara, what did you mean by a good piece of work?" I was more than curious.

"Walker, I'll tell you in a minute. Sara's right, though, you both are stayin' true to purpose and the conversation is valuable. You've been intersectin' with everything they bring up. We have to bring this thing home yet, though, so don't lose your focus." Rev was dead serious, and I felt his admonition in my bones.

Then, Rev explained what happened.

"Evidence suggests that Troy Dennis is protectin' a position. His objections did not fit the points you were makin'. He never engaged with what you were sayin' before he criticized. He was more attackin' you than he was makin' any point of his own. Those are all signs someone is threatened. He likely brought the Enterwise deal to Grey and doesn't want to lose it. Then, there was the off-hand comment."

"Off-hand? Nothing seemed casual to me?" Sharon said what I was thinking.

Sara laughed. "Rev means something different by off-hand comment."

"Yep. Be careful with what I'm gonna tell you. It is only a signal to ask accuracy questions, not certain evidence of deceit. There is a body of linguistic research that studies how our bodies reflect our thoughts. I noticed that Troy was right handed. When people are makin' statements about the future, they tend to gesture in the direction of their dominant hand if they believe in what they are sayin'. It's a way of pointin' to what they really think is in their future. If they use their 'off' hand and point in the off-hand direction, they are relegating their comment to the past. It's possible that Troy no longer believes the Enterwise deal will happen. He pointed to the past when he said Gardner wanted to own InfoBridge. When I put that together with the protective way he's been communicatin', I knew we needed to poke around. I was movin' the conversation toward accuracy, takin' away some of the room for pretense."

"And that's not all, Rev." Sara turned to Sharon and me.

"Rev also achieved two other things. He created a direct connection with Grey based on value. Rev's questions and suggestions made sense relative to Grey's purposes. Rev did not attack, he did not defend. Then, he gave Grey some personal background as an invitation to a relationship."

I chimed in. "That, at least, I noticed."

Sara went on. "Good, Walker. Secondly, Rev reset the relationship with Troy."

Sharon said, "That makes some sense, but could you explain more?"

Rev laughed softly. "Sharon, where I grew up there was a saying: That cowboy is all hat and no cattle. We said that 'bout folks who lacked substance. It seemed to me that Troy was relatin' to you two like you were all hat and no cattle. We need for Troy to have a more accurate idea of you and your resources. So, I switched the conversation from his private agenda back to the meeting we called. Then, I met the antitrust comment head-on. I imagine he's adjusted his opinion somewhat."

Sharon smiled. "Rev, I think you handled it."

"Rev, are we ever going to learn all you've discovered about conversation?" Rev awed me yet again.

"I hope not, Walker. That would mean I stopped learnin' long enough for you to catch up!" We all found *that* laughable.

Sharon's cell phone rang and she answered. "Good, Grey. We'll be right there." It was time to return to the business at hand.

As we walked back in, a new player entered the proceedings.

"Rev, a present for you. I see you're starting again; I hope I'm not too late."

The man speaking was big, nearly Rev's size. His brown hair, sprinkled with gray, suggested he might be about Rev's age, too. The look on Rev's face made it clear that this was a welcome friend.

"Hello, mon frere. I can't imagine a time that is not perfect for Eddie V's meringue-topped bread puddin'. Everyone, this is my friend Larry. He and Guy own this little piece of heaven." It turned out Larry already knew both Grey Davis and Sara, so introductions were quick.

"You folks have work to do, so I'll drop this off and leave. When Rev shows up, we automatically put one of these in the oven. He's semi-addicted, you see." Larry's mischievous smile expressed affection for Rev as well as pride in the gorgeous dessert. Heat waves were rising from the golden meringue and I was eager for a sample.

Larry left, sharing a parting glance with Rev on the way out. The rest of us came quickly to discover the reason for Rev's semi-addiction. As Rev liked to say, "Mighty fine, mighty tasty!" We refilled beverages, and the meeting resumed.

Grey immediately laid out his position.

"Knowing the facts behind Troy's remarks, I do not think that Gardner will be a barrier to a deal between us. However, any pursuit of this deal after today will require some positive feedback from Glen and the other enterprise software companies you mentioned. Rev, did you get any feel for the antitrust issues in an alliance between those companies and InfoBridge?"

"I got a short briefing. I don't think it will be an issue. To make sure, though, I set it up, Troy, for you to get the information firsthand. With your experience in the law and your knowledge of the business, I figured you should have direct contact with the congresswoman. That okay with you?" Rev waited for Troy's response.

"Uh, sure, I'll be happy to do that. Grey, I'll get back to you fast on this. Rev, thanks for setting it up. I'll get the contact info from you before we leave." Troy seemed about two inches taller, his stature in the interaction restored.

Then, Grey wanted to explore the benefits to MightyTek for retaining some ownership. We shared our thinking, Grey and Madeline shared theirs, and then ideas started coming up that none of us had considered. One even came from Troy.

"I see a real possibility for synergy regarding outsourcing contracts. If we can include connecting systems that can't currently 'talk' to each other in our outsourcing offers, we will close a lot of deals. It's also a feature we can add to our services contracts." Troy seemed fully engaged for the first time. Grey loved Troy's ideas, because he really wanted to grow MightyTek's services and outsourcing revenues.

Finally, we worked on the details of a potential deal. Grey, Madeline, and Sara Mac got very active, and numbers of all kinds were written, erased, and rewritten again until we got to a rough agreement. Subject to our signing royalty agreements with the enterprise software firms, we agreed:

- We would pay MightyTek's asking price.
- MightyTek would retain a 25 percent stake in InfoBridge.

- Fifty percent of the purchase price was to be paid in cash and the balance in a five-year note. If we failed to pay the note in five years, the MightyTek share would increase by 5 percent per quarter up to 50 percent.

The McGregor Fund would be the source of funds for both the cash payment and $50 million of working capital for InfoBridge operations.

We agreed on sharing certain distribution channels, on joint marketing of the first software release, and an exclusive two-year agreement for MightyTek to bundle InfoBridge into their outsourcing and services contracts.

We would stay in our current building at a market rate lease.

Grey *demanded* a four-year management contract for Sharon and three others (including yours truly).

Two board seats would go to MightyTek until the note was repaid, one being Grey.

Wow, what a roller coaster! We left Eddie V's in good spirits and with plenty left to do. Six weeks later, we closed the deal. Even considering MightyTek's ownership percentage and The McGregor Funds ownership, there was enough left for Sharon and I to have a small stake and fund a good employee stock ownership plan. Do you know what is weird? If you walk around our building, the day-to-day work isn't much different. We're virtually still a part of MightyTek. I like it. I like it a lot.

Sharon, Sara Mac, Rev, and I had dinner together at Rev's to celebrate the closing of the deal. It was a remarkable evening. We had barbecue brisket, ribs, sausage, fresh spinach and green beans, and melt-in-your-mouth corn bread. The best part, though, was the conversation. Rev said that any of us could interrupt anything to acknowledge a lesson or a person. He called it "appreciative dinin'" and said, "It's the best way I know to renew the cycle of value."

The lessons and appreciations were many. We thanked each other many times for many things, mentioning dozens of important lessons. You can probably imagine the things we said. After all, you've been along for the ride. I'll just share the last few minutes with you.

"Walker," Rev said, "You have my great admiration for fallin' in a deep rut and gettin' yourself out of it in time to change partners and dance."

I think both Sharon and I looked a tad confused. Rev went on.

"Walker, you ever notice when a piece of music grabs you and you start movin' with it without even thinkin'?" I said I did.

"Conversation, well that's like music, too. There are two kinds of music playin' all the time. The ole Bioreact Band plays threat and waste music, and the Intersect Band plays purpose and value music. Waste and value are both dance partners, Walker. Most folks don't realize that they can pick their partner, so they just find themselves movin' to whatever music is the loudest. You were wise enough and strong enough to change partners."

Sharon added, "Good thing, Walker, because all of us got to come to the dance!"

"Hear. Hear!" Sara raised an iced tea glass in honor of the moment.

That was an emotional moment for me. It felt good, though.

We finished dinner with more appreciations and a to-die-for pecan pie with just the right amount of fresh whipped cream. As we were walking outside, amid the handshakes, back slaps, hugs, and good-byes, Rev told me one thing more.

"Walker, you and I have a date to discuss the Catalyst. Call me soon. I have a conversational survival guide to give you, some phone numbers, and a Web address." I promised to call in the next week.

Sharon drove out first, and I rolled down my window to say a last good-bye to Rev and Sara. They didn't hear me. They were dancing and singing in the grass near the parking lot. Do you know that there actually is a song called "Change Partners and Dance"? It's pretty catchy. I hummed it most of the way home.

CHAPTER / NINE

THE BACK ROAD
TO BRILLIANCE

■ ■ ■

"I have learned throughout my life as a composer chiefly
through my mistakes and false assumptions. . . ."

IGOR STRAVINSKY, *THEMES AND EPISODES*

"Wisdom rises upon the ruins of folly."

THOMAS FULLER, M.D., *GNOMOLOGIA*

"Flops are part of life's menu and I've never been a girl to
miss out on any of the courses."

ROSALIND RUSSELL

None of us is omniscient. That fact sets up the great game of discovery. With
the flair and affection children bring to hide and seek, most of us enjoy the
discovery game. However, one of the names of discovery is *failure*. When
failure is looked down on, a natural door to discovery slams shut.

Learning that takes root and grows is fertilized by misstep and mistake.
What have been your most important lessons? Have they arrived as a sudden grasp of wisdom or as a response to disappointment? In our experience, the road to wisdom is a circuitous back road of attempt, failure,
reflection, and adjustment. We would do well to abandon our images of
unimpeded success, because life itself works another way.

■ ■ ■

"In order to go on living one must try to escape the death
involved in perfectionism."

HANNAH ARENDT

Rivers form as water navigates surfaces too hard to penetrate. The beauty of a winding river is due, in part, to the failure to prevail, followed by adjustment. A life well lived has similar characteristics. We all know that. Our compassionate knowledge of failure's rightful place explains the popularity of *Don Quixote, The Red Shoes,* and *Braveheart,* as well as Eddie the Eagle, England's valiant though errant Olympic ski jumper. It explains our enduring fascination with tales of redemption. We know it. We've known it forever. We have known, as a Christian minister once said, "There is no resurrection without death." Why, then, is failure treated like the plague? In *The Communication Catalyst,* we blame it on dismay.

From its German roots, *dismay* means "cut off from power." When we relate to failed intention as an *end,* rather than as *information,* we are dismayed. Here is how you can tell if you are looking at failure as an end: The future looks like more of the same. It is doom that dismays, not failure. What is doom but ending in failure?

In the context of a purpose, failure is information, not an end. We recommend that at least once a year you answer the following questions: What essential purposes are steering my life? What one to three purposes fuel discovery and prevent dismay? Then, failure is the back road to brilliance instead of an unfortunate dead end. For example, the purpose of *The Communication Catalyst* is to harness the power of conversation to accelerate the creation of value. In the context of purpose, all of our mistakes contribute to, rather than invalidate, our development.

We are going to share with you the major lessons that have emerged from where our mistakes have intersected with our purpose. Then, Rev will leave us with ten laws that help us live out of the lessons. As you read this chapter, we invite you to reflect on your own lessons, especially the ones informed by failure and recovery. Which ones resonate with the concepts of *The Communication Catalyst?* We suggest you compile a list of those important lessons. Then, look through the list for themes. Finally, name the most essential lesson to keep in front of you for the next two months. Maintain a two-month focus on that most important lesson, and we predict great value.

Our Top Six Lessons on the Back Road to Brilliance

It's the conversation, stupid. We have discovered the hard way that, to paraphrase John Donne, no person is an island. We cannot even understand ourselves except in the context of relationship. Descarte said, "I think, therefore I am." We have come to prefer, "I relate, therefore I am." We consider the fundamental act of relationship to be conversation, the dance of impression and expression. It is through conversation that we relate to people and events. By purposefully caring for the value of conversation, our relationships are valuable, and the cycle of value is spawned.

From the view of *The Communication Catalyst,* conversation *is* relating. Use the words interchangeably. Count on it: the quality of conversation/relationship is the quality of your life. Conversations for value or conversations for waste—you make the choice.

It's achievable from here. Only a person can kill a purpose, and he or she kills it in a conversation. No circumstance has the power to so kill. In any set of circumstances is *something* that can help our cause.

The faster we admit error, the sooner we make good. Embarrassment, current and prospective, prevents many a lesson. Heaven forbid we should admit mistake and adjust. It is painful to watch leaders preserve an image of omniscience at the expense of learning. It is inspiring to witness a simple, "This was a mistake; this is what I've learned; this is what I will do differently."

Success is the redemption of small and large failures, so forgive already! Who among us has not needed a second chance? If you want to lead a culture of learning and adjustment, you will need frequent doses of forgiveness. "You messed it up. Clean it up in a way that makes the mess worthwhile." (By the way, if you cannot have the forgiveness conversation in the mirror, you will stink at having it anywhere else.)

■ ■ ■

Because conversation is the natural way that humans
think together, it is, like all life, messy.
The practice of conversation takes courage, faith, and time.
We don't get it right the first time, and we don't have to.

MARGARET WHEATLEY, *TURNING TO ONE ANOTHER*

Appreciation is a purpose, not a reaction. Appreciation is the act of discovering and acknowledging value. Do it on purpose. Demand it of yourself. You grant legitimacy and stature to people and events by appreciating their contribution to value. While others search for better people and circumstances, you will unleash value for customers, investors, and employees. As an added benefit, developing your competence to appreciate reduces stress.

Being valuable is more satisfying and, in the long run, more safe than being popular. Being approved of is a seductive emotional drug. Most of us have painful memories of selling out real value for the false security of acceptance. Value occurs at an intersection, and that intersection includes you. If you decide to cater to someone else's approval, there is no intersection because there is no "you" there. To intersect is not to succumb. If you choose popularity over value, you have taken residence in the opinion of another. Those are cramped quarters. Value earns respect. Popularity earns, at the very best, fleeting affection.

Remember, please, that these six lessons are a function of a complex array of mistakes. You are welcome to profit from our mistakes and then make new ones of your very own. The recipe for becoming a communication catalyst is liberally sprinkled with errors made valuable by learning. If you make some particularly valuable mistakes, get in touch. We would like to learn from yours, too.

Still to come is Rev's wrap-up with Walker. Also, you will find a simple diagnostic in Appendix B to help assess the value of a conversation. When you are done, please identify your essential learning focus and turn it into an eight-week adventure. And no kidding, we want to hear from you about the value you create. An easy way to contact us is our Web site: <www.conversant.net>.

Thanks for your interest in *The Communication Catalyst*. We are grateful that you have invested your time with us. Oh, and tell Rev we said "hi."

CHAPTER SUMMARY

The Heart of the Matter

In the context of a purpose, failure is information on the back road to brilliance, not a doomed dead end. Avoiding failure generates pretense and makes us slow to adjust. Returning the investment of failure makes us strong, agile, and wise.

The recipe for becoming a communication catalyst is liberally sprinkled with errors made valuable by learning. We invite you to profit from our mistakes and then make new ones of your very own.

Our Top Six Lessons on the Back Road to Brilliance

1. **It's the conversation, stupid.** Conversation *is* relating. The quality of the conversation/relationship is the quality of your life.
2. **It's achievable from here.** People kill purposes; circumstances do not. In any set of circumstances, there is something that can help our cause.
3. **The faster we admit error, the sooner we make good.** It is inspiring to witness a simple, "This was a mistake; this is what I've learned; this is what I will do differently."
4. **Success is the redemption of small and large failures, so forgive already!** If you want to lead a culture of learning and adjustment, you will need frequent doses of forgiveness. Start with yourself.
5. **Appreciation is a purpose, not a reaction.** Appreciation is the act of discovering and acknowledging value. Do it on purpose.
6. **Being valuable is more satisfying and, in the long run, more safe than being popular.** Value occurs at an authentic intersection and earns respect. Popularity earns, at best, fleeting affection.

Value track: Reflect on your experiences. What lessons have you learned that have been informed by failure and recovery? Do the lessons resonate with the concepts of *The Communication Catalyst*? What themes do you see? Identify the most essential lesson. Maintain a two-month focus on that lesson. We predict great value as you reap the rewards of exploring your own back road to brilliance.

R E V   L E S S O N

· · ·

If You Have to Eat Crow, Eat It Fresh

"Everybody plays the fool sometime;

There's no exception to the rule.

Listen, baby, it may be factual, may be cruel,

I ain't lyin', everybody plays the fool."

AARON NEVILLE, "EVERYBODY PLAYS THE FOOL"

(WRITTEN BY RUDY CLARK, KENNY WILLIAMS, AND JIM BAILEY)

Dusk is a time of transition. The gradual segue from light to dark was a perfect accompaniment to the end of a party and the beginning of a private conversation. We sat at the end of the dock, four legs swaying gently just inches over the water. I stretched and the bottoms of my feet grazed the tops of the small waves.

The breeze had been there all day, driven from notice by the searing heat. Now its notable comfort escorted us into the evening. It was a few minutes before I noticed what was missing. Words. Mindless verbiage filling space and time. It occurred to me that I had passed through my chattering need for Rev's approval. Rich, full quiet covered Rev and me like a blanket on a chilly night.

I'd been at Rev's since early that morning. When I called to arrange for our Catalyst conversation, Rev told me he had Saturday night free. Then he asked if I might be available to give him a hand Saturday during the day. Rev Baker's Barbecue Café was hosting a wedding reception, and Rev said, "We got 250 folks comin' and we can use all the help we can get." I didn't see how I could be of much assistance, but I liked the idea of helping Rev out. I served food and drink, did whatever else Rev directed, and learned a little about cooking.

Did you know that a barbecue is really a roast of a whole animal, like a cow, fish, or pig? I didn't. Rev said that *barbe-a-queue* is French for "snout to tail." He said that some people say it's from the Spanish *barbacoa,* but he personally went for the French claim. Rev told me more about marinades, rubs, and roasting than I can hope to recall. My compensation was snacking on his artistry the whole day long, and it was worthy pay. We took care of people and sang along with the band when they played something one of us knew. It was all inside our senior purpose:

"Take care of the guests, Walker. Just take care of the guests, and you'll do fine."
He was right, I did fine.

A fish jumped about six feet in front of us and I flinched.

"Walker, I guess there weren't many fish jumpin' where you grew up." Rev was
smiling at my involuntary reaction.

"No, Rev, there were not. I ought to be used to new experiences when I'm with
you, though."

"We have had an interestin' time this last couple of months, haven't we, Walker?"

"*Interesting* is one of many words to describe it, Rev. Also *uncomfortable, confusing, inspiring, disappointing, exciting, scary,* and *satisfying*. It feels like I fit ten
years into less than three months."

"You've done well, Walker. Now, I know we've had quite a day, but we've a little
left to do."

"The Catalyst?"

"Yessir, the Catalyst." As Rev spoke, he moved, without effort, from sitting to
standing on the dock. Even as big as he is, Rev is cat quick and nimble. "Let's take
a walk up to the shed. I've got some things for you in the office."

We walked off the dock, and the sounds of the water lapping the lakeshore
faded about the time we passed the magnolias. On the way, Rev said that he was
leaving for a while. He did not give much detail, and I knew better than to ask.

"I'll be a gone a few weeks at least, Walker, and in a time zone that doesn't line
up well with central Texas, so I don't imagine we'll talk for a while."

"Hey, I'll be fine. I don't need a babysitter. Don't insult me, Rev." Where did that
come from? I heard my offended whine almost like it was another person. I looked
over at Rev. His face was calm and unlined, simply waiting.

I shook my head hard. "Whoa. Sorry, Rev. That was uncalled for. I apologize. I
think I just had a bioreactive fit. It was a surprise that you're leaving. I guess I've
gotten used to having you around and available. I really *will* be fine. Wow. That felt
like the movie *Invasion of the Body Snatchers*.

Rev chuckled. "I know you'll do fine. You did just then."

"What do you mean?"

Still chuckling, "I believe I need to let you in on some military history, Walker."

Then, Rev told me about an incident near the end of the War of 1812. During
an armistice, an American soldier shot a crow while he was in British territory. A
British officer surprised and captured the American. The British officer decided to
humiliate the American for his transgression of British lines and forced him to take
a bite of the crow. Then, the officer got careless and the American, his gun recovered, forced his captor to eat the rest of the crow. The expression "eat crow" caught
on quickly to describe the disagreeable moment of admitting error.

"So, Walker, you just ate a little crow. A man I know, Gary Egan, is one of the finest business leaders I've ever met. Back before he retired, he told me that one of his most important lessons was, 'If you have to eat crow, eat it fresh.'"

I laughed out loud. "So if you're a real fool, like me, just catch it and correct quickly, right? Hey, I don't feel quite as stupid, Rev."

"Everybody plays the fool, Walker. Bioreaction is a darn sight faster than you. No dishonor in havin' bioreactions. The evidence of your honor is how fast you own up and move on."

'Rev, I'll post that one on my wall. Maybe I'll even frame 'If you have to eat crow, eat it fresh'."

"It's worth rememberin', all right. Let's go ahead inside, Walker."

We went in to Rev's office and there on his desk was a bulky manila envelope. It had "Walker O'Reilly" written in black ink across the front. Rev picked it up, motioned me to one of the red leather chairs, and sat next to me at the table. He pulled out some papers and a small cardboard box.

"Walker, welcome to the Catalyst. Let's not get too dramatic, though. This is no self-important secret society. These people respect and enjoy conversation, and they like meetin' big challenges with the cycle of value. They stay true to the value of conversation when it's easy and when it's hard. We watch out for one another, we share lessons, and we call on each other if we need to. There is not much formality to the Catalyst. We have some recommendations, though. You interested?"

"Hah! Of course, I'm interested. Please, go on."

"Fine. First, here's the purpose that holds us together."

Rev handed me a sheet of paper on which was typed, in bold letters: **We promise that we can meet any challenge, no matter how difficult, by having the right people in the right conversation.** Below that were four sentences:

1. When something in the Cycle of Value is missing, provide it.
2. Make principles more important than jargon.
3. Value mutuality over difference, research over indignation, and integration over disintegration.
4. Master one law at a time.

I looked up at Rev. "This all makes perfect sense to me, except the 'master one law at a time' part. What's that about?"

"One fella in the Catalyst suggested something years ago and it caught on. Once a year, a lot of us get together and share our biggest mistakes. Together, we turn them into actionable lessons. We call those the 'back road to brilliance' sessions. Two years back, we wrote down the lessons that come up so often that they seem to be laws. Now, we've got people around the world holdin' sessions and workin' together to master those laws one at a time.

"Over the years, we learned that if you try to master everything, you end up masterin' nothin'. It's good to focus on one thing at a time until you're reliable for it. A lot of what you and I have worked on is in the ten laws. It's not everything, not even close. I'll guarantee you this, though: Anyone who is reliable for the ten laws is causin' a monstrous amount of value." Rev was beaming as that last sentence ended. I could tell he had high regard for anyone who mastered the ten laws.

"May I see them?"

"I'll do more than let you see 'em, Walker. This box contains three hours of audio on the ten laws. If you get serious about this mastery business, these'll be a big help. Here are the ten laws all printed up."

Rev handed me a stiff card. On one side was a four-color version of the conversation meter. On the other side were the ten laws. I'll share them with you, plus comments Rev made about each of them.

The Code of the Back Road: Ten Natural Laws

1. **Law of Teamwork:** *The source of teamwork is a common future.*
   Rev: "If you don't have a goal, purpose, or some kind of tomorrow in common, then you can't coordinate efforts today."

2. **Law of Influence:** *People need to influence like they need to breathe.*
   Rev: "People need to be heard and be valuable. Suppress them and their influence will be felt in wasteful ways."

3. **Law of Purpose:** *Great achievement demands being true to purpose in the face of fear and threat.*
   Rev: "You need to decide where you live and where you visit. I like to live in purpose, visit fear, and then come back home."

4. **Law of Listening:** *The test for listening is learning.*
   Rev: "Your ears will produce downright miracles if you learn every time you listen. When most folks listen, they're just ratifyin' what they already think."

5. **Law of Conversation:** *The quality of conversation governs the rate of value creation.*
   Rev: "This is the conversation meter. Be grateful when anyone else gives you sincerity, and then hold yourself to account for accuracy and authenticity."

6. **Law of Appraisal:** *Our judgments are based on perception, not reality; hold them lightly.*

Rev: "The question about judgments is not, 'Am I right or wrong?' The question is, 'Am I valuable or wasteful?'"

7. **Law of Resistance:** *Where you get resistance, do research.*

   Rev: "Folks don't resist you, they resist threat. You step up the force, they'll step up the resistance. Instead, get respectfully interested in their puposes and concerns."

8. **Law of Failure:** *The integrity of failure is return on investment.*

   Rev: "Any failure, no matter how big, will stop botherin' you when you learn enough to make it worthwhile."

9. **Law of Consensus:** *Having influence does not mean having a veto.*

   Rev: "If everyone has a veto, no one has to learn from anyone else. Learn from everyone involved but give the final say to whoever's in position to do what's best for customers, employees, and investors."

10. **Law of Appreciation:** *Appreciation is the soul of high performance, bringing meaning, resilience, and learning to the workplace.*

    Rev: "Appreciate someone's contribution, and you're gonna get more of it. Take it for granted, and you're gonna get less. Folks tend to gravitate toward where they truly matter."

I think it took us about an hour to talk through the laws.

"Pick one that you like, Walker, and stick with it until it's natural."

"I will, Rev. Picking just one will be a challenge. I'll take the coaching, though, and find one to focus on for a month or two." I was trying to decide between appraisal, failure, and resistance.

Rev shrugged as he spoke to me. "They're all valuable, and whichever one you pick will lead you back to all the rest, so it's hard to go wrong. It's best, though, to look for one that fascinates you, 'cause that'll be easy to keep in mind. When folks pick the one they feel worst about, they don't tend to stick with it."

I truly love listening to Rev. He makes a kind of sense that is easy for me to hear.

Rev packed my audios, the purpose statement, and the ten laws back into the manila envelope. Then, he took out one of his business cards, wrote on the back, and slid that in the envelope, too.

"That card has an Internet address and a password. You go in there and you'll have access to all our archives. You'll also see how to add your own stories, Walker. I'm sure you will have some fine ones. Post your name and e-mail address and anything you'd like to know more about. Folks will get back to you quickly. They are fine people, Walker. You start gettin' to know them, and there is no telling the adventures comin' your way."

Rev handed me the envelope with both hands and I received it with both of mine. It seemed an act of deep respect. We were at that small round table, you know. The whole thing felt Arthurian to me. Okay, I know that sounds dramatic. That *is* how I felt, though. I still do.

"Rev, I'm not sure what I've done to deserve your friendship and support. I am grateful."

"Contribution tends to find people who are ready for it, Walker. I recommend you don't bother about whether you deserve it. Bother yourself about what you're gonna do with it." Rev looked deeply into me as he spoke. Somehow, he is deeply compassionate and demanding at the same time.

"Rev, how can I thank you?"

"Share the wealth, Walker."

"I promise to, Rev. Most people won't have the same problems that we've had, but I know the lessons apply in any situation. I'm happy to share the wealth, and I know it will keep me learning."

Rev stood and so did I. We walked outside together, pausing at the door to the shed.

"Walker, I've got some gettin' ready to do, so I'll be stayin' up here for a bit. Give Sharon, Louis, and Ray my best, all right?"

I just stared at Rev, taking in his broad, dark face and bright eyes.

Rev looked right back at me and we held the look for a moment. I started to speak and then stopped after stumbling over my own words.

Rev said, "Walker, sometimes there aren't words that'll do. Best to just let the silence do the talkin'."

He shook my hand, winked, and went back into the shed. I stepped out into the grass and looked up through the trees at the stars. I heard a noise and looked to see Rev opening the windows and shutters in that room with all the sophisticated equipment. I started to move on, heard some music beginning, and stopped. Coming from the shed was the distinct, lilting voice of Aaron Neville. "Everybody plays the fool, sometime, there's no exception to the rule." I shook my head and smiled. I was sure the closing concert was for my benefit.

I walked back toward my car, enjoying the stars and the summer breeze. As Rev says, "There aren't any perfect people, but there are perfect moments."

APPENDIX / A

. . .

GENERIC STEPS
TO THE INTERSECTION

Because the intersection is so central to the principles in *The Communication Catalyst,* we have provided the following steps to follow to reach the intersection. Keep in mind that the conversation meter is your speedometer to measure the speed of your trip to the intersection.

1. What is your initial purpose?
2. Who is crucial to that purpose? For each person, answer:
   - What purposes of his or hers can I respect?
   - What concerns might he or she have?
   - What circumstances and events are affecting him or her?
3. What are the themes that cross all of those views?
4. What is a valuable intersection?
   - A valuable intersection is attractive to the people involved; they want to be in the conversation.
   - A good test: Is it the name of a meeting all parties would want to attend?

APPENDIX / B

. . .

EVALUATION TOOL

This diagnostic is a tool to evaluate the relational strength of your conversations. Follow these steps to increase value creation in your conversations:

Step 1. Identify a project or goal that is important to you.

Step 2. Consider the quality of the conversation as a whole with respect to that project or goal.

Step 3. Select a highlighter pen color for each of the conversation meter categories (pretense, sincerity, accuracy, and authenticity).

Step 4. Go through each cycle of value conversation in the chart that follows. Determine which of the four conversation samples best represents the quality of that conversation within the project team or work group. Using the highlighter color for that conversation meter category, highlight the box you have selected.

Step 5. When you have been through the whole cycle of value, look for patterns that are revealed in the chart and actions you can take:
- If three or more of the conversations are in pretense or sincerity, then focus on accuracy.
- If one specific conversation is rated at the low end (pretense/sincerity), focus specifically on raising the quality of that conversation.
- If two conversations are rated at the low end (pretense/sincerity), focus first on raising the quality of the conversation that occurs earlier in the cycle of value. For example, if intersect and engage are both low, focus first on the intersect conversation.

Step 6: Repeat the diagnostic at regular intervals to note improvement and to renew your learning focus. You can add it to your conversational debriefs.

Cycle of Value	Purpose	Pretense 0–25	Sincerity 26–50	Accuracy 51–75	Authenticity 76–100
Align					
Intersect	Identifying key participants and senior purpose	Dishonesty or lack of disclosure of relevant information	Openly expressing and defending individual views	Carefully researching views and the facts	Understanding and commingling views and facts to discover valuable senior purpose
Invent	Inventing a surplus of ideas to fulfill the senior purpose	Disinterest—withholding full participation	Promoting own ideas; questioning or attacking others' ideas	Carefully listening to each idea to reach understanding	Building on each idea to cause a cascade of increasingly valuable ideas
Invest	Confronting feasibility and committing resources to fulfill senior purpose	Avoiding commitment of resources	Refusing to commit resources	Identifying and troubleshooting the resource and feasibility implications	Expanding the reach of the value to be created while addressing feasibility and resource implications
Act					
Engage	Connecting the senior purpose with the best interests of the people you are counting on	Forgetting or ignoring the interests of the people you are counting on	Communicating the new direction to the masses (e.g., via mass e-mail)	Cascading accurate information through the organization with opportunities for questions and answers	Hosting conversations in which people clearly appreciate value at the intersection of customer, investor, and employee views
Clarify	Clarifying precise expectations to fulfill senior purpose	Assuming that expectations must be clear and obvious	One-way download of expectations	Thorough review of specific tasks and duties and associated expectations	Have relevant people clarify the network of interdependent promises important to the senior purpose
Close	Committing to action to fulfill senior purpose	Assuming understanding equals commitment	Demanding commitment by wielding power	Requesting specific people to deliver specific value by a specific time	Each individual ensuring his/her full commitment to being in action to fulfill the senior purpose
Adjust					
Review	Reviewing performance to-date relative to fulfillment of senior purpose	Being afraid to "slow down" or "lose time" by reviewing	Conclusions from a hasty review (one or two people) published so everyone can see where they went wrong	Thorough and inclusive review of actual events, explanations, and effectiveness	Honestly reviewing effectiveness to reveal valuable adjustments in service of the senior purpose
Renew	Learning lessons and designing a new focus to better fulfill the senior purpose	Quietly hoping things will go better next time	Attributing success or failure to luck or circumstance and unwittingly precluding learning	Actively seeking explanations of performance that reveal actionable areas for improvement	Discovery of a learning focus that resonates with participants and ensures dramatically increased competency and value creation

I N D E X

■ ■ ■

Share the message!

Bulk discounts
Discounts start at only 10 copies and range from 30% to 55% off retail price based on quantity.

Custom publishing
Private label a cover with your organization's name and logo. Or, tailor information to your needs with a custom pamphlet that highlights specific chapters.

Ancillaries
Workshop outlines, videos, and other products are available on select titles.

Dynamic speakers
Engaging authors are available to share their expertise and insight at your event.

Call Kaplan Publishing Corporate Sales at 1-800-621-9621, ext. 4444, or e-mail kaplanpubsales@kaplan.com

KAPLAN

PUBLISHING